BUILDING HOOVER DAM

BUILDING HOOVER DAM

An Oral History of the Great Depression

Andrew J. Dunar and Dennis McBride

UNIVERSITY OF NEVADA PRESS
Reno & Las Vegas

Building Hoover Dam: An Oral History of the Great Depression
by Andrew J. Dunar and Dennis McBride was first published in 1993
by Twayne Publishers as no. 11 in Twayne's Oral History Series.

University of Nevada Press, Reno, Nevada 89557 USA
Cover design by Carrie House
The paper used in this book meets the requirements of American National
Standard for Information Sciences—Permanence of Paper for Printed
Materials, ANSI Z39.48-1984. Binding materials were selected for strength
and durability.
Library of Congress Cataloging-in-Publication Data
Dunar, Andrew J.
Building Hoover Dam : an oral history of the Great Depression /
Andrew J. Dunar and Dennis McBride.
p. cm.
Originally published: New York : Twayne Publishers, © 1993.
Includes bibliographical references and index.
ISBN 0-87417-489-9 (alk. paper)
1. Hoover Dam (Ariz. and Nev.)—History. 2. Dams—Colorado River
(Colo.-Mexico)—Design and construction—History. 3. Construction
workers—Nevada—Boulder City—Interviews. 4. Boulder City (Nev.)—
Biography. 5. Oral history. I. McBride, Dennis. II. Title.

TC557.5.H6 D86 2001
627'.82'0979312—dc 21   00-069074

10 09 08 07 06 05

5 4 3

For Teddy Fenton,
who was the first to listen

Contents

Illustrations

Foreword

Massive public works programs formed an integral part of the New Deal's response to the Great Depression of the 1930s. Projects on the scale of the Hoover Dam put people back to work, harnessed natural resources, and provided low-cost public power. Like the ancient pyramids, twentieth-century hydroelectric dams awe visitors by their sheer magnitude and by a realization of the obstacles that had to be overcome for their construction. While we know much about the pharaohs and presidents for whom they are named, seeing these monuments makes us curious about the people who actually built them. Those who labored on the pyramids remain obscure, but *Building Hoover Dam* tells of their modern counterparts, in their own words. The motives that drew these construction workers and their families into the wilderness, the camp communities in which they lived, the daily construction under which they operated, their triumphs and their hardships, provide a story of epic proportions, matching the dam that they built.

Oral history may well be the twentieth century's substitute for the written memoir. In exchange for the immediacy of diaries or correspondence, the retrospective interview offers a dialogue between the participant and the informed interviewer. Having prepared sufficient preliminary research, interviewers can direct the discussion into areas long since "forgotten," or no longer considered of consequence. "I haven't thought about that in years" is a common response, uttered just before an interviewee commences with a surprisingly detailed description of some past incident. The quality of the interview, its candidness and depth, generally will depend as much on the interviewer as the interviewee, and the confidence and rapport between the two adds a special dimension to the spoken memoir.

Interviewers represent a variety of disciplines and work either as part of a collective effort or individually. Regardless of their different interests or the variety of their subjects, all interviewers share a common imperative: to collect memories while they are still available. Most oral historians feel an additional responsibility to make their interviews accessible for use beyond their own research needs. Still, important collections of vital, vibrant interviews lie scattered in archives throughout every state, undiscovered or simply not used.

Twayne's Oral History Series seeks to identify those resources and to publish selections of the best materials. The series lets people speak for themselves, from their own unique perspectives on people, places, and events. But to be more than a babble of voices, each volume organizes its interviews around particular situations and events and ties them together with interpretive essays that place individuals into the larger historical context. The styles and format of individual volumes vary with the material from which they are drawn, demonstrating again the diversity of oral history and its methodology.

Whenever oral historians gather in conference, they enjoy retelling experiences about inspiring individuals they met, unexpected information they elicited, and unforgettable reminiscences that would otherwise have never been recorded. The result invariably reminds listeners of others who deserve to be interviewed, provides them with models of interviewing techniques, and inspires them to make their own contribution to the field. I trust that the oral historians in this series, as interviewers, editors, and interpreters, will have a similar effect on their readers.

DONALD A. RITCHIE
Series Editor, Senate Historical Office

Acknowledgments

Many people assisted us at every stage of this project, but three in particular have contributed from the beginning. Teddy Fenton, the unofficial historian of Boulder City, has lived in the town since the early 1930s, and still resides in a remodeled and enlarged Six Companies house. Her boundless enthusiasm has for years nourished those interested in the history of Hoover Dam, and we have been fortunate beneficiaries. She shared stories, gave us access to her extensive personal collection of photographs and artifacts, helped arrange interviews, and encouraged us at every step. We are proud to dedicate this book to Teddy, one of Boulder City's authentic pioneers.

Carroll Gardner was the librarian of the Boulder City Library when we began our work, and gave us access to the library's important collection of taped interviews conducted in the early 1970s by the Boulder City chapter of the American Association of University Women. Since then she and her husband, Jack, retired librarian of the Las Vegas Public Library, have assisted us in many ways: critiquing draft chapters, providing lodging, and giving sound advice.

We extend thanks also to Tom King, who gave us access to material in the University of Nevada, Reno, Oral History Project. Duncan McCoy, Carroll Gardner's successor at the Boulder City Library, gave us permission to use tapes from the Boulder City Library Oral History Project. The Special Collections Department of the University of Nevada, Las Vegas, was generous in providing not only access to its impressive collection of oral history interviews and historic photographs and documents, but in furnishing facilities for taping. The staff was patient, helpful, and enjoyable to work with.

The University of Alabama in Huntsville assisted us with a grant through its internal grants program. Colleagues in the History Department at the University of Alabama in Huntsville, particularly Johanna Shields and Stephen Waring, offered encouragement even when Hoover Dam took time from our other projects. Grants and financial support were likewise provided by the Nevada Humanities Committee and the Boulder Dam Credit Union.

Series editor Don Ritchie encouraged us from the moment we first approached him, and offered wise counsel throughout. Anne Jones, Mark

Zadrozny, and Rob Winston at Twayne were always responsive and gave sensible professional advice.

Our families shared in our enthusiasm for the story of the building of the dam. Cathie Dunar read chapter drafts, helped with the preparation of the index, and offered homefront support with the help of Jamie, Kimberly, and Michael. Alveta McBride provided room and board long after most mothers would have kicked their sons out and told them to find a real job.

To these and to all who graciously consented to be interviewed, we offer sincere thanks.

Illustration Credits

Boulder City Library, figs. 16, 18, 64; Bechtel Album Three, figs. 55, 61; Eileen Conners photograph, fig. 21; Carl and Mary Ann Merrill Collection, fig. 44

D. R. McBride Collection, figs. 7, 8, 30, 40

Nevada State Museum and Historical Society, figs. 9, 23, 25

U.S. Bureau of Reclamation, figs. 19, 20, 24, 62; Fenton-Harbour Collection, figs. 5, 27, 28, 29, 37, 42, 43, 45, 66; Ben Glaha photograph, figs. 26, 31, 32, 33, 35, 36, 38, 39, 57; John McCreary photograph, fig. 56; O. G. Patch photograph, fig. 11; W. B. Radford photograph, fig. 60; Cliff Segerblom photograph, fig. 67; Rupert Spearman photograph, fig. 65; Walker R. Young photograph, figs. 3, 4

University of Nevada, Las Vegas, Blood Collection, fig. 48; Davis Collection, fig. 2; Display Collection, fig. 22; Doktor Collection, fig. 53; Garrett Collection, figs. 6, 12, 13, 14, 15, 49, 51, 52; Jensen Collection, figs. 46, 58, 59; Kizziar Collection, fig. 50; Manis Collection, figs. 34, 41, 47, 63; Map Collection, fig. 1; Single Accessions, fig. 54; Union Pacific Railroad Collection, figs. 10, 17

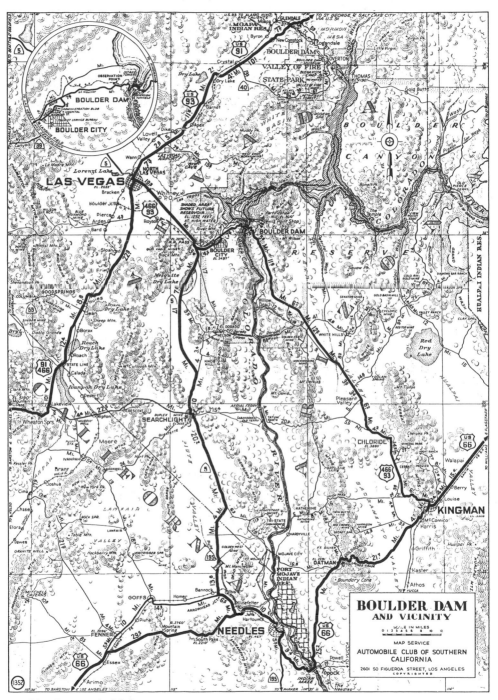

Boulder Dam and vicinity

Introduction

Hoover Dam is one of the monumental engineering achievements of the twentieth century. Even as later dams surpassed it in height, volume, and power production, Hoover Dam remained the first of the great multipurpose dams, providing flood control, water for irrigation, and hydroelectric power to the Southwest. It stands as a tribute to American ingenuity, persistence, and will, and is one of the most enduring legacies of the "American Century." One writer suggested that "When forests push through the rotting streets of New York and the Empire State Building is a crumbling hulk, Hoover Dam will sit astride the Colorado River much as it does today—intact, formidable, serene."[1]

Built between 1931 and 1935, Boulder Dam, as it was then known, dwarfed other dams around the world. It was 726 feet high, 660 feet wide at its base, and 45 feet wide at the crest. The 3.25 million cubic yards of concrete in the dam weighed 6.6 million tons. At the peak of construction, more than 5,200 men worked on the dam 24 hours a day, seven days a week.

But statistics do not tell the story of Hoover Dam. More compelling is the human side, the personal stories that illustrate America's pioneering heritage and industrial resourcefulness and make this a particularly American drama. Cold statistics assume a deeper resonance and a wider context when reflected through the details of ordinary life. Oral history provides this dimension.

Too often the historical record obscures the personal perspective of individuals involved in the day-to-day routine of great events or attributes their achievements to high-ranking officials. Hoover Dam is, after all, named for a president; its reservoir, Lake Mead, for a commissioner of the Bureau of Reclamation. Even the plaques on the crest of the dam that visitors pass as they line up for tours mention only a handful of top officials.

The politics behind authorization of the Boulder Canyon Project and construction of Hoover Dam is a story that has been told elsewhere.[2] In this book government planners, rivermen, engineers, officials, journalists, laborers, and their wives tell their own stories of building Hoover Dam. They describe their plans to tame one of the world's wildest rivers; their desperate search for escape from the horrors of the Great Depression; the rigors of making a life in the desolation of southern Nevada; and their enjoyment of the pleasures of Las Vegas when it was a rough and raucous railroad town. These people came from every walk of life and from every corner of America. Social and economic upheaval brought them together and fueled the drive with which they built Hoover Dam. For some it was just a job, a steady paycheck and a place to live. For others it was salvation.

We have assembled here interviews of individuals ranging from the government's chief engineer on the project to muckers who dug mud and rocks from the canyon floor with picks and shovels. We have used both our own interviews and other interviews conducted over the past two decades.

The supplementary interviews came from projects initiated before we started our work and have given us access to the recollections of people who died long before our work on this book began. As early as 1967 the University of Nevada, Reno, conducted interviews related to the building of the dam and the growth of Las Vegas as a part of the university's ongoing Oral History Program. In the 1970s the Boulder City chapter of the American Association of University Women, in cooperation with the Boulder City Public Library, conducted an oral history project. The invaluable interview with Walker R. Young came from this project. In the late 1970s and early 1980s, Dr. Ralph Roske of the University of Nevada, Las Vegas, encouraged his students to conduct interviews with southern Nevada pioneers and deposited tapes of these interviews in the university library's Special Collections Department. The interview with Murl Emery is one of these student interviews. The quotations from Charles "Pop" Squires come from his unpublished memoir cataloged in Special Collections at the University of Nevada, Las Vegas. Transcripts of most interviews used in this book (except for those in which sound quality was too poor for full transcription) are housed in Special Collections of the University of Nevada, Las Vegas, and in the Boulder City Public Library.

We have edited the oral history transcripts included in this book with two principles in mind: to build a story with continuity and coherence and to retain the phrasing, intent, and character of the original oral testimony. In some cases, in order to provide clarity and maintain coherence, we have changed the order of presentation within interviews or combined statements from different interviews of the same person. Changes in the original wording are noted in brackets, although we have tried to keep such changes to a minimum. While we have tried to limit our intrusion into the narrative, we have included transition notes that explain the context of individual comments, technical aspects of construction, and the dam's operation.

Our goal throughout has been to allow individuals to tell their own stories in their own way.

Big Bend of the Colorado River as it enters Black Canyon, about 1929

I

INVESTIGATION AND APPROVAL: SOUTHERN NEVADA, 1902–1929

"Incomprehensible how they could build a dam there."

*For decades before construction of Hoover Dam began, the federal govern-
ment had wanted to build a dam on the lower Colorado River. After
devastating floods in California's Imperial Valley in 1905–07 stirred
demand for flood control, the Bureau of Reclamation investigated potential
damsites along the river near Las Vegas, Nevada. Reclamation engineer
Walker R. Young led investigations during the early 1920s in Boulder
and Black canyons. Later he became the chief construction engineer during
the building of Hoover Dam.*

WALKER R. YOUNG

The Colorado River had been under study for many years—you might say
from the inception of the Bureau of Reclamation in 1902. Mr. [Joseph
Barlow] Lippincott in 1905 was sent to get a look at the lower part of the
river. Nothing was done at that time, but later they got to thinking about
irrigation, flood control, demands for power, domestic water supply. Dr.
Arthur P. Davis, who was then the commissioner of Reclamation, got the
idea that a large storage should be provided for the lower Colorado River
near the point of use. So he originated the idea. I consider him the father of
the Boulder Canyon Project.

Then Homer [Hamlin], who was a geologist [for] the Bureau of Reclamation, was sent down to explore the river below the entrance of the Virgin
River. He and an assistant, whose name I believe was Wheeler, made a trip

down the river as far as Blythe [California]. He was looking for a damsite that would provide for an immense storage. He reported that there was a damsite available in Boulder Canyon, depending on the results of an investigation, that would meet the requirements. He said that if for any reason it should develop after an investigation that the damsites in Boulder Canyon were not suitable, there was another site 20 miles downstream in Black Canyon.

Mr. Davis, the commissioner, and Frank E. Weymouth, who was then chief engineer in the Bureau of Reclamation office in Denver, Colorado, made a trip down the river personally [in November 1920]. They came back to Denver. At the time I happened to be working in the chief engineer's office. They asked me how soon I could leave for Boulder Canyon. So I started out with Mr. James Munn, who was the superintendent of construction for the Bureau of Reclamation, a man that I had worked with at the Arrow Rock Dam. He was sort of a father of mine. He and I arrived at St. Thomas, Nevada, in the last week of December [1920]. We went down to look over the canyon and came back with the idea that the work should be speeded up, and so reported. I had some experience before this in the investigation of damsites and working at damsites. I became in charge of the investigation. That was Boulder Canyon, the one that was first suggested for Hoover Dam.

Young and his crew established a camp at the entrance to Boulder Canyon, 50 miles from Las Vegas. For two years they conducted investigations and reconnaissance of the river from Boulder Canyon to Black Canyon, 20 miles to the south. Edna Jackson Ferguson's husband, Clarence, was a member of this Reclamation crew.

EDNA JACKSON FERGUSON

It was the latter part of December 1922. Clarence Jackson, known to most people as Jack, had just finished a job in Utah and was returning to Los Angeles to seek more employment. Stopping in Las Vegas overnight, he decided to try his luck at finding work on the big dam that was going to be built on the Colorado River. The Bureau of Reclamation had offices in Las Vegas directing the preliminary investigations into the building of the dam. The man in charge was Walker R. Young. After a short interview Jack was hired.

Investigations were being made at both Black Canyon and Boulder Canyon to see which place would be more suitable for such a giant piece of construc-

Bureau of Reclamation crew at the Boulder Canyon camp. Drilling foreman George A. Hammond standing in the front row, 26 February 1921

Clarence Jackson in charge of the Boulder Canyon gaging station, operating 90-pound sounding weights and a current meter, 27 February 1923

tion. Jack was told to report for work at the camp for field employees at Boulder Canyon. It was approximately 50 miles from Las Vegas.

To reach this camp, one traveled the main highway towards Salt Lake City for a few miles, then turned to the right on a road used and maintained by a large borax mine. This dirt and sometimes gravel road was followed for about two-thirds of the distance. Then for 17 miles to go to Boulder Canyon, one followed dry washes over hills and the tracks and ruts of those who had been this way before. Anyone familiar with flash floods can understand how the tracks and ruts that they had followed going into town could be washed out on the return trip. Only an experienced eye could pick out the correct way to go. The road, if one can call it that, was so narrow in places that sometimes in making a turn one had to make a complete circle, crossing their own tracks to negotiate the turn and be able to get started up the road ahead. All the supplies had to be brought from Las Vegas over this route.

When Jack arrived at camp, he found it well organized with a field office, mess hall, sleeping quarters for everyone, and the necessary equipment to take care of about 30 men. There were no buildings. Only tents were used. The investigations had been going on for several years, but because of the intense heat in the summer months the field work had only been done when it was cooler—I would say from early fall to mid-March.

My husband was given the responsibility of measuring the flow of the water in Boulder Canyon—that is, how many cubic feet of water was rushing through the canyon. This information was necessary in the planning of the dam because of the strength that would be needed to curb the flow of water. Besides taking the flow of the water, surveyors were mapping the terrain, and geologists were measuring and studying the formations of the earth structures.

Boulder Canyon was a beautiful place. The camp itself was situated probably one-fourth to one-half mile from it. At camp large willow trees lined the riverbank, and there was plenty of desert vegetation to make it attractive. Boulder Canyon Gorge was very narrow, and the hills of solid rock towered so high on either side that one could scarcely see the tops.

In March [1923], with most of the work at hand completed, the camp was broken up and the men went their separate ways to compute their findings or to other projects. Only a skeleton camp remained, with my husband and an assistant remaining to carry on their work.

After camp had broken up in March, every day Jack and his helper would walk the distance from camp to the place where they took their measurements. At this point was a heavy cable across the river. Attached to this cable was a mobile tram, and they would climb [in] with their instruments. Of course, the weight of the car made the cable sag in the middle. They would coast to this point, then by hand pull themselves up to the far side. From there they came back slowly, dropping their meters, which were attached by wires to the tram into the water below. One of the meters measured the rate of flow of the water; the other, the depth of the river. The meters would be drawn up, read, and let down a little further on. This process continued until they were back at the point from which they started with the tram. On the return trip, again when they reached the middle of the stream, it was uphill the rest of the way. They had to crank the machine pulley as well as take the readings. When reaching the place from which they had started, the tram was secured, and back to camp they went to compute and record their figures.

Jack and I were married in Las Vegas May 17, 1923. I had been teaching school in Idaho, and the snow was barely gone from the ground when I left there to find two days later a temperature of a hundred four degrees. It was in this heat we traveled to Boulder Canyon, our first home. Our camp was near the river at the mouth of a wide wash. We had an office tent, which doubled as the helper's living quarters; a kitchen–dining room tent; and our living quarters tent, which stood on a knoll near the cooking tent so that it could catch the cool breezes when and if. Later the boys put up a small tent with a steel drum rigged up over it for a shower tent. Water was pumped into the drum, and the sun warmed the water. Sometimes it would be too hot to use. Who knows—this may have been the original solar heating system. For our drinking water there were several barrels which were pumped full of water from the river. It would take a day at least for the silt to settle before we could use the water.

One might wonder how food was kept from spoiling in this climate. A cave, approximately five feet square, had been dug into the side of the hill near the mess tent and timbered up inside to keep it from collapsing. The front was walled up and was about a foot thick. There were two doors leading into it. The first one was an ordinary door. The inner one was about six inches thick, made so it was insulated so that no heat could get through it. When the groceries were brought, there was always a 300-pound cake of ice. The ice went in first, and all perishables were placed on and around it. One had to be very careful not to leave the doors ajar when entering so as little as possible heat could get through. A flashlight or lantern had to be used as there was no light in there.

I had the opportunity to go down through this big canyon in a boat that was piloted by an expert who knew the river well,[1] where the rocks and eddies were. It was an awesome sight. At the time they said I was the first woman to go through there, and that very few men had made this trip. Since then only a few expeditions were made before it was inundated by the waters of Lake Mead.

I claim the distinction of being the first white woman to have lived in this area, and I doubt that there were many after me. Now all this territory is covered by Lake Mead. We lived there until December [1923], the last few months of which my husband had no helper, so I helped with the book work and reports required for information at the office in Denver. When we left, everything was dismantled as that was the end of the investigation in Boulder Canyon.

WALKER YOUNG

We had to build new barges, build new drills, build new boats to take the crew back and forth in this river. The result of that work was that we drilled three damsites in Boulder Canyon. After we got the information from Boulder Canyon, we thought of Homer Hamlin's suggestion of a damsite about 20 miles below [in Black Canyon]. So I went with George Hammond, a man of 60 or 65 years old who was the drill foreman, and Harry Armisted, an old experienced riverman, and his dog Baldy. We three got in a boat that he [Armisted] had built. It was a small one because we knew we had a job getting back upstream. It was a 16-foot boat. George Hammond was a fellow that weighed about 200 pounds. Harry Armisted was not that heavy, but he was an oarsman. All he did was sit and row. We sized [Black] Canyon up on a preliminary basis. When we were there, we discovered a stake that was set by Homer Hamlin several years before. It looked to us that the lower canyon suggested by Homer Hamlin was the best in that site. We recorded that and started back. We almost didn't get back, because the river at that time was running fairly well with those sand waves. You remember from studying the Colorado River what sand waves are. It simply means that the velocity of the water reached the point where it picked up the sand from the bed of the river and made it roll. It would break like ocean waves. When we went down in the trough of one of those waves, we'd get full of sand.

There is some explanation of why the change was made in the location of the dam in Black Canyon rather than Boulder Canyon. As I recall, we discovered that the upper end of Boulder Canyon would be right in the vicinity of a fault. Also, because of this great big storage capacity in the Las Vegas Wash basin itself between the two sites, it turned out it was less expensive to build a dam in Black Canyon rather than Boulder Canyon. At Boulder Canyon there were no locations for a spillway. The thing that turned the tide over was the fact that one day when I was trying to find out whether we could reach the damsite from the top—we'd already reached it from the bottom— I discovered it was [possible] to actually build a railroad from the main line [in] Las Vegas to the top of the damsite. I mean right at the top. There was considerable relief on the part of the chief engineer and his crew when we found we could get the resources, millions of tons of materials, down to that damsite on a standard gauge railroad. As I've said many times, the Lord left that damsite there. It was only up to man to discover it and to use it.

Until the Bureau of Reclamation determined when it would build Hoover Dam, the Colorado River near Las Vegas was home to hard-rock miners, beaver trappers, and rivermen. One of the earliest of these river rats and the best known was Murl Emery, who had lived with his family on the river since about 1917. It was Murl Emery who ferried Walker Young and other dignitaries up and down the river throughout the 1920s.

MURL EMERY

We homesteaded on the Colorado River at Cottonwood Island. The first move was to keep the wolf from the door. We leased Jim Cashman's old ferry that was tied up on the bank on the Nevada side at Cottonwood Island. We had a boat down there, and a marina there many years later. I became the ferryman, because Dad had come to the point that the grass was greener over in Lordsburg, New Mexico. So he took off and left us on the homestead.

I was running the ferry at about 14 years old. So I developed the ability of navigating on the Colorado River. No rapids, just muddy water. It was awfully hard to find clear water to run the boat in. I became the expert at it as time went along. I had to know what I was doing, because I could get the ferry to Arizona and back to Nevada.

Another highlight in my life was when the beaver trappers came down the river. What they would do—about Christmastime each year they would wind up in St. Thomas, Nevada. They would come in there, make a deal with somebody to load up their gear, and go by wagon down the Virgin River to Rioville. Part of their load, outside of the necessary bacon and beans, their lard and whatnot—the load consisted of two-by-fours, one-by-twelves, a bucket of tar, and a handful of nails. They'd just build themselves a little flatbottom boat and make a pair of oars. And that's what they used coming down the river.

I would get word that they were trapping up on a foot trail, or one of these places between Black Canyon and Cottonwood. Once they came down into this area, I had to come home and run the ferry because the beaver trappers were my heroes. They were the world's best. I learned to trap from them. Of course, the most important thing on my mind was food. I would go camp with them, and they would feed me. They would eat—serve beaver, of course. You have to develop a like for that because the like isn't built in.

The reason they came down here was the fact that the Colorado River had the finest beaver in the United States or Canada. Big beaver, minimum dark hairs, so that made it choice. Our beaver pelts was shipped to St. Louis at that time. It was superfine, and I'd get as much as $40 a blanket. As long as we had the beaver, I had no more hard times, because they were good money.

7

The most important thing that I learned from this ferry operation was the fact that the Volstead Act was in effect at that time. That meant one thing: whiskey was the deal. These bootleggers would come out of Nevada down to the ferry, pretty well out in the open, hollering it out, "Anybody on the other side?" Then, of course, we'd tell them no. If there was anybody on the other side, they were certainly under cover. So you'd haul a man across with his load of whiskey. These big old automobiles. The Stanley was one of the favorite ones, one of the big cars built before 1920. The reason that they were hauling whiskey to Arizona was the fact that Sam Gay was our sheriff in Clark County [Nevada], and Sam was quite a guy. Every time the federals would come, Sam would send the word out: "Head for cover." So that made him real popular, and also that depressed the cost of whiskey. Whiskey was $4 a gallon in Clark County. In Mohave County there was a sheriff by the name of Bill Mahoney, and he would give you a hard talking-to. He said, "As long as the law is on the books, I'm going to enforce it." And he knew how, because whiskey in Mohave County was $60. You can well see why the bootleggers were hauling all their whiskey out of Nevada to Arizona.

Anyway, I'm living down there at [the] old Cottonwood ranch, and word came that Al Jorgenson, the drive operator from Chloride,[2] was looking for me. That word had to just pass over the country because nobody knew where I was. So I went over to Chloride, and he said, "Kid, we're going to build a boat to go up the river." That was OK by me. So we started to work building this boat. He wouldn't tell me much beyond that. He wanted me because I had developed the ability to navigate the Colorado River. I could look out on that river and tell you within two inches the depth of the water. I had developed that through living on the river, from the ferry.

I was to be the skipper. So we built this little boat—30 feet long, 6 feet wide. The only thing we had to go by was the old rule of thumb that a boat on the Colorado River must be six times as long as it is wide. That was the most ridiculous thing that ever come up. But that was it. That was how you'd do it. It was made out of one-by-twelves and two-by-fours, just like the trappers'. Thirty feet long, 5 feet wide, tunnel stern. Up to the building of the dam, all our boats were tunnel stern. That was a tunnel-like arrangement at the stern of the boat, usually a third as long as the boat. A propeller was run into this opening so you could navigate. We hauled it down to Cottonwood, down below the ferry line.

I left there and went on up and got up to Boulder Canyon. I got over the roaring rapids, pushed my way over that. We got over Rainbow Rapids. I got over the reverse rapids. I had to get out and pull a little, push and pull a little to get over it. So we got up there. Walker Young and his diamond-drill crew were set up there on the riverbank, in a miserable government camp designed to be in the spot where 95 percent of the blowing sand was—typical

Federal and State representatives at meeting of Colorado River Compact Commission. Santε Fe, New Mexico, 24 November 1922. *Left to right*: W. S. Norviel, Commissioner for Arizona; Arthur P. Davis, Director, Reclamation Service; Ottamar Hamels, Chief Counsel, Reclamation Service; Herbert Hoover, Secretary of Commerce and Chairman of Commission; Clarence C. Stetson, Executive Secretary of Commission; L. Ward Bannieter, Attorney, of Colorado; Richard E. Sloan, Attorney, of Arizona; Edward Clark, Commissioner for Nevada; C. P. Scuires, Commissioner for Nevada; James R. Scrugham, Commissioner for Nevada; William F. Mills, former Mayor of Denver; R. E. Caldwell, Commissioner for Utah; W. F. McClure, Commissioner for California; F. F. McKisick, Deputy Attorney General of California; Delph E. Carpenter, Commissioner for Colorado; R. J. Meeker, Assistant State Engineer of Colorado; Stephen B. Davis, Jr., Commissioner for New Mexico; J. S. Nickerson, President, Imperial Irrigation District of California; Frank C. Emerson, Commissioner for Wyoming; Charles May, State Engineer of New Mexico; Merritt C. Mechem, Governor of New Mexico; T. C. Yeager, Attorney for Coachella Valley Irrigation District of California government setup. Walker Young sees this old boat out in front there. He was flabbergasted that a boat could get up the river.

Flabbergasted and impressed. In the years that followed, while Congress debated the Boulder Canyon Project Act, Walker Young often called on Emery and his family to carry senators, members of Congress, and other influential visitors up and down the river.

MURL EMERY

They had to sell all the congressmen, all the senators that they could. We were real busy at that time, because we were hauling governors and senators and congressmen till they were running out of our ears. My job in my little boat was to leave my camp in the middle of the lake and go up to Boulder Canyon and pick up these various dignitaries and bring them down to Black Canyon and show them the Black Canyon site. We went up there to pick up Carl Hayden, who was a very influential congressman and later senator from the state of Arizona. I was called to go and pick up General [William Luther] Sibert.[3] I waited for days for General [George Washington] Goethals[4] to come to show him the damsite and the area. When he finally did show up, he showed up with a great big basket of food, and big white clean tablecloths, et cetera and so forth. He went outside and laid out his big white tablecloth, brought out his food. All that beautiful food, and he never offered me one stinking bite of it. He kept eating. He would have seen the hungriest ground squirrel in the world if he had just looked up. I didn't like that. He probably didn't like me either, so we broke even on that one. [Herbert Hoover] was no bother and easy to handle. By the same token, he was not the kind of a guy you could start up a conversation with.

Despite the official interest in the Colorado River damsites, the area was still sparsely populated. Las Vegas was a small town, and scattered through the surrounding desert were even smaller communities, including St. Thomas, which would later be submerged beneath Lake Mead. Elbert Edwards, a lifelong resident, remembers what the area was like before the dam.

10

ELBERT EDWARDS

Activity was restricted and limited pretty much to railroading. In some of the outlying communities, there was mining. There was mining being carried on in Goodsprings, and in Searchlight down in El Dorado Canyon. There was farming carried on in the northern part of the county in the Virgin Valley and the Moapa Valley. Moapa at that time, however, was primarily a little railroad station, more devoted to railroading than to agriculture. St. Thomas was quite typical of the small Mormon communities. The town was laid out in blocks, with broad streets, tree-lined, given very much to agriculture, farming on a small scale.

There was also some mining activity going on in hills over in the Arizona Strip—the Grand Gulch Mines, producing copper. The ore was freighted down across the bridge and river into St. Thomas, from where it was loaded on the railroad and shipped out for reduction.

I remember Las Vegas as having one paved street, and everything else was dust. The street that was paved was Fremont. It was paved out possibly to about Fifth Street, and from there on out it was gravel. The business section, of course, pretty well lined Fremont Street from the railroad depot on Main Street east to about Fifth Street. Beyond Fifth Street there was very little. Out on Tenth Street there was a little resort operated by a man by the name of Ladd. He had sunk a well out there and got a good flow of water and had installed a swimming pool that was quite popular with the people of the community at that time.

Dean Pulsipher, a southern Nevada native born in the farming community of Bunkerville in the Moapa Valley, often came to Las Vegas in the days before the Boulder Canyon Project. He later made a trip into the future damsite before construction began.

DEAN PULSIPHER

I used to come to Vegas with my father when I was 8, 10 years old. We used to bring down a wagonload of chickens through the winter months. We'd bring two or three hundred head of chickens. We'd bring them to Las Vegas, and we'd park in one spot. We'd park on Fremont Street. I remember Fremont Street. There was nothing on Fremont Street—all dirt. Not a paved road anywhere.

11

There was only about twenty-five hundred to three thousand people in Las Vegas at that time. We'd park on Fremont Street and we'd sell those chickens—big Rhode Island Reds and Plymouth chickens. We'd sell them for a dollar apiece, three hundred at a time. Some of the people would come in there and take two or three chickens, and they'd tell their neighbors, and we'd sit in that one spot and sell them all. We'd never have to move. People would come to us to get the chickens.

When I came to Las Vegas in 1927, I had to leave the valley over there before I finished high school because my father had gotten sick and we were in debt. He owed taxes. He owed stores, one in Mesquite, one in Bunkerville. I had to come to Las Vegas to go to work so I could pay off his debts and keep my dad and mother. I was just a kid, a teenager out of school.

I started to work for the Clark County Road Department. I was just a helper then. I was a laborer. I worked for $4 a day, and they paid every 30 days, once a month. That's where I got the experience of driving a truck and running Cats [Caterpillars]. Later on I had the experience of going into the repair shop, overhauling trucks and cars. I was maintaining this road from Las Vegas all the way out to Searchlight. We had a big Cat. There was three of us. We had a big ol' Cat, a hand-controlled blade. We didn't have hydraulic lifts then. We had to crank to lower and raise the blade, trim the wheels. And we had a cookshack, a four-wheeled (made out of hard rubber tires) cookshack. We stayed in that, camped and slept in that, ate in that. If you see *The Grapes of Wrath*, that would be it. Here we had the cookshack, the Cat, the blade; then we had about a 1923 or '24 Dodge touring car we had to take along in case of emergency so we could get to town.

We started in the spring of 1929 to build a road from Railroad Pass down to the [Colorado] river. There was just a cow trail going down there. Two tracks for one car. If you'd meet a car, you'd have to pull off the road and let the other car by. That's all it was, from Railroad Pass to the river. We followed that old road all the way down to the river. Using the Cat and the blade, we made it wide enough so that two cars could come along to pass each other without one having to pull out of the tracks. All I was doing was throwing rocks off the road. I was just a flunky.

The only person who was living in that area at the time was Murl Emery, down at the river. Murl came along about twice a week to go to town to get groceries and gas. He'd stop and talk to us. He told us one day—we had to work six days a week; then we had Sundays off—he said, "If you guys will come down, I'll take you down in a boat to where the dam is going to be built." These other two guys wouldn't go. I said, "I'll come down. I'd like to come down and see what there is down there." So on a Sunday morning, I got myself in the car and went down. At that time he had one tent, and he had a canvas over some mesquite brush there. If I remember, he had two boats, about 14-foot boats. He had a Star or a Durant motor in them, I don't remember which one it was—all wooden boats. We got in that boat, and we started down the river. We were chugging along, maybe 10, 15 miles an hour. We got down below where the lower portal tunnels are now. We turned around to come back, and he said, "Would you like to drive this thing?" I said, "Sure." I had never been in a boat before in my life.

So we started up there through the canyon. Right across from where his boat dock was [above] Black Canyon, the river [passed through] what they call the east-west bend. It went [by] the Vegas Wash and [hit] this big black ridge over there. When it'd hit that big black ridge, there's a whirlpool going in there. It was spring, and it looked like you could walk across that river. The river at that time was only about half-covered with water. The rest of it was sandbars.

I started back, and away from the whirlpool. He said, "Keep moving, keep moving. Don't get out in that sandbar and get us stuck." We got out in the middle of that big whirlpool, and we stopped there. We didn't move. I looked around at Murl, and he's sitting there with a big grin on his face. I said, "You better come and take ahold of this and get us out of here." All he did was come up and pull the throttle on that thing and took us right out and we went back over to his boat dock. I can remember that as if it was yesterday.

It was incomprehensible how they could possibly build a dam in there. It was beyond my means to see how they could even start to build a dam in there. That canyon was full of water—there were no sandbars down there. I thought that's an impossible task that they'll ever accomplish that.

Arriving in Las Vegas in 1905, Charles P. "Pop" Squires was a major booster of the Boulder Canyon Project. Publisher of the Las Vegas Age, *Squires spent more than 20 years pushing for a dam on the Colorado River. Squires's daughter, Florence Boyer, remembers her father's effort.*

FLORENCE BOYER

My father was an early, untiring advocate of the building of the Boulder Dam, and I am sure no single person devoted more time and effort towards that project—both through his newspaper and personally—than did Charles P. Squires.

Beginning in 1920, when he was appointed [Nevada] Governor Boyle's representative to the meeting of the League of the Southwest, until the final ratification of the bill for the construction of the dam, he worked unceasingly for the project. He spent a great deal of his own time and money in working for the final passage of the bill but felt that it was well spent, since it seemed to ensure a prosperous future for his beloved Las Vegas, which he had helped to create.

My father went to the meeting as a representative of Governor Boyle and took with him as delegates Roy W. Martin, Jim Cashman, and E. W. Griffith.[5] They spent five or six days drawing up resolutions. My father prepared most of the resolutions which were accepted. Then they decided to have another meeting in Denver in April, with the governors of the seven Colorado Basin states present.

Father attended that meeting too. There they called him "Governor Squires," because he was the representative of the governor of Nevada.[6] He served on the Committee on Resolutions. He attended most of the subsequent meetings and wrote several accounts of the activities of the commission.

He described all of the maneuvering of the various groups in his memoirs. I don't know whether he told this in his account: it was my father who insisted that in the distribution of water Nevada be allowed 300,000 acrefeet. Nobody at that time thought we'd have much use for it, but he insisted that it be put into the compact. He spent most of 1928 in Washington, lobbying for the passage of the Boulder Canyon Project bill.

CHARLES SQUIRES

In the long fight for the passage of the Boulder Canyon Project Act, certain characters are worthy of special mention. For Nevada [Senators] Tasker L. Oddie, Key Pittman, and Congressman Sam Arentz were particularly active. In California the people of the Imperial Valley particularly were enlisted in the cause, as well as the Los Angeles Bureau of Water and Power. In this bureau there were several men without whose aid this work could not have been accomplished. Among those were W. B. Mathews, attorney for the Los Angeles Bureau of Water and Power, and William Mulholland, the distinguished engineer who built the great aqueduct from Owens Valley to Los Angeles.

During all those years Senator Hiram Johnson, Senator Black, and Congressman Phil Swing were the Californians active in the fight for the Colorado Project. Swing represented the Imperial Valley, which was so threatened with destruction by the floodwaters of the Colorado. That accounts for the fact that the bill providing for the building of a dam in the Colorado River was long known as the Swing-Johnson Act, having been introduced by Congressman Swing in the lower house and by Hiram Johnson in the upper house of Congress.

At the start of the campaign for the project, it was feared that it would become a partisan issue and thereby lose much of its strength. At that time

Calvin Coolidge was president, Herbert Hoover secretary of commerce, and both houses of Congress were Republican. Key Pittman, a Democrat, came out boldly for the project. After that there was no question of partisanship. The truth is that at times I, as a Republican, was a little bit jealous of the very active part that some Democrats were playing in the promotion of our pet project.

One morning in Washington, through the efforts of Senator Oddie, I was given an interview with President Calvin Coolidge. He was very pleasant and polite and allowed me to tell the whole story of the needs of the Imperial Valley and the California cities and of the benefits that the vast amount of electrical power created would bring to the whole Southwest. Up to that date the president had given out no public word as to whether or not he favored the project, and when I finished my discussion, I was sure that I had him completely convinced. I said, "Now, Mr. President, isn't that a wonderful project?" expecting him to say, "Why, yes, it is a wonderful project, and I favor it." But instead he said, "Yes, Mr. Squires, that is a very great project." I could get no word from him as to whether he would approve the bill or not. I felt for a time that we weren't very sure of the support of the Republican administration, although Mr. Hoover assured me in confidence that the president really was very much in favor of our bill.

In December 1928 Congress at last passed the Boulder Canyon Project Act. President Calvin Coolidge signed the bill on 21 December, triggering a wild celebration in Las Vegas.

ELBERT EDWARDS

Las Vegas had been looking forward to that for a long time. The business community recognized that as holding the potential for the future of Las Vegas. They had followed it. Pop Squires particularly—he was editor of the *Las Vegas Age* at that time—was one of the enthusiasts. For that matter, all of the business people, the chamber of commerce people, were pushing it, and doing all that they could giving support to the California interests, who were primarily pushing it because of their need for water control, for flood control, and for power production, and, of course, also for their need for water for industry and culinary purposes.

So the people of Las Vegas, recognizing that the future of the community rested on new industry coming in, were very enthusiastic for it, and when that bill was signed, they just broke loose with everything they had in celebrating. The volunteer fire department turned out in full force, leading the parade. Bootleg liquor just flowed like water.

LEON ROCKWELL

When the bill was passed, that's when the excitement was. Nobody thought that it might happen, now or maybe 50 years from now. When the bill was signed, we got the fire truck out, and—my God, everybody that could hooked onto it! In carts and baby buggies and everything else—just like they was nuts. There was people that got lit that never had taken a drink before.

CHARLES SQUIRES

Somebody hit upon the clever idea of having a meeting on the banks of the river as a thanksgiving for the passage of the bill. Perhaps 100 people made the hard drive from Las Vegas over the sandy, unimproved roads and knelt in the sand on the banks of the river while a prayer of thanksgiving was offered.

FLORENCE BOYER

This plan was broached by a fellow who was working on the *The Age* for us at that time and who was quite a publicity stunt operator. I was always a little ashamed of it, because it was purely publicity—they had cameras there and everything. I had this feeling about having the paper back of the thing. It was one of those things that newspapermen do.

DEAN PULSIPHER

Everybody in Las Vegas was out celebrating until the wee hours of the morning, and I was one of them. I was out there celebrating until I had to go to work. That was the making of Las Vegas. That made the West here. That made the whole western part of the United States, including Las Vegas.

I remember you'd go down the street, and there were so many newcomers. You'd see there's a newcomer, there's a newcomer. People started coming in then.

People began drifting into Las Vegas soon after passage of the Boulder Canyon Project Act. One of these was Elton Garrett, who was eager to seize the opportunity offered by the Hoover Dam project. As a newspaper reporter, he closely followed early preparations by government officials and Las Vegas merchants and entrepreneurs.

ELTON GARRETT

I landed as a hitchhiker on January 15, 1929, having traveled a gravel-dirt road from southern California to Las Vegas. I wanted to get into a newspaper spot where I could hit the typewriter and make it last. I knew I was going to have to make the job, and I knew I could do it.

At first I got with Pop Squires and his newspaper office on Fremont Street with my Graflex. I told him I had been a copyreader on the Seattle *P.I.* [*Post Intelligencer*] after getting my degree at the University of Washington. Pop Squires and his editor helped me into the presence of one big shot of Las Vegas after another. I took a picture of these fellows. This got me acquainted a bit, and within two weeks I had a part-time job on Pop Squires's *Las Vegas Age*. The photography faded into the background. I was writing news and handling advertising to some extent.

Walker R. Young was the [Boulder Canyon Project] construction engineer. He came and had an office on the third floor of the Beckley Building in Las Vegas before they got the building built out here [Boulder City] where his office would be housed. Raymond Walter;[7] members of the Six Companies, Incorporated: Frank Crowe,[8] Charlie Shea,[9] the Bechtels,[10] any and all of the members of the board of directors of the Six Companies. These fellows came to Las Vegas, and as soon as [Boulder City] was being built here, they came here. Charlie Shea with his floppy hat. We got acquainted with each of these fellows as they came in.

The chamber of commerce in Las Vegas was actively promoting, as you would expect them to do, whatever would heighten the adequate facilities to take care of people who would be streaming in. They knew people would stream in as workers, as tourists, as journalists from afar who wanted to get in on the act.

17

Indeed, a tourist industry was already developing in Las Vegas and along the Colorado River in anticipation of dam construction. Ray Cutright came to southern Nevada in 1930 and took a job running tourist boats on the river.

RAY CUTRIGHT

Mr. [Glenn] Davis[11] and I arrived in Las Vegas, Nevada [on] August 1, 1930, from Chicago for the express purpose of building Boulder Dam—which I actually never worked on. Not even one day. Shortly after arriving in Las Vegas, I got a job operating [tourist] boats on the Colorado River. The boat was owned by Mr. [O. B.] Ayers. Our principal job was to carry passengers down to the damsite and bring them back safely to the landing dock.

The boats we operated were homemade, flat-bottomed boats with a tunnel built in the bottom contoured to curve the water [as it went through], which would keep the propellers and the rudder above the bottom of the boat so they didn't hit rocks and things to damage them. These boats were powered by automobile engines. The one I operated had two Studebaker engines in it. In navigating the river you only navigated by what you could see on the surface, because you could not see through the water at all. And you operated only by the currents to guide your boat back and forth.

We'd take the people down to where the dam was going to be built in Black Canyon, swing the boat around in the middle of the river, and try to explain to the people as much as we could the nature of what was going to happen.

On the Nevada side of the river, high above where the top of the dam was going to be, was a white flag. Twelve hundred, fifteen hundred feet above the river, something like that. A lot of people were from Chicago, so we'd tell them that they could take and put the Wrigley Building on top of the Palmolive Building and still not reach where that flag was at. Of course, they couldn't quite believe this. Also on the boat we'd carry a few rocks. We'd offer to take all the people back to the dock and give them their money back if anyone could throw a rock to either shore from where the boat was at that time, in the middle of the river. Somebody would always try it and give a big heave with the rock, and [it] would land about 50 feet off the boat. So they'd take another rock and heave again, with the same results. After this you had no problem telling them that at that point the river was some 600 or 700 feet wide. And in my estimation it takes a pretty good person to throw a rock 300 feet—it's just almost impossible.

So then we continued to talk to them about how big the dam was going

News reporter Elton Garrett, about 1930

Murl Emery, about 1930

to be. At that time we were informed that Boulder Dam would contain more concrete and more steel than all the other 55 dams the government had at that time. We told the people it would take a train at least 135 miles long to haul the cement that would be used in construction of the dam. We said these things to impress on their minds the size of the project that was going to be undertaken. Then we'd start back upstream after cautioning the people to sit still in the boat, kind of balance it out so it was sitting flat—because if you get too much weight on one side, that side would act as a keel and you'd have no more control over it.

Every trip on the river was an experience all its own, because you never went to exactly the same place two times in succession. One time I went down the river and started back up with my load of passengers and a sandbar had formed clear across the river. It took me three tries to get over that sandbar.

When they started to work on the dam, the tourist trips were discontinued and no one was allowed down in there except the workers on the dam.

Like Murl Emery, Cutright also took government bureaucrats up and down the river, maneuvering through some treacherous reaches.

RAY CUTRIGHT

I took some engineers up the river one day to Boulder Canyon, which is about 20 miles up above [Black Canyon]. On the way up there, 'long about Fort Callville,[12] the river widened out in a real rocky sort of place, and it was quite hard to get a boat through there without doing some kind of damage. But we made it by taking it easy and going just almost rock to rock. And then not too far above that, there was a huge rock ledge which run clear across the river from one side to the other, and there was no way around that rock ledge. The water run over that rock ledge just as it goes over a spillway on a dam. You'd head the boat right into the ledge and just about the time the bow of the boat would touch that rock, you gunned the throttle real hard and the boat would almost leap up on top of that [ledge] up there into nice calm water, just as beautiful as it could be, nice, deep, cool water. Now, that was quite a thrill, to go up over that rock ledge. And it was just as much of a thrill to come back down, because you had to go over it; there was no place to stop and look around. You headed for that rock ledge and down you went. Just below that you'd run into the rocks where the river spread out.

Now, those rocks only showed up like that in the wintertime when it was

Silver Spike Ceremony on the Boulder City branch of the Union Pacific Railroad at Boulder Junction, 17 September 1930

frozen up in Colorado, when the river would be flowing about, oh, 5,000 cubic feet a second, something like that. But in the springtime when the floods came, the river would go up to as high as 200,000 [cubic] feet of water a second or more. And at that time you had no rocks to contend with. You'd have trees and trash and rubbish and stuff but no rocks. They were all covered up. All you had to contend with was strong, riley water.

On 17 September 1930 Secretary of the Interior Ray Lyman Wilbur officiated at the Silver Spike Ceremony near Las Vegas, an occasion that marked the start of construction of the Union Pacific Railroad branch line from Las Vegas to the Black Canyon damsite. Wilbur named the dam for Herbert Hoover at this ceremony, sparking controversy over the dam's name that persists today. Reporter Elton Garrett was there.

ELTON GARRETT

There was a circle of newsmen with cameras taking a picture of the secretary of the interior when he got off the Union Pacific train on the main line of the Union Pacific at Boulder Junction. Big crowd. They were all equipped—the circle of news photographers holding back the rest of the crowd. When the secretary was ready to drive the silver spike, circled around behind him were senators and congressmen and publishers. They're in the pictures. I remember shooting pictures of the secretary. He missed his first blow at the spike—missed it completely. He was not a spike driver; he was an administrator in a college.[13] That made a difference, didn't it? Ray Lyman Wilbur took another swipe at it, and he landed it and drove in the silver spike.

He surprised everybody there with the announcement "This is going to be named Hoover Dam." The Boulder Canyon Project Act had used the name of Boulder because they had expected to build the dam at Boulder Canyon. While it was changed to Black Canyon, it was still Boulder Dam in the headlines. But the argument, as you know, went on. People who wanted it to be Hoover Dam were happy. People in another political party who resented it backed Secretary [Harold] Ickes later in changing back to Boulder Dam. Then there came the day that Harry Truman's administration saw Congress switch it back to Hoover Dam, officially. I did like the old name, Boulder Dam, but I now write it "Hoover Dam" because that's official and that's correct.[14]

2

SETTLEMENTS: BLACK CANYON AND VICINITY, 1929–1931

"It was so terrible hot."

The stock market crash of October 1929 and the depression that followed put millions out of work. Throughout 1930, as factories, mines, and offices closed, fearful Americans looked to the federal government for relief. Although construction of the branch-line railroad to the Black Canyon damsite commenced in September 1930, the government was in no rush at this early stage to begin construction of the dam itself. But as word spread across the country that Hoover Dam was one of the few places work might be found, people began drifting into southern Nevada. By 1931 thousands of desperate families crowded into Las Vegas hoping to find jobs at Black Canyon.

LEO DUNBAR

You've got to realize that when people found out that the project was going to be built, they flocked in here from all parts of the United States. This was the Great Depression, the period of 1928 to 1932 or '33. The fact that there was going to be work here induced people to come in here—not only the men, but their families came with them. They just picked up whatever they had and loaded it into a truck and drove here, and had hopes of getting a job. There had been thousands of people that had moved in here. They had moved down on the river; they had moved into where Boulder City was supposed to be. I imagine a thousand people had camped just on the other side of what is now Railroad Pass, on the flats there.

New arrival in Boulder City, about 1931

JOE KINE

The thirteenth day of July 1931 is when I arrived here. I was baching it in a little one-room place in Joplin, Missouri, before I came. Before that I worked in the mines in Oklahoma. The mines closed down, and I was out of a job. I picked strawberries to make a little money. I tried selling Real Silk Hosiery [a popular brand in the 1920s] and a few things like that. But I heard about this going on out here, so I bought a Model T Ford for $10 and drove it out. Finally I sold my Model T Ford after I got here, for $2.50. I wish I had it back now. I could get in parades, and all that.

Everything was really a-buzzin'. When night came, people was sleeping just anywhere they could find. I parked my little old Model T Ford along the highway, and I was going to fix myself something to eat and maybe put down my blankets and sleep there when a man called Pistol Pete come a-dashing down there and run me off. So I moved over across where the highway's at, over into the desert there. Nobody bothered me over there.

BOB PARKER

In early '31 doctors told my folks that my sister, who had had pneumonia two winters running, had a spot on one lung the size of a dollar. We'd have to take her to a warmer climate. So we set out in a Model T Ford from Grand Junction—two brothers, two sisters, and my dad and mother in a two–door Ford with all our belongings. It took three days to get down there on the roads and the snow. When we got to Las Vegas, we went to visit with John Page.[1] He suggested that Las Vegas weather in southern Nevada was as good as Arizona weather. This was a hot climate, and if we were satisfied that it would help my sister with her lung problem and asthma, we could stay here and he'd see what he could do about getting me a job. If we were going to have to go to work somewhere, we might just see if we could get on down here at Hoover Dam.

MARY EATON

We came from Kansas. We were victims of the depression, as were many others. [My husband] was a pipeline inspector for these big gas lines that they built from Chicago to Texas. They quit doing the pipelines, and we didn't realize—we thought this might be something that happened, and it would be back to work in two or three weeks. But it went on and on and on, and in fact they never did resume the gas lines for many, many years. My husband found out that they were going to build Hoover Dam—Boulder Dam. This was the only place we knew that there was any work.

LEROY BURT

In 1929, at the start of the depression, I was working in a little hamburger joint in Salt Lake City called Snappy Service Lunch. These hamburgers sold for a nickel each. That's what I was doing in 1929. In October of 1929 I was married. I was 19 years old. In 1929 I was transferred to manage one of these little hamburger places in Long Beach, California. Of course, my first baby came along, so we came back to Salt Lake City in early '31. I came on down here because my father had the contract to plaster the first 12 government houses on Denver Street.

TOMMY NELSON

What I was doing prior to that time—I'm a musician, a trumpet player. Things were pretty rough back in that era—people couldn't afford to dance. So things were really tough. I was jumping around the country with some bands. We played a lot of jobs on what they call percentage: 60 percent for the band, 40 percent for the house. A lot of these were one-night stands. A lot of times we just didn't make it. I went into marriage rather early in life, age 19. I was having it doggone rough, believe me. I had a guarantee after I got married, supposedly, at $25 a week to go into Grand Junction, Colorado, and play with a band. Now, this was a jitney dance, 10¢ a dance. I was having a little trouble collecting my wages, and things was getting a little rough. My father was down in this area, so he told me, "If you come on down, I can get you a job." So I did.

WILFRED VOSS

It was very interesting to be down there. You found men that were managers of concerns, presidents of banks. They were down there working so they wouldn't go on relief, just like this fellow right here. I wasn't about to go on relief.

HARRY HALL

I came here from Kaw City, Oklahoma. They were tearing down some 55,000-gallon oil storage tanks there, and that was the end of the job. When we finished that job, we had a new Chevrolet sedan, and we decided to come out here. It was quite well known that this was the only place you could get a job. Jobs were very hard to come by, so we decided to come out here and try our luck.

JOHN GIECK

I was roughnecking down in Long Beach and Culver City. If you got $3 a day, you were lucky—if you worked at all. I heard about them building Boulder Dam, so I thought I'd give it a try. I had a '29 Model A Ford, and I borrowed $80 on it to come up here. I owed about $80 worth of meal tickets down there and about $130 worth of room.

They didn't have an employment [office] yet. You just went out on the job and hustled the foreman. I followed one foreman around named Chilson, and he sent me down to the dam three times. Every time I went down there, it was so hot guys'd be passing out and I'd get scared and come back. I finally followed Charlie Williams around five or six days—he was the carpentry boss. He finally gave me a job—told me to go out there and report to Cecil Lotspich, building houses. He told me, "Now, we have a schedule here. If you keep up with the schedule, you'll have a job tomorrow. If you don't, you won't." For the first two weeks, I got 50¢ an hour.

> *Thomas Cave Wilson, a reporter from northern Nevada, came to Las Vegas to work for Charles P. Squires's* Las Vegas Age. *He remembers the arduous trip he took from Reno to Las Vegas in the summer of 1931— and what he saw when he arrived.*

THOMAS WILSON

[It was] 1931 when I went to Las Vegas. I got on a Pullman car which was standing on a siding in downtown Reno by the express company. Had a Pullman porter—berths were made up. Went to bed. Just a car by itself—a Pullman. Sometime during the night they hooked it on a train. And when I woke up, we were not far from Luning. And at Luning—that was as far as the Pullman went—we changed to a dirty baggage car with seats in part of it, and not as good as a bus.

And we rode into Tonopah in that. At Tonopah we had breakfast. There was a stage where I bought my tickets. The stage was a big black limousine and, I think, carried nine passengers. I remember they put a five-gallon thermos jug on the stage, with ice water. And I thought that was very considerate. It was August and hot. But we never got any of that water. That was for the radiator.

It took us all day to get to Vegas. We got to Las Vegas in late afternoon—maybe 4:30—and came down the street, and I was sitting behind the driver. And I asked, "Is there going to be a parade or something?"

He said, "Why do you ask?"

I said, "Well, the streets are just black with people standing on the sidewalk—all these crowds."

He said, "Oh, those are men waiting for jobs on the dam." And they were!

BRUCE EATON

I can recall where the Union Plaza [Hotel] is now was the old Union Pacific depot, and there was quite a park out in front of it. And in this park and the park around the old courthouse was where most of the unemployed spent most of their time.

When these people arrived in southern Nevada, they found a construction project barely under way in one of the hottest and most inhospitable deserts in the world. Caught unprepared by the depth of the depression, neither Las Vegas nor the federal government was yet able to employ, house, or feed these hungry thousands. The social and economic impact on Las Vegas was tremendous. John Cahlan, who came to work in 1929 for his brother Al Cahlan, publisher of the Las Vegas Evening Review-Journal, *remembers the flood of refugees.*

JOHN CAHLAN

If you haven't lived through it, you can't imagine what would happen to a little railroad community of 5,000 people having about a good 10,000 to

20,000 people dumped on it all at one time. There wasn't any money available! You had to provide schools for the kids. You had one high school and one grammar school. You had to provide facilities for the community. The water company couldn't supply water, because their charter wouldn't allow them to provide any for any places outside of the original townsite. Believe me, it was terrible! They just didn't know what to do. I mean, nobody knew what to do, because they were here, and some of them could get jobs on the dam, and some of them couldn't. You had problems—people problems. We just did the best we could.

The Red Cross and Salvation Army were very active here. They did very good work. They would supply clothes and meals—the usual things that the Red Cross did. The Salvation Army established a—I don't know what they call them, but there was a captain or someone who was the head of the organization, and they helped out.

Usually the people who were on the road with their families went to the welfare department. If they had families and had someplace to go, I would send them over to the welfare department. Mrs. Fleming, who was the head of the welfare department here for the county, would give them enough money to get gas and food to get someplace else. But very little cash was distributed, because they were afraid that if the cash was distributed, it would be placed in the wrong hands. They'd go spend their money someplace where they shouldn't. If any of the Mormons were in trouble, they could go over to the bishop's place and get food. Other churches would provide food, clothing.

Bruce Eaton came to Las Vegas looking for work. He recalls the lengths to which local authorities went trying to find money for city and county coffers.

BRUCE EATON

They were in such need of finances that they were picking up money anyplace they could get it legally. We had not been in Las Vegas two hours. We were in the park by the old courthouse under the shade of the big cottonwood trees that used to be there—it was the coolest place in town—trying to get cool. Middle of June. And we were approached by two police officers. They wanted to know where we were from, how long we intended to stay, what we came for. We told them we were looking for work. We were advised that

10 days after we started to work, we would be expected to have a Nevada tag on our automobile. We were permitted that much grace.

At that time we paid a poll tax, and [for] everyone that went to work here the county negotiated with the contractor to withhold the first $4 you earned on the project to go for poll taxes. And that continued until it was outlawed.

John Cahlan also remembers the great increase in crime Las Vegas suffered when its population boomed.

JOHN CAHLAN

When I first came to Las Vegas, I came down with the first chief of police. Prior to that time they had two constables—a daytime constable and a nighttime constable. We didn't have anything but a volunteer fire department. We had a police force that had three members on it before the dam started. But they never had any problems, because there wasn't too much crime then or too much disorder.

There was very little crime in Las Vegas, mainly because of the fact that if you committed a crime, there was no way to get out of here. Between here and Reno you had Beatty, and between here and Kingman you had Needles, and between here and Los Angeles you had the agricultural stations. You couldn't go out in the desert and escape, because if you did, you never came back.

By the time that the dam started and the influx started, we had a police force of maybe 15 to 20 men. It was expanding all the time. We had an awful problem with the vagrants who came in here from other parts of the country and expected to get jobs right away. They couldn't get jobs right away. They had no money, and we had to get them out of here. Some of these people would get hungry, and they'd go break into some houses so they could get money, or steal stuff from a grocery store.

They had a holding tank in the city jail, which was on Second Street in the vicinity of where Benny Binion's Horseshoe Club is now. They had one room that was 15 by 40 maybe—no facilities. It was called the Blue Room. It had no plumbing fixtures at all. It had a floor that slanted into a big cesspool, and they'd wash it out maybe every two or three days. Anybody who was incarcerated more than a day or two never wanted to see it again. It was compared by some of the people to the Black Hole of Calcutta. They'd just throw them in there and keep them overnight and then give them a floater the next day—get them out of town if you could. Anytime you would sentence them to the Blue Room, you were a cinch not to see them again for at least five years, because the stench in that place was just absolutely terrible! It was made to accommodate maybe 10 or 12 people. On some weekends they'd have as many as 150 in there, and they would be from wall to wall, some of them sleeping on top of the others. It was very, very bad. As I say, the people of the community weren't accustomed to handling these sorts of things, and the only way to do it was to get them as far away out of town as possible. Let somebody else take care of them.

The merchants put money together and hired people to watch their stores at night. You see, there again the community had no money to do these things, didn't have enough money for a patrol at night. The merchants would confer very much with all the members of the city commission. I mean, Las Vegas still was a small town, and everybody knew everybody else. Whenever the merchants wanted to complain, they'd go over to the city commission and complain, and the city commission would either grant it or tell them they couldn't do it. That was the reason the "merchant police" was formed, because the city just couldn't afford it.

I was very close to the city commission, and the city commissioners appointed the city judge. They decided that they needed an alternate judge to preside when Judge Frank McNamee was away. He used to make trips over to Europe and be away for a month or two. So they appointed me as an alternate judge: I would serve when he was out of town. The police department was very happy that I was appointed as the judge. The hobo jungles were over in back of what now is the Union Plaza Hotel, and there used to be many, many vagrants who lived over there. When I was presiding on the bench, the police would go and round up the vagrants over there in the jungles, arrest them and bring them in, keep them overnight and bring them in to see me the next morning. So they were very familiar with their surroundings in the Blue Room. I would ask them whether they pleaded guilty or not guilty—no visible means of support. If they pleaded guilty, I would say, "All right now. I'll give you a suspended sentence of 10 days in the Blue Room. If you're out of town by sunrise, everything will be all right. I won't be able to do anything to you." If they pleaded not guilty, I wouldn't give them a chance to get out of town. They'd have to spend their 10 days in the Blue Room. Every time that I was on the bench, the police officers would go out and round them up. For maybe six weeks, maybe two months, we wouldn't have any of the panhandlers and the beggars and those kinds of people on the street.

John Gieck, who was one of those who came to Las Vegas jobless, recalls one incident when some of these panhandlers and beggars stole food.

JOHN GIECK

They'd take anything they could get ahold of. Couple of guys got ahold of a crate of cantaloupes and took them out where men was looking for jobs. They went at 'em like a bunch of pigs.

While Las Vegas was trying to cope with its economic refugees, the government had begun to prepare for work on the dam. At the top of Hemenway Wash near the site of Boulder City, the Bureau of Reclamation built Government Survey Camp No. 1 in August 1930 to house its surveyors and engineers. By early 1931, as unemployed men and their families arrived looking for work, this survey camp became a squatters' settlement known as McKeeversville.

TEX NUNLEY

I started with the government at Yuma, Arizona, in 1929. I was transferred to Shoshone, Idaho. Then I was transferred back here. I was one of the early ones. There were a few here before I came, but just a few.

The old government camp was set up with the tent camp and all, but that was all. With the tent camp the government had a mess hall and tents for the men—four men to a tent. The tents were built up. They had floors. It was walled up four foot high and screened in, and had canvas over the top where you could put the awnings out or could drop the awnings down, depending on the way the wind was blowing. That was what I found. I imagine maybe 40 government people were out here at that time. They were all engineers.

It was what later became known as McKeeversville. Where McKeeversville originally got its name was from the cook in the mess hall there for the government. His name was McKeever. He set up a tent just over the hill. He and his wife lived there. That's where McKeeversville started. His name was McKeever, and they named it McKeeversville.

BOB PARKER

[My father] stayed over there in the government camp. Eventually he and McKeever and a few others moved over the hill and set up tents, which became McKeeversville. A lot of the families that moved out here moved over

Government Survey Camp No. 1. Boulder City townsite on hill in background,
4 September 1930

River Camp, 1931

there, boarded up their tents, and finally made makeshift homes up there. That was known as McKeeversville for years.

At first [we lived in] a tent. Then we kept adding to it and boarding it up and finally put a roof over it. I scavanged a lot of scrap lumber for them, and we finally made a makeshift home over there, like most of the rest of them that lived up there. Eventually it became kind of a rag camp, you might call it. It wasn't anything to brag about. Some of the homes weren't too bad. For a while we didn't have any running water. Well, we could look across the road and see our chick sale [outdoor privy, also spelled chic sale]. Right across the road. That's what we had in those days. We didn't have any rent-a-cans or anything else over there.

STEVE CHUBBS

McKeever was a cook and a bull cook. A bull cook is the same as a janitor. They named the town after him. He used to steal a lot of whiskey. He used to steal my whiskey.

HOBART BLAIR

For three years I lived in McKeeversville. We lived in tents there, and it was rough. It got so dang hot [that when] you'd pick up the knives and forks, you'd want to put your gloves on. We had two tents, eight-by-ten foot; put a floor in them; put walls up three or four feet; and put a canvas over the top. We ate in one tent and slept in the other. My wife and I and our son, Eddie. We had the outside two-holer. We used gas lanterns and cooked on a kerosene stove. We had to close down the flaps on the tent when the wind blew so the stove wouldn't go out, and that made it unbearably hot. We had to haul our water for the first year, and after that they piped the water and we could go outside to the faucet and get us a pail of water. Bob Cowan and I lived next door to each other, and we borrowed a government truck one day, went down to the Six Companies warehouse, and they gave us a bunch of ten-by-twelves [lumber]. We built us a garage. We had us a little queen stove, tin stove, we used for heat—put two or three little sticks of wood in, [and] it'd get pretty hot. We put a barrel on top of the garage, and we'd haul our water and pour it in the barrel up there. We'd let it heat from the sun and we'd take a shower. It was rough, but it was worth it.

DOROTHY NUNLEY

I was over there just a few times. It seemed to me like people had a lot of fun there, but they still had just shacks and outhouses. They didn't have any indoor plumbing or anything. But the times I was over there was in the evenings, and they'd be around a big campfire, singing and having a great time, really.

While the Bureau of Reclamation built Government Survey Camp No. 1, Six Companies established River Camp as a residential barracks for its employees. Clinging precariously to cliffs at the entrance to Black Canyon, the dormitories, kitchen, and mess hall of River Camp were connected by steep flights of wooden stairs. The camp simmered in the heat during the summer of 1931. Only 17 when he came to southern Nevada with his family, Bob Parker arrived with a letter promising him a menial job as a swamper's helper in the River Camp mess hall operated by the Anderson Brothers Supply Company.

BOB PARKER

Harold Anderson gave me a letter to take to the hiring office. When I got in there, they read this letter from Anderson. They started laughing. I couldn't understand what they were laughing about. One of them said they'd heard of a swamper, but they'd never heard of a swamper's helper before. They sent me down to the River Camp in early June 1931.

They called us cliff dwellers down there, because the dormitories were built on stilts at the side of the canyon. The mess hall was down on the road level, and they had wooden stairways up the side of the canyon wall there to these dormitories up in the canyon there. The first dormitory on the hill was the cookshack dormitory, where the cooks and all the waiters stayed, and there were three or four other dormitories behind us. We traveled up and down that hill on those wooden steps three or four times a day, going back and forth to the mess hall down on the road level below.

It was a very well-laid-out kitchen, except it was very hot down there that summer. The temperature got to 112. It was the coolest it got at five o'clock in the morning for six weeks straight. In that kitchen, with all those big ranges and cookstoves, it was a fright in there. In those days we didn't have any air conditioning; we didn't even have any swamp [evaporative] coolers. If I hadn't been a young fellow, I'd have never managed to make it. I broke out in prickly heat just like I had scarlet fever, and that's ruptured sweat glands. That sweat—when it would get in those sores, in your hair especially, it would drive you off your rocker. The only way we got any sleep was in the afternoon, when we got a few hours off before we served the dinner meal. We'd go up there and take cornstarch and scatter it in the sheets so it would absorb the sweat and keep it out of those sore pores for an hour or two, and then we'd have to head for the shower and wash it all off.

I scrubbed the kitchen floor, and mopped the floor, and hauled out the garbage to the trucks and loaded it in the trucks. There were big GI cans, and, I'll tell you, I learned I had muscles I didn't know I had with those big GI cans full of garbage. When I wasn't doing that, I was helping the fry cooks around there, just a general roustabout. We had to wear white clothing—all white clothing. Anderson's would get our measurements and buy the clothing. We'd pay them for the clothing. They did our laundry. They paid the swampers and all the rest of the labor crew like me $60 a month—board, room, and laundry. We worked 14 hours a day, seven days a week. If we got a day off, it was because we were sick. To take the day off, you had to have a pretty good reason.

We lost four down there because of the heat in the canyon. Anderson's lost four men from heat prostration. One of them was our boss. I forgot the name they called him. He made out the menus and was the boss over the chef and all the stewards. He kept his books in the reefer [refrigerator], where they kept the produce at about 40 degrees. They never kept it freezing, but they kept all the produce in this one room off the kitchen at about 40 degrees. He wore a great big peacoat, and he'd go in there and make out his menus and make out all his orders for groceries and what have you, and then he'd come out into the kitchen, and had to go through the kitchen to go back to his office. He got in that habit. One day he went in there—about the middle of July, as I remember—he went into that produce reefer cooler and came out about four hours later. He took about six or eight steps down through the kitchen in front of those big hot ranges, and he collapsed and died right there on the spot from heat prostration.

We also had what we called the Ice Brigade. When somebody there in the canyon, a Six Companies man or one of ours, became overcome with the heat, we dashed out there with these ice buckets and we'd pack them in ice. If their heart took it and they survived, OK. But if their heart stopped, that was it. We sent for the undertaker.

Dr. John R. McDaniel, who was associated with the Las Vegas Hospital, conducted preemployment health examinations for the Six Companies for $250 a month.

DR. JOHN R. McDANIEL

The first day I went out there to examine the men was down at [River Camp]. They had a thermometer hanging outside in the shade, but the darned thing only registered 120 degrees and it broke the first day I was down there.

Most of [the men] had been starving pretty much before they got here, and it was amazing, the number of people who had high blood pressure. I suppose they were worried they wouldn't get a job. Working out here too had something to do with that. But after two or three days, their blood pressure would come down.

The most notorious of the construction settlements grew at the bottom of Hemenway Wash on the shore of the Colorado River where it enters Black Canyon. This was Williamsville, known as Ragtown—or as Hell's Hole. The site developed near Murl Emery's boat landing, where the ferry linked Nevada with Arizona. Because it was close to the Black Canyon damsite, people believed they had a better chance of finding work. Their illusions did not last.

VELMA HOLLAND

We left Las Vegas and came out to the river, down to Williamsville,[2] later known as Ragtown. The moon was shining on that river, and it was the most beautiful silver strand you ever saw in your life. It was about that time that that song was popular, "Where the Silver Colorado River Played." Well, there it was. I seemed to get a thrill out of it. I knew the song, and there was the silver Colorado. We came in and took enough off of the truck to pitch beds. We went to bed. We got up the next morning. I looked out, and right down there it was awful—tents, big wood-colored stuff that had looked so beautiful the night before in the moonlight.

HELEN HOLMES

When you went down from the top of the hill down to the river, you could feel the heat. Sometimes you'd feel like you couldn't get your breath. It just seemed like it was so terrible hot.

When we arrived down there, there was nothing but tents, and one building that had been built for the man that was sort of in charge of men going to work. It was right at the edge of the water. There were about 500 tents there over quite a large area clear back to the bank. Some didn't really even have a tent, and a lot of them with little children.

Before we left Wyoming, my husband bought a tent, if you could believe it, for $15. It had nine feet in front, and you tied the awning to your cross to hold it. The awning had to be supported to hold it up. If the wind blew and caught this awning, the tent would go down. It had a bed that rolled up and a little campstove.

I imagine the first week or two, or maybe even month, we wouldn't go very much or do very much at all except just live, exist.

I just don't know how I stood it. There was very little fresh food or meat or anything at the little store that was run by Emery. The ants were absolutely our worst problem—the heat and the ants. We had a little card table we used, and you had to put the legs in a little can of water or the ants would beat you to the food. They were there before you could even realize it. I remember one time hanging a ham up from the ceiling down on a little twine or rope, and the ants could still find it.

At that time there was not even a well. Later they dug a little place back from the water's edge, and the water would seep in there and seemed to be a little clearer. You would go down to get a pail of water, and then it would settle, and there would be sediment in the bottom.

There was quite a lot of dysentery. Everyone was busy lining up to go to the Maggie and Jigs at that time. Just outside toilets. We would take our scraps and bury it in the sand. There was all sand and rocks, and there was mesquite bushes. Where I hung clothes was on top of mesquite bushes. You were really just existing.

At night it was so hot that you had to wet sheets to be able to rest because you just couldn't sleep, it was so hot. If there was a breeze and they would dry, you'd get up and wet them again in order to be able to sleep. During the day you just washed your face off. The coolness of the air or the breeze would make it cooler for you. I don't recall that it was so terrible, but now, looking back, we certainly never could go through it again.

People were coming and going so rapidly. Maybe some would be there a few days, and maybe some would be there longer. Maybe some would never find a job.

MURL EMERY

I moved all the scrap lumber I could find down to Hemenway Wash, and we set up a camp down there, right in the middle of summertime. [We ferried workers in] these little boats, and there were only 50 passengers, some of them less than that. That was a 24-hour job. And while that was going on, we had converted our little sight-seeing soda pop joint into a store at Rag-town. That was our big job, this operation with our boats running 24 hours a day, and all of a sudden this lousy store came to the point that we [needed] two trucks hauling supplies.

[People] came with their kids. They came with everything on their backs. And their cars had broke down before they got here, and they walked. No one helped them. I was the only person they could come to, the only person they had access to. The government would have nothing to do with them. The Six Companies would leave them. So we began to feed these people. Some of them had no money. Truckloads of provisions every day and coming out feeding these people. I kept a lousy set of books. Everything was on honor. It worked. I wound up with [only] two checks I never collected. I'm satisfied that they were two men who were lost and not accounted for.

The most vivid memories of Ragtown come from Erma Godbey. Erma's husband, Tom, who had lost his job in the mines of Silverton, Colorado for protesting wage cuts, moved his family to Oatman, Arizona, where there was still a gold mine in operation. As the depression worsened, Tom and Erma wondered whether they might have better luck on the dam project.

ERMA GODBEY

We had heard a lot about the Boulder Canyon Project while we still lived in Colorado and took the *Denver Post*, because the regional offices of the Bureau of Reclamation were in Colorado, and there was a lot about the Boulder Canyon Project in the *Denver Post* for several years. Also there were men who had helped do diamond drilling to find out where they could build a dam that had later come up to Silverton and worked in the mines, that we had talked to personally, so we thought what we'll do is come over here.

My mother and stepfather came down from Colorado to visit us. They were driving an old seven-passenger Dodge touring car. We had no car, so we had them drive us over here. We put a mattress and two baby cribs and two baby mattresses on the top of the car and tied them on. Then all of us got in the car. We brought a few cooking utensils and very few clothes and some bedding with us—and that's all. We had four children, and my baby was only five months old. We came from Oatman down to Needles and around by way of Searchlight.

It was terrifically hot. My God, it was terribly hot and dusty. None of the roads were paved in those days. It was just ungodly, it was so hot.

We got into where Boulder City is now, down by where the airport used to be; that's where the Six Company camp was. It was all tents. We stopped there and asked about a job. They said we just have a tent mess hall here, and we have tents for the men that are working, and you'll have to go down into the river bottom. So we still had to keep on driving. We went down to what is now the middle of [Lake Mead].

It was called Ragtown, but it was officially Williamsville, after Claude Williams, who was in charge of it. It looked like anyplace that is just built out of pasteboard cartons or anything else. Everybody had come in just in a car, with no furniture or anything. My mother looked around. They had to go back to Colorado. She said, "Well, I'll never see you again, I'll never see you again." I said, "Oh, Mom, we're tough. Remember, we're from pioneer stock." After all, my mother had driven cattle from Texas on horseback to Colorado when she was 11 years old. I said, "We're pioneer stock; we'll last." But she cried, and she left us.

All we could do was just put our mattresses on the ground and get ready to go to sleep, because it was pretty doggone late. We ate whatever I brought along as a luncheon, because we had no stove or anything. Later on, the next morning, we built a campfire. We just laid on the ground. We did set up— the baby five months old—her small crib, and let her be in the crib. The other little girl that was only two, she slept on the ground with her brothers.

We were right in among all these other people that were already camped there. Some had tents, but a lot just had canvas or blankets or anything that they could have for shelter. There was one little fellow that they called Johnny-behind-the-Rock. There was a great big boulder as you came down Hemenway Wash to go into Ragtown. He just kind of moved around where the shade was. He didn't have any tent or anything. He just kept moving wherever the shade was that the rock made.

What I had to do—I had blankets made out of pure wool that I had had made up at Utah Woolen Mills. They had cost me $32 a pair, which was a lot of money in those days, when men were only making four bucks a day wages. We got ahold of some clothesline, and we had some safety pins. We put some poles in the ground and pinned these beautiful wool blankets with safety pins to these poles to try to make a little bit of shade from the terrible heat. It would get to be 120 by nine in the morning, and it wouldn't get below 120 before nine at night. It just seemed like the river just drew the heat right down there. You could just see the heat dancing off of the mountains, the black cliffs down there. I would wrap my babies in wet sheets so they could sleep. But for my littlest baby, the one that was only five months old, Ila, I would put the wet sheet around her crib so the air would blow through it. But it wasn't enough.

It was about four days that we were like that, just with the blankets for shade. There was a little camp real close to us. The man who lived in that tent work[ed] in drilling the diversion tunnels. He wasn't a miner; he just was somebody who needed to have a job. When they would blast in the tunnels, they would just set the blast off as the men came off shift. Then the next shift would muck out, but the blast would go off between shifts. This man was so anxious to get in to work to earn his wages that he went in a little ahead of some of the other men, and the blast hadn't finished going off. Just as he put his shovel down to muck out, a delayed blast went off and it made the handle of his shovel go like this [gestures] and it disemboweled him. His wife—the only thing she could do was to have the body sent back home to her relatives or it would be buried in Las Vegas in the old cemetery— that was the Woodlawn Cemetery at that time. Then she'd just have to move on, since she had no way of making a living or anything. So we bought her tent. That way we had a small tent, but it still wasn't big enough for anything but maybe to do a little cooking in it.

We had no furniture. Nobody had furniture. But every once in a while, whenever we'd get a powder box, we'd have something to sit on. We'd invite somebody over; we had a chair. I don't know why in the world I took my ironing board with me, because there was no way in God's world that I could iron any clothes, but I did take my ironing board. Eventually we got two powder boxes. I set them up in the tent, and I put the ironing board across, so that way we had a bench.

We had to haul drinking water from the river. They had dug a couple of holes a little bit in from the river, and the river would seep through the sand and it would be pretty good. But, of course, when people would dip a lot into these wells, it would get riley again, so you'd have to let it settle. My husband didn't want to drink that water, and I didn't either. I had brought over my copper boiler, so I had something to put water in. He would take the boiler and swipe water from the mess halls when the cooks were busy feeding the men.

I didn't give [my] nursing baby enough water to drink. I gave her about the same amount of water that I had given my other babies that I had raised up in Colorado. She pretty near became dehydrated. So one night when all my other three children woke up and wanted a drink of water, I picked the baby up to nurse her and she just knocked the cup I was drinking right out of my hand. It was a 10-ounce white granite cup. It spilled on her. My husband said, "Mama, I think the baby's thirsty." We gave her a drink, and she drank 10 ounces of water. She drank it out of a cup, and she never did take water out of a bottle after that.

We had to go down to the river and bathe. I wore my dress but no petticoat

41

and stuff, and we'd wash up underneath and do the best you could without becoming naked for other people to see us. One day I was holding the baby by one leg, and I darn near lost her in the river. My husband managed to rescue her before she floated on down the river. I couldn't swim.

People would dig a hole in their tent floor. They would put one of these powder boxes down in the hole, and they would try to keep things a little bit cool that way. We hauled water from the river and had to let it settle to wash clothes and things. And here I had a baby in diapers. We didn't have Clorox and stuff like that in those days, so I had to boil the diapers on the campfire.

They did have outside toilets that the government furnished. The rangers would put slaked lime in them about twice a week. The only thing you could do with garbage was to burn it. There was no garbage removal or anything. Everybody just had to burn their garbage on their own premises as best they could.

They would go to work at 7:00 in the morning. It was so terribly hot by noon that men were passing out with the heat. So they decided that they would go to work at 4:00 in the morning and work until noon. Another shift would come on at 4:00 in the afternoon and work until midnight. But nobody would work during the very heat of the day between noon and 4:00. So then my husband had to be at work at 4:00 in the morning. That meant I had to get up at about 2:30 in the morning and get some breakfast going for him and get his lunch packed. I was still using the campfire. The very first money that he got, we got somebody to go into Las Vegas and we got a Coleman campstove. We had a carbide lamp—that's what miners use, you know. And we had the carbide crystals. So what I would use at night was the carbide lamp.

The reason I left Ragtown was not only the heat. Four people died—four women died in one day. That was the 26th of July [1931], and it was terribly hot. There was a woman that was 60 years old and a girl 16 and another woman that I don't know how old she was or anything much about her, and then there was a woman that was 28 that was just three tents from me. Her husband was working the swing shift in the diversion tunnels. They had come out from New York State. She was sick. He had done the best he could. He left her with a thermos bottle with ice. We could get ice once a day where they brought the ice in. They had a big dog, a big police dog. She just got to feeling terribly bad, so she tied a note on her dog's collar and told him to go get the ranger. He knew what she'd told him, but where was the ranger? Mr. Williams was anywhere. He probably wasn't in his office when the dog went hunting for him. In the note she had asked Mr. Williams to come and get her and take her to the river so she could get in the water to get cooled off. By the time Mr. Williams got to her after the dog got to him, she was just lying across a folding cot and she was dead. They told we women that

42

were close. There were three of us that went over into her tent. We kind of straightened her up on the bed.

They sent the other ranger or somebody to get her husband out of the tunnels. The woman had been dead for probably an hour by the time he got there. He immediately tried to give her artificial respiration. Then he looked at we three women, and he said, "Anybody going to Alaska? Anybody want to buy a fur coat?" We all just batted our eyes, hearing this in over-120-degree heat. Who in the heck would want a fur coat? But we got to thinking later that what the poor man was trying to do was get enough money out of the fur coat to bury his wife. They couldn't even move her into Vegas right away, because there wasn't any transportation. They had taken the other three people earlier in the day into Las Vegas. I went back to my tent, and I told my husband, "We've got to get out of here. We've just absolutely got to get out of here. I've got to get somewhere I can get the babies to a doctor if need be, and also myself."

Far worse than the primitive conditions of life in McKeeversville, River Camp, and Ragtown was the heat. The summer of 1931 was one of the hottest on record, and heat is the overriding memory of those who lived and worked at Black Canyon that year. Dozens of men, such as Neil Holmes, fell to heat prostration.

HELEN HOLMES

The men were going out with the heat. They called it passing out. Summer temperatures went terrifically high. The ambulance would go up so many times with the people. I don't remember if there were too many that died, but they'd have to pack them in ice and take them up. Of course, that siren— oh, it scared you 'cause you wondered if it might be your husband.

NEIL HOLMES

For a month during the summer, 30 days, the thermometer never went below 100, day or night. It was from that on up to 138. That was doing a lot to us.

I went to work as a pipe fitter. They gave me a crew, and I went to work at four o'clock in the morning and worked until noon. Along about the twenty-fourth or twenty-fifth of July, I got a little bit too hot. They had a truck run into the compressor plant at the lower end and broke out some pipe work. So they got ahold of me along about five, six o'clock in the morning to go down and repair that job. It took us until noon to get through with it, which was time for us to go home. We got too hot down there in the sunshine.

HELEN HOLMES

It seemed to me like it was late in the afternoon. He had come home and just didn't feel well. He just perspired all night long, just soaked with perspiration, and he just was weak. He didn't have to be taken to Las Vegas in the ambulance, but he did have heat prostration. I got ice from the little store and put ice on him. He thought the best thing to do was to go to the mountains to try to get feeling better. I don't remember how he got off his job and was able to leave, but maybe he had made some arrangement before he got home. We drove up into Las Vegas and saw a doctor, then went up to the mountains for about two weeks before he was even able to do anything at all. It was just lucky that he wasn't one that passed out. If they lost consciousness, they would just pack them in ice and take them into a hospital or into Las Vegas. But the thing of it is some of them didn't survive or recover.

Dr. Clare Woodbury was one of the physicians in Las Vegas who cared for these men.

DR. CLARE WOODBURY

At that time very little was known about heat exhaustion. During the summer months, for a while they brought in sometimes 10 and 12 men at a time unconscious and incontinent. We had no electric thermometer then, but with an ordinary thermometer their rectal temperature went up to 112 degrees. We had half a dozen bathtubs filled with cold water and ice floating in it. As soon as they come in, we put them in the ice water and within an hour their temperature was reduced to near normal. Then we gave them the intravenous fluids they needed. Before that the mortality was about 50 percent or 60 percent. After that they all recovered.

WALKER YOUNG

I had temperatures taken myself that I'm positive were correct. When we were down at the damsite itself in Black Canyon, we did have temperatures recorded. At this particular time we were building the forms for the sedimentation tank which supplies the water for Boulder City. One side was the shady side, and the other was in the sun. I went over in the shade and sat with my thermometer and watched the crew. It made a temperature of 140 degrees. The foreman in charge sat with me. You know what his job was? He watched the men in his crew and when one of them staggered out, he told him to come on over and sit down here for a while. He'd sit there 15 minutes. After they'd got accustomed a little bit to the heat, then they'd go to work again. So there's one instance I know it was 140 degrees.

While heat disabled many of the first workers on Hoover Dam, and even killed several, it also offered opportunity for scientific study. Dr. David Bruce Dill, a Stanford-trained physiologist, came to the Boulder Canyon Project at the invitation of the Bureau of Reclamation to study the effects of heat on workers. Dill's research at Boulder City and in the Mohave Desert led to publication of his classic study Life, Heat, and Altitude *in 1938.*

DR. DAVID DILL

I was in Europe in the summer of '31. On returning from Europe I read in the ship's newspaper of the death of 13 workmen in the construction of the dam here in the summer of 1931. That made us think that we might be able to have research on the problem of high temperatures here in the following summer. In the fall I got in touch with Secretary [Ray Lyman] Wilbur of the Department of the Interior. I had met him. He was the clinician when I was first at Stanford. I wrote to him and explained to him our interests and had no problem getting approval. He then notified the people in Washington and here at Boulder City, so everything paved the way for us.

We had a young M.D. in our laboratory, John Talbott. I arranged for him to come out here in advance of our study in February [1932]. He won the approval of the physician employed by Six Companies in the hospital they built for his study of all heat patients that came in the hospital during the summer of 1932. So when we arrived in 1932, we shortly had a laboratory set up where we did physiological and biochemical studies. Our subjects were ourselves and also many of the workmen from the dam who volunteered as healthy, normal workmen.

But the great difference between that summer and the previous summer was that with no air conditioning the previous summer, many workmen lived down in the canyon where it was much hotter, and there they sweat day and night, not only during their work but during the rest of the day. So that accounted for the deaths that first year. When we arrived in '32, they had air-conditioned dormitories, air-conditioned mess hall, excellent food, and motor transports to and from the dam. So what we found was that while there was very great stress of 8 hours' work at the dam, the conditions were favorable for their recuperating during the other 16 hours. Our studies of them showed that with an occasional exception, the men kept in excellent physical condition that second year of 1932. It takes no more than two or three days for a man doing hard work to become fully adapted. His sweat glands function normally, excellently, after two or three days. His sweat becomes a little less concentrated with time. Body temperature regulation is excellent. There's no problem with that.

WALKER YOUNG

It was very interesting to me. They had people from the white-collar gang go out and play several sets of tennis. They put an apparatus on their arms to collect all the perspiration so they could take it out later and measure it. They played so many sets, so many minutes, so many times; then they'd measure the amount of water in that man's system that had to come out— or did come out, anyway. Then they employed or paid a number of Six Companies employees who were working on the job. They reported in every day after working their shift to get the same sort of measurements, testing the effect [of the heat]. One of the experiments was they put men on the highway leading a dog on a rope and sent them walking down Hemenway Wash and back. It turned out the man could stand it better than the dog. That's because the dog has only one place to perspire—his tongue. So the man outdid the dog.

DR. DAVID DILL

There was one lack that we recognized. The evidence had been advanced in the literature that workmen in high temperatures often have a deficiency of salt, develop heat cramps. So in some other places this was already being recognized, but it hadn't come to the attention of the surgeon here. He had a big sign up in the mess hall: THE SURGEON SAYS DRINK PLENTY OF WATER. Dr. Talbott persuaded him to add to that: AND PUT PLENTY OF SALT ON YOUR FOOD. So that was the only step that we took to protect the men against loss of salt in their sweat. There were no deaths in '32 from heat and, as far as I know, not in subsequent years.

BOB PARKER

That summer of '32 they brought in doctors from back east. Dr. Dill was one of them. These doctors went out here in the desert. We'd see them out there with their shorts, walking around in the heat. Pretty soon they came up with the idea that the heat prostration that we suffered so bad from the summer before [and] the deaths that were occasioned down there was due to lack of salt in the body. So they came up with the suggestion that we use salt. That's the first deal with salt, right here on Boulder Canyon Project. We put two to four ounces of salt in all the lemonade in the mess hall for these men who were working down there in that heat in '32.

It was too much—bad food, bad water, the horror of life in Ragtown, the unbearable heat—and on 7 August 1931 the Six Companies threatened to cut wages for muckers who cleared debris from diversion tunnels being blasted in the canyon walls. The Industrial Workers of the World (IWW), a radical labor union popularly known as the Wobblies, called a strike against the project. Glen E. "Bud" Bodell, a tough, cigar-chewing deputy sheriff who came to Vegas from Ely, Nevada, in June 1930 to take charge of security for the Bureau of Reclamation, remembers the Wobblies and the strike.

BUD BODELL

The sheriff's office was policing [the dam], but they were having trouble. It was during the Panic, and these Wobblies were coming in by the trainload and busload, and they established two camps. One was called Texas Acres and the other Oklahoma City. All those deep-hole miners from down around

47

Mother and children camped in the desert near Las Vegas while father
looks for work on Hoover Dam, 1931

Ragtown, 1931

Pitcher, Oklahoma. They were not the ones who were doing trouble. It was the ones from Butte and Anaconda [Montana], up in that country, and Chicago, where the Wobblies were pretty thick. Seattle, Washington. They'd load onto them trains and ride into Vegas. They had a feeding hall down here for them, where they were supposed to get a meal a day. The city and the Red Cross were feeding them. They was sleeping around on the floor of the Big Four Club on Second Street, and the Boulder Club, the backs of cars. They'd get up and go get their meal, then double back at noon. Finally [Police] Commissioner Roscoe Thomas[3] came to me and told me to pack 'em up and ship 'em out; they could ride back where they came from. So [we] loaded them up and took them out to the [California] state line and left men there to see they didn't come back.

BOB PARKER

The IWW, which we called "I Won't Work," represented the International [Industrial] Workers of the World. They were down here trying to stir up trouble and organize the workers at Hoover Dam. They were agitating and trying to get things set up so that they could dictate to the Six Companies and the government about a lot of the labor rules.

ERMA GODBEY

I don't think they were really unionized here. But they were going to cut the wages on the muckers in the tunnels. And they were only getting $4 a day anyhow, which was nothing. You could live on it in those days, but you couldn't hardly. The other men that did the other kinds of work knew that if they were successful in cutting the muckers' wages, they would cut their wages too.

BUD BODELL

They were paying miners at the dam $5 a day and $4 a day for the muckers. 'Course, they fed them awful good—three meals a day and all they could eat. The Wobblies had nothing anywhere they were, so they all hopped freights and came out here because it was the only job in the country. And the Teamsters were organized. And when the carpenters came in, they were convinced the Wobblies were trying to take over the job. So there was the strike that shut it down.

HARRY HALL

I'm not sure just what the reason was. I think they wanted better conditions, but conditions were not improved as far as I could see. It started uptown. It started up in Boulder City. We weren't aware of what was going on down in Ragtown until they came down and told us to leave. They ran all the people out of Ragtown. They just told us to leave, period. The other employees were restricted to the dormitories—the single men.

JOE KINE

They rounded up everybody that was working there and took them all off. Everybody. They tried to get everybody. Then the foreman, or whoever it was, would go out and vouch for those guys, and they'd come back in and be working.

TEX NUNLEY

It was the Six Companies workers that were striking to get a little better wages. They couldn't have had any better food. I guess it was money and maybe a little better working conditions on the job. They gave [government workers] shotguns and put them out here and there to guard. Don't let anyone come in or out. I was just a rodman. It was the bigger shots that had the guns.

MURL EMERY

All working men were fenced out of the area. A big fence, with guards, about halfway between Boulder City and Railroad Pass. All of the working men were sent outside, and their families were left down at Ragtown. So I had all these women and kids—no men down there—to feed. The Six Companies came down with two ton-and-a-half pickups loaded with food, and they did give it to them. But they had motion pictures of it, taking pictures of feeding these families. I had those same trucks going back and forth to Vegas for days and days while all this was going on. But I forgot the motion picture. And, of course, a lot of things happened that are hard to live with. These people, they just wanted to work.

ERMA GODBEY

They threw the gate up out here by Railroad Pass, and nobody could get back in unless they had a job. Anybody that didn't have a pass couldn't get through the gate, and anybody that got through the gate and didn't have a pass couldn't get out. [My husband] didn't have a job. It took a whole month. We didn't have any money coming in and didn't know when we would have more money coming in. But we were luckier than most people, because we had insurance that we could borrow on, that we had paid on before, when Pop was working in the years before the depression. We borrowed some money from that so we could buy groceries.

Thrown off the job at Black Canyon, construction workers swarmed into Las Vegas.

BOB PARKER

They had a few fights over there. I remember the muckers and the truck drivers got into it over there on Fremont Street. They were having a big battle, a knock-down, drag-out. It took the police a while to get them under control. Some of the gambling halls were worried they might storm the money cages. I remember the Pioneer Club had machine guns showing up in the money cage just in case they broke in there. It could have gotten out of hand, but it didn't amount to much. It was mostly a drunken brawl. Things settled down pretty well after the police got all the drunks off the street.

The Las Vegas Evening Review-Journal *found itself in a quandary: it had to cover the strike because it was news, but publisher Al Cahlan was firmly antiunion and antistrike. Al's brother John explains the paper's position.*

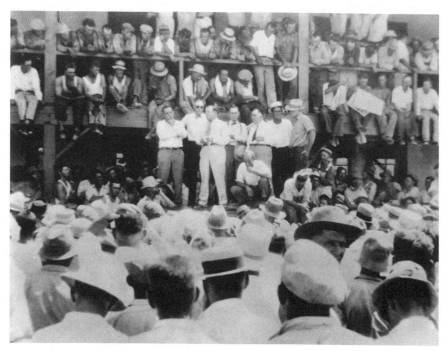

Strikers gathered in Boulder City, August 1931

Soup kitchen in Las Vegas for strikers, chef Jack Smith preparing mulligan stew and rice pudding, August 1931

JOHN CAHLAN

The unions lost their hold in Las Vegas when they had the [railroad] strike in 1922.[4] The people who were here were just absolutely fighting mad about the rail strikes, because the Union Pacific moved all of the employment out of the city of Las Vegas. They practically moved all of the railroad shops out of Las Vegas. When the people [at Hoover Dam] struck, there was a slight movement of people from the rest of the country to come in here and take the strikers' place. It stirred up a lot of problems. The chamber of commerce naturally was against it, because it was going to affect the future of the city of Las Vegas. The people in the city of Las Vegas were determined that the labor unions were not going to get a big hold on the community.

The paper was with Six Companies. We didn't give the strike much space. The thing that we felt at that time, and I'm sure that my brother joined with me, is that any of these people who were trying to do anything that would give Las Vegas a bad name, they would not be covered. I mean—I just let them go. We had editorials in the paper that warned against any advance of the Wobblies. Everybody felt that Las Vegas was a town that was not going to be affected by any of these Wobblies or strikes or anything else, because of the depression. Any of those Wobblies who came up were floated out of town. We didn't even use their names, I don't think. As I say, the idea that people in Las Vegas had at that time was if any of the troublemakers are in here, get them out of town! They could stay in the Blue Room until they rotted.

Ragnald Fyhen came down here. He was a labor organizer in Reno. He was pretty straight union. He was just coming down to organize [the Las Vegas Central Labor Council]. I knew Fyhen very well. I knew him in Reno. His Central Labor Council was supposed to represent all of the laborers in Las Vegas. I don't know that he got out onto the dam, because I think he was barred from the reservation.

Fyhen came down here with big ideas. I talked to him just shortly after he came down here, and having known him in Reno, he opened up pretty good to me. He said he was down here to organize the labor force, and that he was going to get the workers on Boulder Dam organized, and he was going to be the boss. He had big ideas, and they just didn't work. He was kind of on the outer fringe of the inner guard of the labor unions in Reno. Reno, of course, was a lot older than Las Vegas and had existed on a lot of the labor problems.

But it was the depression. The people who were working on the dam were feeding their wives and children and having a fairly good existence. They weren't interested in unions. Fyhen used to come into the office all the time. He'd go in and talk to Al, and I'd be out working. I know that Al didn't care too much for Fyhen. He was going to do something that was going to cripple the community by calling a strike. They were not very successful—not at that time. They became stronger later.

The strike lasted about a week, although Bud Bodell managed to bust IWW agitation within a few hours.

BUD BODELL

I put a couple of men out in their camps. They came in, went to work—we had cards for them. And then we began to know every move they were going to make. Their plan—and we knew their plan—was to get in at night and cut all the gas lines on the transportation trucks. We found out through the undercover men I had down there what time they'd be in. I didn't have enough men, so the AFL [American Federation of Labor] offered me its help. They gave me 10 or 12 men. So sure enough, about one o'clock in the morning [the Wobblies] came in and cut the gas [lines] on two trucks. Unbeknownst to me, all the [AFL] guys had been supplied with rubber hoses. They came in on [the Wobblies] in the garage and [beat them], tried to stop them. They didn't want them in there.

We brought [the Wobblies] into Vegas and put them under arrest. The rest of them had congregated in the mess hall. Someone informed the Teamsters and the carpenters, and they arrived at the mess hall and went to work on the Wobblies. That's the last trouble we had with them.

Whether the strike of August 1931 was successful is open to question even today.

ELTON GARRETT

To a certain extent it did help. Management tried to be reasonable, and at times they improved conditions for the workers. They didn't give in to them and say, "You can have all your wishes." They didn't do that. The depression gave this whole country a climate where management could dictate terms pretty much.

[Frank Crowe], as superintendent, had various administrators who handled

Boulder City's first police station. *Left to right*: Fred Jensen, Glen E. "Bud" Bodell, Ted Jensen, 1931

the details. He, of course, rode herd on those who ran herd on the others. There was a sort of pyramid of management, of course. He didn't go out there and say, "You guys, get off that soapbox and come back to work." He didn't do that. He had others that negotiated. I would say he was intelligent enough that he worked out the kind of negotiation that would get them back on the job and get the dam finished, and get their bonus. He was intelligent enough to bring the ends together and make it work.

STEVE CHUBBS

They had just gotten over [the strike] when I arrived, and they were weeding out the troublemakers that were here. They called them Wobblies. I think some of the big shots mingled with the men in old dirty work clothes and found out what kind of conversation was going on. I think that's how they found out some of them.

A lot of these Wobblies were really hard workers. They were the type of men that did drilling and blasting, and that's hard work. They weren't loafers. Looking back on it, I think they did a good job. My own personal opinion is that they needed the troublemakers to make the contractor do what he should for the men. I'm not Communist, but I think a man ought to have decent working conditions. They finally had to install drinking fountains down at the dam, and the water was chilled, cooled. They had cool water down there. That's one thing that they gained by the strike.

The Bureau of Reclamation built a gate at the entrance to the project lands and stationed armed guards around the clock. Workers had to register at the state employment office in Las Vegas and could no longer get jobs in Boulder City or at the construction site. Without a job they could not enter the reservation.

BOB PARKER

Walker Young decided that the government was going to decide about all of the safety regulations and every other thing involved with the building of Hoover Dam. So after they struck, he just closed the job down. When he closed the job down, he moved everybody off the project except government employees and those of us that weren't involved with the labor. He moved them off, set up a gate out there with the government rangers, and to get back in here you had to get a special pass and you had to have a badge. Someone had to take the bull by the horns in order to get this job under way and not have a lot of labor problems and one thing and another, which we have so much of today. You have to hand it to Walker Young, although the union branded him as a dictator and a führer and a few other things. If it hadn't been for him, this dam might have been 10 years being built and cost twice as much as it did.

3

CONSTRUCTION CAMP: BOULDER CITY, 1931

"The idea was to get the town built."

The government wanted Boulder City built and settled before Hoover Dam construction began, but the depression rushed the schedule. Unemployed men who arrived at Black Canyon in 1931 started work before their families had a place to live. Thousands lived in camps like Ragtown and McKeeversville, but the scattered tent settlements were only temporary solutions, unsightly and unhealthy. The government wanted them cleared out and pushed Six Companies to build Boulder City as quickly as possible. Bureau of Reclamation engineer Walker R. Young chose the site for a construction camp large enough to accommodate 5,000 people.

WALKER R. YOUNG

Establishing a townsite near the dam was almost out of the question. Above the dam there were mountains standing around, and the areas for erecting a tent camp were rather cramped, especially considering that tremendous transmission lines had to go from the damsite through that same area. We knew that we were working in an area of extremely high temperatures. There were air currents to be considered in the hope to control temperatures.

We also wanted to get the employees into a different environment. We knew it was going to take some time to build the dam. Work was to go on 24 hours a day every day of the year except a couple. We wanted them to

Laying out the Boulder City townsite, 13 March 1931. *Left to right*: C. A. Williams, Six Companies construction foreman; H. S. McDowell, Six Companies construction foreman; R. C. Thaxton, Bureau of Reclamation engineer; Frank Crowe, Six Companies construction superintendent; John Page, Bureau of Reclamation office engineer forget all about the work at the damsite, what they were going through down there, and get away where they'd have a family life.

The location that was finally selected for the townsite was on the summit between Hemenway Wash and the vast area where the dry lake is now [Eldorado Valley]. In order to test that out by actual trial before we finally made the selection, we located our survey camp [Government Survey Camp No. 1] at approximately the same area but outside of the specific area we had in mind for Boulder City. It was over near where McKeeversville was built. We found in our investigations that the temperature was at least 10 degrees lower than at the damsite. We also found that the air currents, particularly from the lake area, from around Hemenway Wash, created almost a continual breeze—very slight on some occasions, very stiff and very severe in other instances. It wasn't a very attractive site for us, but better than anyplace else in that particular area. We went there so many times, and all we found when we went was greasewood and sagebrush, a few burros, tarantulas, centipedes, snakes—not particularly attractive.

After we decided this camp should be located at that particular location, we brought a consultant in. The Bureau of Reclamation employed a townsite man, an architect out of Denver, S[aco] R[ink] DeBoer. He also was a landscape man. He came to the location, and he and I personally went over that for several days, considering what kind of a layout we would have for the town. Out of that, of course, the location was finally approved by the proper authorities. He immediately went to work building the town.

The layout of the town has been talked of in many publications as a model town, and it was intended to be. It was intended to be a comfortable place to live, as near as that was possible in that particular place. It was decided that the town would be built in the shape of a triangle, with the [Bureau of Reclamation] Administration Building as the official headquarters of the bureau at the point of the triangle. The idea was that that shape would fit future plans better than a rectangular shape or a square. The recreational part of the city and the school area would be next, away from the point. Farther out would be the business district. Below the business district would come the residences, principally for the contractor's forces.

It was anticipated that after the construction of the dam was completed and the powerhouse in operation, Boulder City would become simply a residential area for operators. That's why the permanent buildings were built for the government forces, whereas temporary buildings were built for the contractor. Residences built of brick for the government employees were located up near where the Administration Building was, but looking down toward the lake.

JOHN CAHLAN

There is quite a story regarding why Boulder City was set where it was. At the time Ray Lyman Wilbur was secretary of the interior and in charge of the Bureau of Reclamation, which was building the dam. Wilbur came out to see what was going on in this area. Las Vegas was being considered as the railhead for the dam supplies. Wilbur came out here, and, being a president of Stanford University some years before, he was supposed to be quite blue-nosed. The people of Las Vegas, wanting the city to become the railhead because of the business that would attend the settlement of the community, were very interested in seeing that Wilbur didn't see any of the vices that were so rampant in the city of Las Vegas at the time.

On the day scheduled for Wilbur's arrival in a private car, the word went out from the police department that all of the houses of prostitution on North First Street would be closed and there would be no liquor sold in the community until Wilbur got out of the city. So he was taken on a trip through the city of Las Vegas and out to the damsite. And during the time that he was on the trip, Paul Shoup—who was the son of the president of the Southern Pacific Railroad, upon whose special car Wilbur was traveling—and several newspapermen who were with the secretary wanted to know if there wasn't a possibility that we could get him some whiskey, or a drink or something. They were dry. So being very obliging to the newspaper people and the son of the president of the Southern Pacific Railroad, we arranged to have the Arizona Club, which was one of the places on Block 16, which was the prostitution area of Las Vegas, opened up. We all went down and had several libations and went back to the car shortly before Wilbur arrived. So we all said our good-byes, and everything seemed to be all right until Wilbur announced the next day that he was [building] Boulder City to house the workmen because Las Vegas was no place for people to live during the construction of the dam. I never did find out whether Shoup and all the newspaper boys told him about the visit down to Block Sixteen and the whiskey they got, or not. Anyway, they didn't get the railhead in Las Vegas.

Among the first structures in Boulder City were Six Companies and government dormitories for unmarried workers.

WILLIAM D. McCULLOUGH

I seen a guy was smokin' a pipe and wore glasses, a big guy, and I walked over and asked him for a job. He said, "What can you do, lad?" I guess I was about 25. I said, "Oh, I'll do anything." This guy's name was Charlie Williams, and he was in charge of all the building of the dormitories and everything in Boulder City except the government buildings. And later on he was in charge of a lot of the stuff down at the dam. [Williams] said, "See that old guy over there holdin' his teeth in?"—and he was, too. "Go over and talk to him." That old man's name was Kissel, and I went over and said Charlie Williams told me to see him. [Kissel] said, "Well, just go ahead and go to work." And I did. I went to work in the carpentry shop, helping build the dormitories and the mess hall. The dormitories was two stories high. They had great big showers for 15, 20 people at a time. Each man had his own room, his own single bed and Simmons mattress—very good, and they changed the linen there whenever you wanted it.

ELTON GARRETT

Ten [Six Companies] dormitories were built, each like a letter H. A cross between two rows was a connecting—shall I say bath area—for the use of people from all four of the wings. I lived in one of those dormitories for a while before other housing was available for me. I had a room. I stacked it up with newspaper stuff and junk.

When Dormitory 3 had been finished—I forgot which leg of the H I was in—but I had a room in Dormitory 3, right across the street from where the [Boulder City] company store was. I could go to the recreation center and see the guy who had tried to be heavyweight champion,[1] who was supposed to be responsible for the recreation center. I could hobnob with him, buy a Coca-Cola, play pool with one of the boys. Even Frank Crowe would come in there once in a while. We had a chummy sort of a relationship all the way around. It was fun.

CARL MERRILL

The room was about twelve by twelve. They didn't know who I was when I came in here. They knew I came in and I had a job when I got here. So the local powers-to-be put me in what they called one of the premium rooms, which they save for the big shots. I enjoyed that room for about a month, and they found out I was just a peon, so they moved me into another room, which was about eight by ten. The only thing it had in it was a bed. It was one of those spring-type cots. They furnished your linen and blankets. Our wages were $60 a month and board and room. So that room was provided as part of our salary.

DENZLE S. PEASE

After I got put on the payroll, I moved into the Six Companies dormitory. The rooms were single rooms, very drab—everything in 'em was the same color. They had good beds, steel-framed beds with good mattresses. And they had a semblance of air conditioning, but it wasn't enough to take care of the heat and make the room comfortable during the hot weather. Part of the time I was working graveyard or swing shift, which would mean that I would have to sleep during the daytime, and this was a situation which was practically intolerable.

BRUCE EATON

The men who were fortunate enough *not* to have their families living here with them, if that's how you want to put it, and who had to live in the dormitory had a decided advantage. They did have a cool place to sleep; they had a good place to eat.

> *The Bureau of Reclamation built two dormitories for its employees. Unlike the spartan Six Companies dorms, Government Dormitory No. 1 was a spacious and comfortable stucco villa overlooking the area where the lake would rise.*

TEX NUNLEY

They had two dormitories. Number 1 was up by the Ad[ministration] Building. I moved in there as soon as it opened up. Two men to a room, $15 a month, and everything was taken care of: the sheets and towels, everything. The bed made, everything.

Government Dormitory No. 2 was a two-story frame structure presided over by Hattie Peterson, whose husband, Charles Peterson, later became Boulder City's police chief.

CURLEY FRANCIS

I got acquainted with Hattie when I lived in the government dormitory. Buck Blaine and I had one of the rooms that had two men in it. Both of us were single. When Hattie Peterson said there would be no girls upstairs, she meant just that. I don't think there was any girl that ever got up there, because Hattie Peterson kept a pretty tight rein on everything that went on in the dormitory.

We had one particular man in there that I believe had lead poisoning. He was a painter. He was sick for quite a while. Hattie Peterson saw to it that he never went without food. He couldn't go anyplace to eat. She saw that he got his meals. She'd even tell us fellows that could go out and get something to bring home for him to eat. He was well taken care of. I think that this was one of the things that made Hattie Peterson's dormitory so outstanding. We were all individuals and very special to her.

Six Companies and the Bureau of Reclamation began construction of homes for workers with families in the late summer and fall of 1931. Once begun, construction moved rapidly. By the beginning of 1932, hundreds of small frame houses stood in neat rows across the sand flats of Boulder City below the Administration Building.

JOHN GIECK

They started building them on Avenue B and Wyoming Street. They built the three-room houses first, then the two-room [houses]. Last built was the dingbat houses—the one-room houses down below New Mexico Street. They was precut: the studs and rafters and everything. They had two carpenters [per house]—no helpers—and they had 12 hours [to build each] house. They had to lay the foundation, put the flooring in, frame it, and put the siding on and put the roof on and then [tar] paper it. That didn't include the finishing work: the screens, the doors and windows, or the sheetrock inside. They

Six Companies dormitories, about 1932

Bureau of Reclamation Dormitory No. 1, about 1932

started building houses in June 1931, and I helped finish the last one in March '32.

ROSE LAWSON

I came in November [1931]. For six months before that, we had been working in Oregon. Up there we had pretty rugged housing. But people had passed around the *Reclamation Era* with the pictures of the houses that were being built here for the foremen, and since my husband would be a foreman, we thought, "Well, that's how we're going to live when we get to Boulder City." But we soon found out that we were not up the ladder for any of these houses.

There were people just scrambling for houses. Always a big lineup of people begging for houses and applications for houses. My husband was here two months before he got the house, and then I think somebody put in a good word for him, because there never was enough houses. And, of course, there were so many people already living here that wanted houses. They tried to get those people new houses as fast as they could. But at the time I got here, the Six Companies houses were being finished and moved into at the rate of eight houses a day.

I got here after the road to Boulder City was finished, but there was a detour at Railroad Pass. When I drove into Boulder City, there were people working everywhere: on streets, on buildings. Of course, I went out on the wrong road, even though I did have a good map. I asked some people where Avenue F was. They turned out to be a Mexican road crew and couldn't speak English. I finally found my house, and when I got into it, it was dark. The power was off. We had a power shortage every few evenings. The power shortage lasted into the night, and it was morning before I saw my two-room house.

It wasn't finished. We didn't have any plumbing; we didn't have any water. We did have electricity—one outlet in each room and a light hanging from the ceiling. We had a stove, a gas range. You lit it with a light; no pilot light. The house was built exactly like a shoebox: two rooms with a little porch. They were sitting on sand. Two steps, you were out into the sand.

We had to haul our water from a tank car out on the railroad. It had been brought in from Las Vegas. Soon our little shower rooms were finished. There was a toilet in there, but no washbowl. So for several years we brushed our teeth and washed our faces in the [kitchen] sink. I think those showers were about the most precious things in Boulder City. Many, many mornings in the summer, I jumped out of bed and then took a shower before I even thought of starting breakfast. Then in the afternoon you'd have another shower. Then when you got ready to go to bed, you'd have another shower. Many times you'd never light the [water] heater at all. The water would be warm enough for a shower.

There were less cupboards and no closets in our houses. But there were piles of lumber all over this town when they were building houses. So at night, the men used to go out and steal lumber to build cupboards. The lumber would be pushed under the house to keep it from getting wet if there should be rain—which there never was, of course—and, I guess, probably to keep it from being in the sun. So my husband crawled under the house to get some boards to build a cupboard and put his hand down on a great big cactus. His first thought was, "My gosh, I've been grabbed by some kind of animal!" He backed out from under the house and saw the big cactus hanging on to his hand. He had to pick out—there were a lot of quills. The cactus was curved at the end, and when you stick it in, it doesn't pull out as easily as you think it does.

Of course, I only had one child when we moved here. She slept on the couch here in the kitchen. We slept on the double bed in the living room. Then spring came. We shoveled out the porch, and got the sand all out of it. Then we moved our bed out on the porch. She wanted to sleep out there too. We moved her cot to the end of the porch, where she could sleep. From then on we slept on the porch. During the summer it was our bedroom.

HELEN HOLMES

On October 8 [1931] we were able to get a one-room house. There were quite a few houses built in Boulder. There were few when we came, but they put them up real rapidly. The houses were just shells, really. At that time the electricity and the water wasn't even in that house. The house was finished, but there was no painting or anything like that done. The only way you could get in was through the alley. There was nothing but about a foot of fresh sand. You had to stay right in that track or you got stuck. We still had the outside toilets. But it wasn't very long, possibly a few days or a week, before we had electricity. I painted the living room, papered it and all, spent so much time, thinking we were going to live there forever.

There was one quite large room. I would imagine it might have been 12 feet, or maybe it wasn't over 10 feet. That's where we lived and where our bed was. Then there was a small kitchen. There was a sink in it and a stove, and we had a small table. Then there was a bathroom. It was a shower and a toilet—very, very small. They had this screen porch for sleeping—room enough for a small cot.

We had one of the first coolers. It was simply just burlap on the outside of the window, and you put a hose [there] and you let it drip around and keep this wet. Then you had a fan in the window that circulated air into the house. We had seen this done in Needles, California. We had been down to visit a friend that we had known here. She told us that people were using these. So I believe that we had the first one in Boulder.

We didn't have any heat. I remember the first winter, we had a little kerosene [stove]—possibly a foot and a half high, and round. It had a round burner on it. But you had to watch because the flame would creep up. One time when I had gone out, I came back and my kitchen was all full of smoke. This burner had crept too high, and it just smoked the whole kitchen.

MARY EATON

The floors were terrible. The floors were just plain old pine wood. I had no flooring, so I had to keep the children off the floor as much as I could because they'd get slivers in their little behinds and legs.

WILMA COOPER

These houses were put up in one day, child. You think you can put a house up in one day and have it look like anything? They never were comfortable, because there was no insulation in 'em. And the sheetrock inside was so thin—you sneeze on it, you'd blow a hole in it. But they were never meant to stay here. It was all supposed to revert back to desert when the dam was finished.

We'd sleep out on the screened-in porch that was exactly the width of a double bed. The sand blew incessantly. They always warned me that if you slept on your back, you always flopped over and turned your head down before you opened your eyes in the morning, or you'd get sand in them. Anyway, I put up with that about so long; then I went out to the dump and got some pasteboard boxes and come in and lined those screens on the porch. Then we had the screen and the canvas and the pasteboard boxes flopping in the breeze all the time. The wind blew incessantly—it was a noisy place to sleep.

I kept after my husband to move that partition between the screened-in porch and my front room—just move it in two feet; then at least I could walk around my bed. But he was always busy doing something else. So I got mad one morning after he went to work and tore that partition all out, moved it in two feet and had it back up again by the time he got home at four o'clock. He was dumbfounded. He didn't know I even knew how to use a hammer.

And we didn't need an alarm clock. Where the ceilings came down to meet the walls, they didn't meet. When the sun shone in, it hit our face, and we knew it was time to get up.

The floors were that old three-inch pine, and the wind and sand'd blow up between the boards. I had sinus trouble so bad we decided we'd get some linoleum to lay down. Then when the wind blew, that linoleum'd slide this way and that way. We got tired of chasing the linoleum around the room, so we decided to anchor it down with metal tape around the edge. Then it was like slow motion, and the wind and sand would poof out around the edges of that linoleum rug we had. It was fun, I'll tell ya.

ROSE LAWSON

Every house was exactly alike. You couldn't tell your own house. It was always a joke in the olden days about somebody coming into the wrong house. Men coming home from work—if they weren't thinking, they'd come into the wrong house. I do know of cases where people got up in the morning and found a man sleeping on their couch. But they'd just wake him and ask him what he was doing. "My gosh, this is not where I belong!"

The Six Companies cottages were meant to be demolished after Hoover Dam was finished, but the government's brick houses on the granite ridge overlooking Hemenway Wash and the Colorado River were built as a permanent neighborhood. Leo Dunbar, a government hydrographer from Montrose, Colorado, lived in a tent at Government Survey Camp No. 1 in McKeeversville until he could move his family into one of the brick houses.

LEO DUNBAR

Early in July of 1931, the Denver office asked me if I would be available to transfer to the Boulder Canyon Project. My wife and I talked it over a bit. We had been hearing about the terrible conditions down here on the Boulder Canyon Project, about the rattlesnakes, the high heat, the people dying of heat prostration, along with the lizards and tarantulas, scorpions, and the rest of the things. We debated, Mrs. Dunbar and I, a long time about even accepting coming down. But on the other hand, I was very happy because we knew by that time that it was going to be an immense engineering project. That was my line, and I had hopes of sometime being on it. So I said if I could leave my family in Colorado until I had a place to bring them to and a home, it sounded pretty good to me.

So I came down. I think I arrived the 27th of September 1931. I asked if I could have leave just previous to Christmas to go back and bring the family down if this house was going to be finished for me. On the 22nd of December '31, they told me that the house would be ready for me in a week. If I would be back in a week, I could have the house and it would be ready for the family.

When we arrived, it just happened to be the last day of December 1931— New Year's Eve. We pulled up to the house. The government had shipped my furniture and things down for me. It was piled in the front room of that house, bedding on the floor and the rest of the furniture on top of the bedding. The house was just finished. The plaster was wet.

There was a fireplace in the house. We went out and gathered up all kinds of wood, which was very plentiful because construction was going on at that time. They loaded that fireplace full of wood and touched the thing off. There wasn't a speck of that smoke that would go out the flue. It all came out in the house.

The Government's brick houses along Denver, Colorado, Park, and Utah streets were substantial structures, but the rapid pace of construction caused problems later.

WALKER YOUNG

The town was laid out after a good deal of thought but not too much time for experimentation. The idea was to get the town built, not whether everything was exactly right. It turned out that in excavation for the foundation [of the government houses], we ran into a type of a clay there which had swelling characteristics. Later there were some rains to the extent that the clay got wet [and] took its natural tendency to swell. That raised the house. Those houses raised sufficiently to put zigzag cracks in the joints of the brick. They had to go back and correct that.

MARY EATON

They did a lot of poor planning. Their houses weren't all that well planned, the government houses. You'd think they'd have the very finest in plans, but. . . . For instance, you'd have to go clear across the room in the dark to find the light switch. It just looked like somebody didn't know what they were doing.

I think we lived on a cockroach bed on Denver Street. It was terrible. We'd go someplace and come home and turn the lights on, and they would just scamper in the kitchen. All those houses along Denver had the same problem.

Unfortunately, if the husband in the family didn't work for Six Companies or the government, company housing was closed to them. Families who wanted to live in or near Boulder City stayed in McKeeversville, moved from place to place as space was available, or took whatever slapdash housing they could get.

DOROTHY NUNLEY

I thought this was the weirdest place I'd ever seen. It was going night and day; everything was open all night. I wasn't used to a town like that. The houses were all alike. There wasn't any landscaping except at the government houses and the government lawn. I thought I could never stand to live here.

I moved to an Olympic house. The Olympic houses were built in 1932 for the Olympics in California, in Los Angeles. Somebody was smart enough to buy them and bring them up here. They were put together later. They were built in from the highway [at] New Mexico Street, about two blocks. There was a very tiny combination front room and kitchen, and there was a tiny bedroom and a little bathroom. The bathroom didn't have a window in it. So my husband one day took a knife and cut a window in it. It was made out of something—I think they call it Celotex. It was pressed paper, or pressed wood, something like that.

They were the hottest places, and the coldest places in the wintertime. We had a little stove, kind of a round potbellied stove. I think they called them laundry stoves in those days. They were metal—I think probably tin. I'm sure they weren't iron. Anyhow, you had to heat them in order to heat your water for bathing or washing. I had a little oven in the middle of the stovepipe. I never did learn how to work the thing just right. Everything I put in it burned.

70

ALICE HAMILTON

We arrived in a duststorm. The road from Las Vegas to Boulder City was just a dirt one-track road. Boulder City was bare of greenery. I was aghast. It was terribly warm. I really thought I had come to the jumping-off place. The Six Companies houses were being built: row upon row of little white cottages. Government homes were in place, and the government buildings were in place.

The lists were very long for the Six Companies houses. People waited for sometimes a year before they could get into Six Companies housing. A good many of them lived in Las Vegas in the beginning, until housing became available to them.

Of course, there were priorities, and since [my husband] Al was not employed by the Six Companies, I would always be at the bottom of the list. I went immediately to work for Six Companies myself, but that still made us not able to get a Six Companies house. When we first arrived in Boulder City, Al had leased the home of Wilbur Weed, who was the government landscape artist. He had taken leave of absence for several months because of ill health. It was furnished. We brought very little with us. So for the first few months, we were very comfortable. I think we were in Wilbur Weed's house for five months before he returned.

I have lived, I think, in eight different homes in Boulder City during the time I have been here. I even lived at the men's dormitory, the California-Nevada Power Company's[2] dormitory, for some time when we could not find a place to live, a very small dormitory where their linemen and single men lived. We had a lot of fun. Of course, I was very young and I was the only lady about. We had a community shower and facilities, so whenever I wanted to take a shower, I always posted Al outside the shower door to let the men know it was occupied.

There simply was not enough company housing, and so the government set aside several blocks on the eastern edge of town—Avenues K, L, and M—where workers could build their own houses. Tom and Erma Godbey built the first privately owned house in Boulder City.

ERMA GODBEY

On February 1 [1932] it came out in the paper that there would be an area set aside for privately owned homes. They didn't even have the lots surveyed

71

yet. I had them survey me the third lot down. The restrictions finally got through from Washington what the houses would have to be: it would have to have an inside flush toilet, it couldn't have a boxcar roof [or] a tar-paper roof, and it must cost at least $250. Our carpenter was a man that had worked for New Mexico Construction, but he was putting the roof on the Browder Café. So we stopped and talked to him, and when he got through with the roof on the Browder Café, he would work on building our house. He said, "Have you got any plans?" My husband said, "No, but my wife will draw some." So I went home and I took the back off a tablet, and I drew plans for a small house. I said how long each side was supposed to be, and where the doors were to be, and the windows and everything.

The original part of the house was built out of all scrap material. My husband had just finished helping to build the [water] filter plant. We got quite a bit of this material from there. Also the Edison Company that built the towers that brought the juice in that built the dam had a tent mess hall close to the dam, but they were getting rid of it. We got their mess hall tables, which were built with pine floor, and my living room floor was those eight mess hall tables. And I got other things that had been used for cement forms and everything else.

While Six Companies, government, and private houses rose in different areas of town, the New Mexico Construction Company put in streets, gutters, curbs and sewers, employing a technology whose time was passing.

THEODORE GARRETT

Instead of using power equipment to do the leveling and grading, they used mule-drawn Fresnos. In case you're not familiar with the term *Fresno*, this was pulled by a three-horse team of mules. It was about six feet in width. It was just strictly a dirt mover, a scraper. One man handled a Fresno. It was on skids, and it would go back and forth. That's the way the dirt was moved in the leveling process. That probably was about the beginning of the end of the horse-and-buggy days.

Erma Godbey's husband, Tom, worked for the New Mexico Construction Company driving a four-up and a Fresno.

ERMA GODBEY

A four-up is four mules, and a Fresno is a scoop that you scoop dirt with by hand, and the mules pull it. You hold it down and scoop the dirt and say "Whoa" to the mules, and you dump it. Tom, being as he was a Missouri kid and his dad had had mules, he knew how to drive mules. It takes a bit of doing to drive mules. They were using the very latest equipment building the road down to the dam—that was LeTourneau Construction—big earth-moving machines. But New Mexico Construction was using mules and Fresnos.

MARION ALLEN

They didn't have too many tractors in those days. You'd take one on that sand, and you'd lose it. The mules went right over the top.

WILLIAM D. McCULLOUGH

They did have one conveyor, one ditchdigger, but it broke down nearly all the time. It was kind of slow. We live on [Avenue] M, and this is just about where they kept their horses and mules, right here.

By early 1932 Boulder City's houses and streets were in place, and a business district began thriving along Arizona Street and Nevada Highway. People still, however, had to contend with the weather. Fierce wind, sandstorms, and extreme heat and cold were especially fearsome for those still living in tents, but all of Boulder City's early settlers had to adjust to life in a miserable climate.

MILDRED KINE

In January [1932] they had this terrible windstorm. My husband was still working graveyard. He had come home about eight o'clock in the morning and gone to bed. The wind came up, blew the door open. I couldn't keep the door closed. I tried to put everything against the door I could. Finally I

One of the first privately built homes in Boulder City on a lot leased from the government, 6 July 1933

Billy Buck in the backyard of his family's Six Companies cottage at 631 Avenue I, about 1934

put the table against it, and it kept it shut. Then the old ridge pole in the middle started whipping back and forth. It came loose from the floor. I had to run out and get one of the neighbor men and come back and he pounded nails in. My husband was so tired and so sleepy that even with this fellow pounding those great big nails in, he never woke up at all. He didn't know a thing about it.

Then we had a hard windstorm come through about that same time. It blew many of the tents down, and all our belongings blew away, and even the roofs on some of the houses that they put up in Boulder City had blown off. Our tent stood it—I guess because it had the boards up halfway, and the board siding and the board floor.

HOBART BLAIR

There was people living up in Bootleg Canyon out west of Boulder City where they'd caught a bootlegger with a big still. They was living in all kinds of tents and shacks made of corrugated tin and powder boxes. We had a big wind here one day—must have been 70 miles an hour. I went over to McKeeversville, and a friend of mine said, "You ought to go up the wash with me and see what happened." So I went up there, and every one of those tents and shacks was just flattened.

EDNA FERGUSON

In the early days the sandstorms were really bad. There was so much sand because of all the activity and construction, street building and so forth. One day our older son was in school down at the other end of town, and the wind began to blow. The sand was all stirred up, and nothing could hold it down. It grew worse and worse. It was like a sand blizzard. We knew our son could never make it home. We were getting ready to go after him when his teacher's husband delivered him to our door. They had dismissed school and were taking all of the children home safely.

MADELINE KNIGHTEN

We used to look down in the Six Companies area and feel so sorry for the housewives down here. They'd put their lovely washing out on the line and a sandstorm would come up. We'd look down and see their washing blowing in that wind, and then we'd feel so sorry for them.

MARY EATON

I used to hang my diapers out on the line, and, with the wind, they would just twist around the line until they were worse off than when I put them out there. I've still never gotten used to that wind.

HELEN MANIX

When we first came to Boulder City, it didn't look very good. There was no grass or trees. There was dust, dust, dust everywhere. The houses were not built to keep the dust out—there were screened porches, the dust would blow through, and oftentimes we'd have to shake our bedding at night before we could get in to go to sleep.

TERESA JONES DENNING

We lived at 635 Avenue F, in a one-bedroom house, and it looked like all the others up and down the street. I'll never forget the first night we moved out there. There was no grass in Boulder City at that time. It was just sandpiles. The first night, it blew so hard when we got up in the morning we took a flat-bottomed shovel and actually shoveled the dirt out that had come in on the floor.

While there was little anyone could do against the wind and blowing sand, Boulderites were inventive in contriving ways to keep cool in the summer.

ALICE HAMILTON

I didn't cope very well at first. I can remember the first time I tried to walk downtown. I finally became so hot that I sat down on the curb, and finally some person, I can't recall who, came along in a car and picked me up and took me home. I just couldn't make it, it was so terribly warm. Then I can remember the first Fourth of July I spent in Boulder City. I spent it in the bathtub. I filled the tub full of cold water. I took one of the bed pillows, sank it down into the water, and sat on it.

We all had tiny porches on the houses. We used to put a bridge table out on the porch and play bridge. We always had a big pitcher of lemonade or cold water. Then we would put a dishpan under the table full of water and we'd put our feet in the dishpan. That's how we tried to keep cool.

We used to take a large bath towel and wring it from cold water and put it over ourselves. That's the way we slept part of the time. Of course, wetting the towels was really not a good idea. It caused pneumonia and arthritis.

Men slept under their homes, a lot of them. Most anything to try to keep cool.

JAKE DIELEMAN

The dormitories were really hot boxes. You didn't get a good day's sleep—but you could snatch a few hours. We'd wet a sheet, strip, wrap it around us, and crawl underneath the dormitory floor. It was cooler under there than inside. In a couple of hours, your sheet would get warm, so you'd get up and wet it again.

MADELINE KNIGHTEN

We used fans and lots of opened windows. We had wet rugs on our wooden floors. We'd hang big wet bath towels. We'd pin them into the windows with safety pins on the screens, and let the breeze blow through. It helped.

VELMA HOLLAND

We didn't have a refrigerator. I had orange crates on the kitchen window with a burlap sack over it. We took a five-gallon can and set it on top of that, with little holes [so that] the water would drip down. I kept lettuce and carrots and things in there.

MARY EATON

I just could not believe how people could live in that heat. I got pretty well used to it [but] not entirely. We had a floor fan, and I used to take a pan of water and put the floor fan behind it, hoping that that would make it a little cooler. It didn't, really, but it kind of gave you satisfaction to know you were trying to do something. A lot of people just took the hose and turned it on the roof and just wet the roof down. Another thing—you'd just turn the hosing on the floor, and that would kind of keep it wet and it seemed a little bit cooler. We'd also take a shower and go to bed wet.

LEO DUNBAR

[For] the first cooling system I had, which a number of us put in here, we got five-gallon oil cans, and took part of the top, part of the ends of them out. You cut a hole in the center and hang some towels in there, put a little bit of water in the bottom of what was left. We could rotate that thing a little bit, and if we had a fan, we'd put it at the end of the five-gallon can and blow the water through there with the idea that we'd get a little bit of cooling. That was the evaporation system we had at the beginning.

Keeping cool was the challenge most remember, but keeping warm in winter was a real problem, too.

LEO DUNBAR

We were not allowed to use electricity for heating at that time. All the electricity coming in from the southern California area was for purposes of construction, not for heating for houses or anything like that. We were lucky, though, because in the house was an electric range and, of course, a large oven. We put large rocks in the oven and heated them during the day, and wrapped them up in newspapers and put them in our beds at night.

WILMA COOPER

For heat we had a little potbellied stove that might have been 12 inches around in its biggest part and maybe three feet high. We was always poorer than church mice—everyone was in the same position; nobody had anything. We weren't any different than anyone else. So we'd go off across the desert and we'd pick up dead cactus, old sacks, dead twigs—whatever we could get—and bring 'em in and start a fire in that potbellied stove to heat water enough so we could have a cup of coffee. That old stove'd get red-hot—you was sure you was gonna burn the house down. But there wasn't anything for coals, so when the fire went out, it cooled off right away.

Landscaping soon began to adorn Boulder City, and early settlers would later speak with pride of their "beautiful oasis in the desert." The Bureau of Reclamation hired Wilbur Weed as landscape architect to determine what would grow in the town's desert climate.

BOB PARKER

The government did the only landscaping that was done here on a big scale. All the government houses, all of the parks, down around the city offices: the government landscaped them all. They set up a nursery down there below Colorado Street, between the water [filtration] plant and the truck route. They brought all these shrubs and whatnot in there and kept them in the nursery until they could get the lawns started and get trees started. In some areas of the town, like up there on Denver [Street] near Nevada Highway, that's all solid granite up there. They blasted cups out to plant those trees in. They brought in sand from these sand dunes we've got down here in the desert: blow sand. They hauled in a lot of steer manure by the truckload and tried to build up the soil to where they could get something to grow in it.

The first big problem that came up was in early 1932. They brought in all these shrubs and trees. Then they had a great big freeze and snowstorm that killed about half that nursery. Then they had to start over again.

EDNA FERGUSON

The bad winds came from the south. Our house, being at the north end of the city and on a side hill, caught a lot of the sand that blew up that way.

The government gardeners tried so hard to get the lawns started. These sandstorms would come along and cover up the new grass. One time they had to dig down a foot to find the grass level. They tried four times before the grass could hold its own against the elements.

NADEAN VOSS

They had one-by-twelves around each yard to hold the sand in so the wind couldn't blow your yard away while they put in grass seed. You were supposed to water every two hours until the lawn came up. Otherwise you were going to get fined for the seeds that were lost.

WILMA COOPER

Grass was very precious at that time. We were trying so hard to keep our 15 or 20 sprigs of grass growing. One time after we'd got a pretty good stand of grass growing, we had a terrible sandstorm and it was just like a snowdrift across our lawn. We didn't have a shovel; we didn't have anything to do with. My brother was here visiting me, so he and I took pie tins and paper sacks and went out and loaded the sand and hauled it out to the alley. We saved our grass.

The Six Companies, however, did not landscape its part of town but left such decisions to workers who lived there. Landscaping became a line of social demarcation in Boulder City: federal workers to the north had better jobs, better homes, and green lawns and trees; the Six Companies laborers lived in tiny, look-alike cottages with only the barest landscaping.

MARY EATON

[For] the people in the Six Companies, there was nothing except things like cactus and hollyhocks. There were people used to having a garden. They had radishes and onions and lettuce and some of the common things. But it wasn't easy to do a garden in Boulder City.

ROSE LAWSON

A lot of people went out and brought in cactus. Cactus was a novelty to people from the Middle West and different parts of the country. So we brought in two or three small barrel cactuses, and I planted them right over next to the house so that no one would run into them and get hurt. One evening several of us were sitting on the back steps. My daughter and her little girlfriend wanted to get outside, and they didn't want to climb over us, so they jumped out the window. The neighbor girl landed on the barrel cactus with her bare feet. They had to have the doctor take the cactus out of her feet. I felt so bad about it.

EDNA FRENCH

We wanted so much to have a lawn, and wanted so much to have something that would make shade for [my daughter] Helen and her little playmates to play under. So Helen and I went down to the [sewage] disposal plant a number of different times, taking paper bags, and carried back little pieces of Bermuda grass, which will come up here on the desert if there's water. We started up a little lawn on our front yard, not very large, about eight by ten, I suppose. But since all the houses looked alike, if anyone would ask, "Where do you live?" instead of giving the house number, very often we'd say, "You go down Avenue F until you come to the little plot of grass in the front yard." The children enjoyed that very much. To provide a little bit of shade, we planted castor beans around the house. Castor beans grow very quickly, and in just a few year's time they are almost treelike.

> *Both the government and the Six Companies offered huge savings on water bills to encourage people to maintain lawns and gardens. The more water people used, the less it cost.*

MARY EATON

The water rate was really great. I believe your water was $3 a month if you had a lawn, so most of us tried to have something. It wasn't much, but we had some grass out there.

MARY ANN MERRILL

[For] those who put in lawns, the water rate was much, much lower than if you had just the sand. I think your bill was $5. If you had a lawn, it was $3.50. I wish it was that way now.

STEVE CHUBBS

If you didn't have a lawn, you got the A [water] rate. If you had a lawn, you got the B rate. One of my jobs was to go around and see if people were entitled to the lower rate on water. If they had a lawn, I'd go back and tell [the Bureau of Reclamation] to cut the price down.

Once it took root against the wind and heat, the broad, verdant park below the Bureau of Reclamation Administration Building became the gathering place for families on hot summer nights.

ROSE LAWSON

After the warm weather came, as soon as it started to get dusk, women and the kids—and a lot of the men too—headed for the park. On every street in town, you'd see people with baby buggies, kiddie cars, and tricycles, heading for the park. People would stay there until they had to put their children to bed. Many of the people didn't have children at home, and the men would sleep up there.

LILLIAN WHALEN

In the evening during the summer, many, many people would go up on the government lawn and spend three or four hours until probably ten-thirty at night, when it would cool down a little bit. Then they'd go home and wet their sheets and spread them on the bed and try to go to sleep.

WILMA COOPER

During the hottest part of the summer, up here on the government lawn they'd have just a big church service. One church would open with a prayer; and another one, their choir would sing; and another church's minister would give the speech. Each church would have a part in it, and sometimes it'd be two hours long. And sing—my stars, everyone in town was up there, so you couldn't find a place to stand on the lawn. Everybody sang, and it was beautiful. That went on for quite a few years. All the churches worked together. And now any one church puts something on, everyone in town patronizes it. This all goes back to that early time years ago when we was all in the same boat together. We can't forget those hard times.

Within a year of its groundbreaking, Boulder City resembled an ideal American town: neatly planned, clean, safe and secure against the threat of the depression beyond the reservation gate. Erma Godbey remembers the community gathering for its first Christmas in 1931.

ERMA GODBEY

The first Christmas was at the Anderson Mess Hall. Anderson fixed the goodies for the children. As I remember, there was an apple and an orange each, and some candy. Then they decided to have a program. There was a girl—her name was Betty Campbell. She played piano. They had a piano in the mess hall. They wanted my littlest one, my Ila, to be the baby in the manger, but I knew she'd be scared. So they managed to get hold of a big doll to put in the manger scene. Then all the little kids that had been going to Sunday school sang "Away in a Manger." The New Mexico Construction Company that was building the streets and sewer system for Boulder City had a group of young men. Those men were the Wise Men and the shepherds, and they actually brought frankincense and myrrh. They were burning them as they came down the aisle of the mess hall that night. We never expected anything like that.

The floor of Black Canyon with the river diverted, 1 December 1932

4

TURNING THE RIVER: BLACK CANYON,
1931 TO NOVEMBER 1932

"By dawn the riverbed was dry."

Before work could begin on the dam structure itself, the Colorado River had to be diverted around the construction site. The Six Companies drilled four diversion tunnels, each 50 feet in diameter and three-quarters of a mile long, through the solid rock walls of Black Canyon. Drilling the diversion tunnels was itself a monumental engineering feat. Tex Nunley was among the first to begin this work.

TEX NUNLEY

I was a rodman there. That's where I fit in. I painted a cross right in the center on the face [of the canyon wall]. We took a 50-foot tape and went around, painted a line all around. They had to drill out a 56-foot hole. The tunnel, when they were finished, was 50 foot in diameter [because] there had to be 3 foot of concrete all the way around.

They drilled about a 9-foot hole at the top. The engineers had to give line when you started in that tunnel, give line all the way through there, and where it came out down there. When a curve came on the line, you'd put in stakes. They had to know where the tunnel started and where that tunnel would come out at the end. If one went way over here and the other one some other place, you'd be lost.

Of course, this tunnel above, on the top, it fit in with the rest of the 50-foot tunnel when the other part was drilled. They drilled that first for air.

They wanted to get as much air in there as possible to drill the big part of the tunnel.

Once the pilot tunnels had proven the alignment, the diversion tunnels themselves could be drilled. The unprecedented size of these tunnels and the tight construction schedule the Six Companies followed required innovation. Bernard F. "Woody" Williams, assistant construction superintendent, devised a truck-mounted frame to speed drilling holes for dynamite charges. Huge and ungainly, the Williams "jumbo" nevertheless proved successful. Neil Holmes was a pipe fitter who helped build the first experimental jumbo.[1]

NEIL HOLMES

It fell to me to pipe up that first one. They built that out where you could put 32 or 36 machines on that one truck—drilling machines, jackhammers. They were liners.[2] They had air and water piped up on this truck.

The carpenters built the frame on this International truck. Then I had to go in and pipe it up and put manifolds on so that the miners would have air and water. So whenever they moved, the air and water moved right with them. They had to have that air and water [because] they couldn't drill dry holes. They had to have water to keep the dust down.

Then they found out that that worked all right, so then they built four new machines—made them out of steel. Instead of just a wooden frame on them trucks, they built steel frames. They knew the wooden one wouldn't hold up, because vibrations would shake it all loose. They were built uptown here and then hauled down there.

JOE KINE

The jumbo was for drilling. They'd back that up against the wall and drill out all the holes, then move it over and drill out another set of holes. Then we'd all jump in there, blow out the holes, load them with dynamite, and shoot. There was no such thing as a powderman. Everybody was a powderman. Seems like no matter what it was, we always got the work done.

They left a flat face on the bottom [of the tunnel] so it would make a good road for the trucks to drive on to haul the muck out.

MARION ALLEN

While I was working as a nipper, you worked on the drilling jumbos. Underneath the Williams jumbo was six liners right by the wheels underneath the deck of the jumbo. I think there was 26 machines on there altogether; I'm not positive of the number. There was 6 of them underneath. The miners under there, I think, was the ones they didn't like, because all the water and everything came down on you.

That was the nipper's job: to hand these fellows [drilling] steel under the wheels under the jumbo there. It was a good safe place too. If something caved in, it might get the ones above you, but not you. The nipper had to work under there and hand them the steel that laid on the ground. It paid $5. I was always trying to get on one of those machines. They paid $5.60. That 60¢ was important money.

STEVE CHUBBS

I went down and worked as a grunt down at the dam. A grunt is an electrician's helper, stringing wires to the loaded headings. They'll drill these holes and then load them with dynamite, and bring the primer wires out and tie them to a bigger wire. They had great big long sticks, and they'd shove the primer back with that. The holes were, I guess, 10 foot deep, perhaps deeper. It was my job to go down there with an electrician and hold the flashlight while he twisted the wires together. Then we'd run down to a conduit, to an adit,[3] and the electrician set the shot.

Most of the accidents in the drilling was caused by the men tapping the primers too hard. They have a primer which they don't use anymore. It was mercury fulminate. It's pretty touchy. You put your primer in first with a wooden stick, cautiously. You put the dynamite in behind it or in front of it. Then you bring the wires out and tie them together. The men got too rough, and the dynamite went off and killed a man. We had electric shovels, and we had a man down in front of the shovel. He was an oiler.[4] The shovel hit a primer that hadn't gone off and killed him.

Miners and mucking machines at work in the pilot tunnel for Diversion Tunnel No. 4, 12 October 1931

Trimming jumbo in Diversion Tunnel No. 4, 12 April 1932

Marion Allen came close to death one night when he walked into the wrong tunnel before a blast.

MARION ALLEN

I think I must have been a little thick, probably still am. Red [McCabe] sent me in to tell the shovel boss that was mucking out—to give him some message to move his truck. An electrician and his helper always put off the shots. When they came out of this tunnel, one of them was supposed to stand there, and the other one would go over and hook up the wires. Everybody was out by the time they'd shoot. For some reason there was nobody. I walked in this tunnel to go back there. I got back quite a long ways, and everything is quiet. I had that feeling that something's wrong here. I thought, "I bet I'm in the wrong tunnel." I turned around and started to run. I had probably run a hundred feet when "Boom!" I just went floating out the tunnel. I got up and looked around like you do when you fall down, first thinking, "Did someone see me?" I had the biggest headache you've ever seen in your life.

I went to work the next night—I was on swing shift—and Red said, "You don't look good. You better go home. I'm going to get you a ride home." He sent me home. For three or four days, my head rang. Oh, man. I could hear that blast for a week. It must have been several years later when I took a physical, and the guy said, "Both your eardrums are cracked." They never said nothing up here. I went to the hospital too, but they never said anything about them being cracked. They just figured if I could hear, I was all right.

Once the rock had been blasted away, debris had to be hauled out before work could continue.

STEVE CHUBBS

They'd bring the shovels and the trucks in. They called it muck. Ever hear the word? It was mostly broken rock. But it was an old word they picked up someplace. So they used to refer to the hauling out of the rock as mucking—mucking out. They'd muck out the rock and haul it away.

THEODORE GARRETT

The muck had to be hauled up the hill on either side of the river. On the Arizona side we went straight up the riverbank to a dump area that was on a canyon heading into the river.

HARRY HALL

I got a job working graveyard as what they called a pitman. They were scaling the diversion tunnels at that time on day shift. Graveyard shift would go down there with a 2,300-volt electric Marion shovel and muck out the material that they had shot during the day shift. My job was to back the trucks in so the operator on the shovel would not have to swing too much to load the trucks. They had lights that illuminated well enough so you could see what you were doing. The truck drivers had a throttle on the running board, so they could stand up and look and drive it backwards. They were corn binders we were using—pretty rugged trucks.

TOMMY NELSON

My first job was in the diversion tunnels. These big trucks in there spill off a lot of rocks, and my assignment was to keep the rocks out of the road. I've got to tell you something rather humorous here, to show you how dumb I was. A big rock had fallen off one of the trucks. My foreman came down, and he said, "Nelson, go up to the tunnel and get a jackhammer, and come down here and break up that rock." I hated to admit to him that I was so dumb that I didn't know what a jackhammer was. But I had an inkling of an idea that he was talking about a drill. So I went down to the tunnel, and I came back with what I thought he wanted. He came by and he said,"Nelson, did you find that jackhammer?" I said, "I couldn't find a jackhammer, but I got a drill," and I pointed to it. He said, "How come you're not running it?" I said, "I don't know how." He said, "You know, I thought I was giving you a break. You have a Scandinavian name, and most Scandinavians are pretty good hammermen." So then I told him what I was, and he took it a little easier on me.

With so much going on in the narrow confines of the tunnels, tempers flared when one crew got in the way of another. Pipe fitter Neil Holmes remembers a war he fought with the truck drivers.

NEIL HOLMES

The truck drivers weren't very popular around here. If we had a pipeline going along the side of the tunnel, it seemed like they would try their best to get that pipeline with one of the wheels, and they very often got it. We'd have to take that pipe out and replace it. A lot of the times, they would make a turnaround in there. Them tunnels were 50 foot in diameter, and they could turn around in there, but they'd have to go up the side of the wall a little. We had the pipe up on the side of the wall, maybe five or six feet, hanging on the walls. They would try to get up and get that pipeline. I've seen them go up high enough to get it, too. They would go up and use that pipeline as a bumper to turn their wheels.

More often the competition was good-natured.

MARION ALLEN

The main thing was this challenge. You had to beat the other crew. It didn't make any difference what you did, but you had to beat that other crew. You had to get more footage. "We got two more feet than you did!" This was the whole conversation. It didn't make any difference. Those miners would run into that tunnel, drill all these holes, and run back out again so they could shoot, just to beat the other crew.

Even when crews were cooperating, they still met unexpected setbacks. Torrents of muddy water flooded the tunnels when the Colorado River overflowed on 9 February 1932.

NEIL HOLMES

In February 1932 they had a flood come down the Colorado River. It lasted two or three days, and it flooded our tunnels out, our big tunnels. We had to get the tunnels all cleaned out and pump the water out. Some of that water was too heavy to pump. There was so much mud in it that they had to haul muck in there, spray in the water, and then haul the muck out again. It was too heavy to pump, and it was too light to get out any other way. That took several days, and it ran into probably three or four weeks before that was all cleaned out to where they could go back to their regular mining again, their drilling. You'd wade in there and it would be three and four feet deep in the bottom of them tunnels so that you couldn't pump that muck out. So they had to get all the sand and muck and rock in there to absorb that, and then hauled it out with the shovels.

Construction of the diversion tunnels was dangerous work for the laborers who drilled and blasted the rock, drove the trucks, and shoveled the muck, but it was an equally daunting task to supervise the job. Keeping track of thousands of workers 24 hours a day and keeping to the construction schedule were largely the work of two men: Frank Crowe and Walker Young. Crowe was construction superintendent for the Six Companies, and Young was the government's construction engineer. Both provided vivid memories for those who worked under them.

MARION ALLEN

My father was in Wyoming near Jackson Lake when this young fellow, [Frank] Crowe, and Bob Sass—two brother-in-laws—came along looking for a site to build a dam for the Bureau of Reclamation. This was back about 1906. I wasn't born until 1906, so nothing could happen before then. Being about the same age as my father, they all became great friends. Mr. Crowe finally decided on the site of the dam after several tests. From then on they were in contact over a period of years.

In 1921 [Crowe] came into the valley—my father was a rancher there—and asked him what he was going to do. My father said, "We're going to move to California." He said, "That's wonderful. I'm going to build Boulder Dam." This seems farfetched; I tell my daughter and some younger people about it, and they say, "How would a man know that he was going to build a dam that hadn't even been started?" But Mr. Crowe was quite a planner. He had been with the Bureau of Reclamation for years. After the Bureau of Reclamation quit building their own dams, he went with a private contractor. Murl Emery, on the Colorado River, was telling me that he remembered five years before the dam, when he first met Crowe. He took him down the river, and Mr. Crowe looked over this site of the dam.

Another little background: Walker Young and Mr. Crowe had worked together in the bureau, and so apparently Mr. Crowe was getting firsthand

Frank Crowe, 1932

information of the surveying that was going on in the early twenties or even before, since Walker Young was in charge of that. He had a desire to build this because it was the biggest project that was known to that time. He had planned for years and years. He had looked at all the canyons; he had been up and down the river a dozen times, I heard afterwards.

Frank Crowe. I only knew him for 20 or 25 years, and I didn't know him. He was that type of a person. He was a very deep person. Even his girls, Pat and Betty, said that their father was so bashful that he hardly ever kissed their mother in front of them. Now this was the type of a man he was.

Yet I remember when my brother died on the Shasta Dam. He [Frank Crowe] came down to see my dad, and he said, "Val, you might be short a little money. I better give you a couple hundred." Dad said, "Well, I don't need it." He said, "You take it along. Pay me back whenever you get to it." People, how many hundreds of people that he would help out if somebody—especially [if] a man got killed, the breadwinner. He was always right there.

But on the other hand, he'd get you a job, like he got me a job here, but if I'd have got fired or laid off the next couple of days, it would have been too bad. And that's the type he was. He'd give you a boost, but you'd better look out for yourself.

BOB PARKER

Everyone who worked down here knew who Frank Crowe was. He was all over the job. His workmen, he knew them by their first name, nearly every one of them. Even we who did not work for him, he knew who we were. Once he learned your name, he never forgot it. Frank Crowe: his trademark was a white shirt. He came to work every morning wearing a brand spanking newly ironed white shirt. His daughters told me when they were here in 1950 that that's one part that their mother played in the building of Hoover Dam. She never let him go out of the house on any morning without a clean white shirt on, and that was his trademark—that and a large Stetson hat. Any time you saw a white shirt and a large Stetson hat coming, you knew that was Frank Crowe. Very tall and erect, kind of a stately looking person, a very likable fellow. But he never forgot you if you ever crossed him. Men that had worked for him 15, 20 years, before this dam started, if they ever did anything wrong, he knew it. He remembered it; he never forgot. He had a memory like an elephant, Frank Crowe.

ELTON GARRETT

Frank Crowe was a genius for organized thinking and for imparting organized thinking to other people. Frank Crowe knew engineering. He knew dam construction through experience. He knew how to motivate. He knew how to be friendly with the guy that was tamping the powder into that hole. He knew how to smile at a good gag, such as, for instance, when somebody asked him, "What's the date that you're going to do so-and-so?" He said, "I don't know. I haven't been to the recreation center yet to ask 'em." This was the sort of thing he was capable of. He not only was an engineering genius; he was a people genius. That went a long ways.

But not far enough to impress Leroy Burt.

LEROY BURT

Can I tell you a little story about Frank Crowe? When we were working on the plugs, we had a catwalk between the Arizona side and the Nevada side [of Black Canyon]. We were working back in the valve houses, putting concrete around the big pipes that came out. We had a water-cooling fountain on the Nevada side, but they didn't have one on the Arizona side. I'd take four or five water bags over and get them full, and bring them back. I'm coming back across, and here's this gentleman standing there that I never saw before. He said, "Can I have a drink of that water?" And I said, "The water fountain's right over there, sir. If you want a drink, just help yourself." When I got back over there, somebody asked me, "What did that guy want?" I said, "He wanted a drink of water. I told him to go over and get one on the Nevada side." He said, "Do you know who that was?" I said, "No, it doesn't make any difference to me." He said, "That was Frank Crowe." I figured he was just as healthy as I was; he could walk over and get himself a drink if he wanted to.

SAUL "RED" WIXSON

[Crowe] had an awesome job, and if he wasn't in his office, he was down at the dam. It'd never surprise me to see him down there at two o'clock in the morning, looking around. He didn't want to listen to what was going on down there. He wanted to see it with his own eyes.

I never saw [Crowe] get excited about anything. If something went wrong, he was there to get an eye on it, to explain what was wrong, fix it. He was there to help you, not to fire you. One thing he knew was men. Everyone has a different temperament, and he knew how to treat you. For instance, he never bawled me out, 'cause he knew I was the wrong kind of a guy to bawl out; I'd eat my heart out. And there was other guys he could nibble at a little bit. One time he said to me, "I got to nibble on Jack 'cause he's got to be pushed along a little bit." He respected his men. He was appreciative.

And Charlie Shea'd come down—he was on the Six Companies board of directors and took information back and forth to their office in San Francisco—and he was usually with Crowe. We'd always say, "Here come Crowe-Shea! Here come Crowe-Shea!"

MARION ALLEN

The real contractor, the real push, was old Charlie Shea. He was a character and a half. He was another one like Crowe. How could you could describe

95

a man like that? Very quiet. He'd sit down beside of you and watch you work there for an hour and never say anything. But he was wondering what was going on, and wanted to see what's going on.

If I have time, a quick story anyhow. This fellow came from down in the South somewhere. In the South he was working on a job [where] he wore a tie. He came out, and he's got a tie on, a nice shirt, and a blue vest. He's a [concrete] finisher. See, that's up above a laborer scale. We got on the truck, and he was talk, talk, talk. I was talking to him, and he said, "See that poor old man down there? Good gosh, somebody ought to help him on the bus." Charlie [Shea] is sitting there with his old raggedy hat and his old sweater. Some of the guys laughed. I said, "Well, Mr. Morgan, that's Charlie Shea. He's the resident contractor. He's in charge of this whole project." "What? That old man?" He shakes his head. About that time Crowe drives up in his Buick. "Oh, that's his chauffeur, huh?" "No, that's Mr. Crowe. He's the general superintendent." Then he got to shake. He says, "I've never seen people like this. You know, back where I come from, people in those positions never come on the job. They send somebody else." He couldn't figure this western business out.

If Frank Crowe was the guiding presence on the job, mingling with the workers in the canyon and recreation hall, Walker Young was a silent leader behind the scenes.

BOB PARKER

Walker Young was a man that was a stickler for detail. The day after I went to work, I had a letter from Walker Young. It told me what my duties were, who my boss was, and who I was to see if I had any problems. That detail you don't find in a man that's the head of a project as big as this. He knew every man that worked down here. I think before the job was done, he knew most of the Six Companies employees.

At night, after I went to work down in the canyon, after I left the warehouse to work in the mixing plant down in the canyon, I would be on duty in maybe swing shift or graveyard. I'd be there in the lab office, where we did our paperwork on the concrete slump tests and all that. There wouldn't be anything said, but I'd turn around and he'd be sitting in the chair in the office. Sometimes he'd speak and talk a leg off of you. The next time he came down to sit in the chair, he might not say three words all the time he was down there. But he was watching everything that was going on. Sometimes he wouldn't leave until after midnight, coming back to town. He'd spend all day in the office, then after dinner come down there and watch the work going on in the canyon. That was Walker Young.

One night I had trouble down there. One of the mixer concrete batcher men in the concrete plant was goosing the concrete batches with water. That would make the concrete a lot thinner. They poured a lot faster; you didn't have to tamp it as much. When I caught this batcher doing that, I climbed his frame about it. He said I couldn't prove it. I said, "If I catch you doing that one more time, we're shutting this plant down." I was just a kid in those days, a young fellow, but I told him what was going to happen if he kept on goosing that concrete with water. So he told me that he was going to call Frank Crowe. I said, "Better yet, I'll call Walker Young and Frank Crowe both, and get them down here." I said, "I'm not afraid. Walker Young will be right down here in 30 minutes if I call him. You'll have to answer to Frank Crowe because I know Frank Crowe and Walker Young are just like peas in a pod. They are here to work together and get this job done."

Both Walker Young and Frank Crowe were on the spot to ensure the success of the Boulder Canyon Project, and completion of the diversion tunnels was their first test. As drilling continued through the winter of 1931–32, it became clear that often workers' health was not the first consideration.

HARRY HALL

Later on they had air piped into the tunnels, but there were a lot of exhaust fumes from the trucks so that the condition of the oxygen in there really was not too great. The most oxygen we had in the air was 16 percent, and I'm sure it was less than 16 percent. Miners used to take canaries and put them in a cage, and when the canary looked like he was about gone, you'd better get out of there because there was less than enough oxygen to exist on.

They didn't realize that the exhaust fumes were as dangerous as they were. Later on there were some people that claimed—and I'm sure that it was true—that they had various side effects from those noxious fumes. I didn't notice it. Of course, I was younger than a lot of them, so that some things that would bother other people might not bother me.

CURLEY FRANCIS

Driving trucks through these tunnels, there was a gas problem there, real bad at times. We usually could tell by looking at the lights in the tunnel. If they had a big blue ring around them, we would know the gas was getting pretty rough in there. But fortunately for the truck drivers, you would be driving through it and come out the other end. Usually if you got too much gas, that's when you would get sick—when you came out into the fresh air. And they [took] you on up to the hospital.

TOMMY NELSON

A string of lights through those diversion tunnels that were attached to the wall looked like somebody striking matches from the carbon monoxide gas from those trucks running back in there. I'll tell you, it was tough. Were that dam being built today, as to those diversion tunnels, I'm afraid OSHA would have closed it down in 10 minutes. That gas was terrible.

JOHN GIECK

On the first of April 1932, I was sent down to the dam to do carpentry, building forms for the concrete in the [diversion] tunnels. Trucks and tractors working in there, carbon monoxide. I went to work down there one night, and there was 17 men in [my] crew. The next morning myself and 3 others was all that [was] left—all the rest was taken out sick. You look down that tunnel and them lights was yellow. It was rough.

MURL EMERY

One night I was called out to go down to the boats. A major catastrophe— go down to the boats. So I dashed down and jumped on the first boat that left and got down to the upper portals. They were hauling men out of those tunnels like cordwood. They had been gassed. I laid them on the bottom of the boat, along the seats and whatnot. I don't know how many was gassed. They were sick, real sick. They weren't dead. They were real sick from being gassed working in that tunnel along with the running trucks and this and that. So they hauled them out of there. And that diehard Frank Crowe in the courthouse swore that to the best of his knowledge, there never had been men gassed underground working.

The number of casualties from gas in the tunnels prompted the Bureau of Reclamation to send a team from Washington to investigate. Bob Parker was in the hospital for a hernia operation, and he remembers being questioned.

BOB PARKER

What they were investigating [was] whether there was any truth that all these people dying of pneumonia were actually being gassed in the tunnels. I was in [the hospital] at the time. They came through there and asked me how I was getting along. I told them fine. Then they wanted to know how I was getting treated. I said they were feeding me pretty good, and I liked the nurses. I was going to get out of there pretty quick. I thought that a lot of that ballyhoo that they were listening to in Washington was propaganda. I said as far as I'm concerned, I was quite well satisfied with the doctors, the nurses, and the whole works. I don't think they found out anything of substance.

JOHN CAHLAN

They did have several people out there who were working in the tunnels who filed suit against Six Companies. They charged that because of the carbon monoxide gas that was in the tunnels they had been seriously affected one way or another. One guy charged that he had lost his sexual powers because of the carbon monoxide gas. The same attorney was representing all of these clients, and he figured that if he could win one suit, then the Six Companies would settle the rest of them. So the Six Companies decided, well, all right, if we're going to fight this thing, we're going to fight the toughest one to beat, and they picked this one. The trial went on for weeks and weeks and weeks. Bud Bodell, who was the investigator for the Six Companies, tied this guy up in knots because the plaintiff had gone to Los Angeles and made dates with women. A special investigator followed the complainant to the hotels and listened in on conversations with these women, proving the guy was just as potent as anybody could be. They had a parade of witnesses at the trial and all these women that he had made progress with. So he lost the case. The court dismissed all the rest of the complaints. They never even tried to fight them.

MARY EATON

The way we felt was [that] the men became ill from the gasses in the tunnels. It was too much. So they sent them to the hospital. Of course, it affected their lungs and would go into pneumonia. But we always felt [the diagnosis of pneumonia was] because there would be compensation to pay otherwise: if you said they died of gasses in the tunnels, they were obligated to compensate you, to compensate the family. So they'd just say pneumonia, and they'd get by with that. We never felt that was fair.

TEX NUNLEY

You had to be dead, absolutely dead, down on the job to get killed on the job. If they ever got you in the hospital, you didn't get killed on the job; you just died. Bad luck.

Once the diversion tunnels had been holed through, they still had to be trimmed to a smooth, uniform diameter of 56 feet and then lined with 3 feet of concrete.

STEVE CHUBBS

I worked with a gang of laborers, and we had to clean up the rock before they poured the concrete. The rock had to be clean. My job was to use a shovel and pick up as much rock as possible. Then they'd wash the rest of the rock up with high-pressure water. I only had that job about 10 days. I got fired—thank goodness.

CARL MERRILL

The labor crew that I became a part of, their job was to clean up a pour before they poured the cement. In other words, they had it so clean, every bit of gravel and sand and dirt had to be off of these rocks. It was clean enough really to eat off of. These pours had to be this clean. They used water, a high-pressure hose. Then the last thing you did was mop it up with sponges. They'd get it that clean, and then they'd come in and pour the concrete, then do the next one.

NEIL HOLMES

After the tunnels were all drilled out, we started in on the cement work, and that was quite a project. At first they had to go through and pour the invert, the bottom of the tunnel. Then after that was poured, they built what they called a sidewall jumbo that they poured the sidewalls with.[5] They built that on a track that was laid in the invert. That jumbo was moved ahead. After you poured one form, they collapsed that form, brought it in four or five inches, and then moved it on ahead to the next place, then set that at the proper spot and poured another one. That cement was brought in there on trucks and lifted up with a hoist. They poured that cement in there that way.

Then after that was built, after that was all formed up, they had to build another jumbo for the top [of the tunnel], the arch jumbo, they called it. That was hauled in there, and most of that was blown in there, either pumped in there or blown in there to make a complete circle. That was quite some project for four of them tunnels that had to be built up that same way.

CARL MERRILL

I stayed in the tunnels most of the time. I went from a laborer to a hook tender. We were still in the tunnels and had to get concrete back in there for the liners. They would set these great big rotating drums down on trucks that would back into the tunnels to where they were pouring. Then it was up to me to get that batch of concrete up in the air. This one had a monorail running down the top of the tunnel. I would hook the cable with hooks onto this [concrete] agitator, and then they would move it back in the tunnel, just like on a skyhook. They brought it back when they emptied it, set it on the truck, I unhooked it, and the truck took it back up so they could hook it from the outside [and] take it up to the concrete plant to refill it. Just a vicious circle.

It was extremely warm. Concrete is normally hot. And it was extremely warm back there. I remember when we were pouring the plug—I think it was in the number 3 tunnel on the Arizona side, the one closer to the river. They say the temperature got up to 150, 160 degrees back in there, and men were working. They'd go back in and work for 15 minutes, come out and rest for 15 minutes, back and forth like that. It was very hot.

We used to bring the concrete in and they'd dump it into the concrete pump. Now this pump, you either hooked up a six-inch or an eight-inch line to it, and you actually pumped the concrete up into where you wanted it. Wherever you laid the pipe, this is where the concrete went.

Before this they tried to pour this concrete into hoppers and then put it into an enclosed steel case, which had air entering it through several different places. They tried to blow this concrete through the lines with air. But they found out that the concrete separated too badly, so they abandoned that and went to the pump. From the pump they went to the monorail. They used every method in the world that they knew at that time to get concrete back into those tunnels.

They tried to pump—they could get away with inch-and-a-half rock. We called it inch-and-a-half aggregate. This was the size of the rock that was in the concrete mix. If we tried to go to a three-inch aggregate, usually we got into trouble. There were valves that were going back and forth that would let the concrete through. Then they'd come to a Y here, and went out one line.

A lot of times that Y, these rocks would get stuck right there, and then we'd have trouble. The whole thing had to come down, because you had to get it washed out before the concrete set up in there. That's when the work started. If it happened, we'd cuss and raise the devil when they started sending that three-inch rock through there, because we knew we were going to have problems. We'd try to finish our shift and get out of there before they'd hit, and let the next shift have the problem.

STEVE CHUBBS

It was hard work for the men because they had to be up there with the vibrators [to keep the concrete from separating]. They vibrated it with air vibrators. They would shimmy and shake and shiver when you turned the air on. Have you ever run one? Oh, you missed something. You ought to run one. They beat you to death.

The sloping sides of the tunnels made concrete finishing difficult and were a real test of whether a worker deserved the aristocratic wage of $6 a day. Marion Allen talked himself into a job as a concrete finisher in the tunnels.

MARION ALLEN

There was a fellow by the name of Broughten who was another friend of my dad's. He had charge of the concrete. I had been in the concrete business, the construction business, quite a while. I wanted to get back on finishing. Another thing—it paid $6 a day. I had got up to $5.60—then, with that 40¢, boy! So I went up to see him.

This Jack, he was a rough old character—a rough character, not so old. Forty was old, you know. Jack said, "What are you, claiming to be a finisher. What did you ever finish?" I said, "I've had plenty of finishing." "Aw," he said, "you know, a finisher came out here today, and I sent him down to get some tools." The company furnished the tools. "He got a shovel and went in the tunnel." He made me mad. I said, "Jack, Dad can tell you I'm a finisher. But I'll tell you—if you're not satisfied, I'll work tomorrow and forget to put me on the payroll." "OK, be here in the morning." Then I put about four and a half years on the finishing crew.

[My] first finisher's job was finishing the inverts on the bottom of the tunnel. When we went down there, I could see what Jack was talking about. I think there were about 18 finishers when I got down there in this tunnel. Of course, a lot of them had finished their breakfast, I imagine. But they were all trying, these poor buggers, to do something. These slopes that would come up. If you've ever seen anybody trying to finish concrete on a slope when it's real soft, they start patting, and the first thing, it's on the bottom. You'd get it pulled up fine. Then you'd turn around, and some guy's patting and it's all down on the bottom.

The next day I came out there, there were only half the finishers there. There were only about eight. Three days later there were only five of us there. About two or three days more, there were only three of us. We got along pretty fair that way.

The Six Companies built cofferdams at either end of the damsite: one above the site to force the river into the completed diversion tunnels, and one below to prevent water from backing up into the construction site.

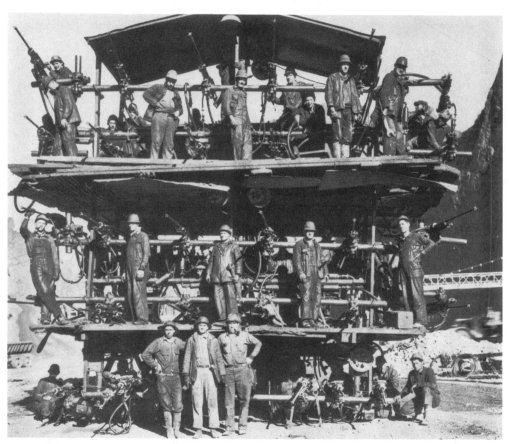

Drilling jumbo, 20 April 1932

STEVE CHUBBS

Building the upper cofferdam was really a problem child. They poured a concrete facing on it, to take care of the river's surge. It seems to me that my uncle worked all night for that cofferdam—worked all day and all night. It's a slow job, building a cofferdam, because for each layer of 12 inches that you put down, you have to tap it with a sheep's foot. Have you ever seen on highways this gadget that goes around and taps the soil? Well, they had that. They couldn't tap it when it was underwater, but after it got up aways, then they'd start tapping it.

MARION ALLEN

They talk about the heat, but we were working on the face of the cofferdam. I was working, and we were floating off the top, just a float job on the top of the cofferdam there. All at once this concrete is hard. I lifted up my float, and it's all frozen. I told a young inspector there, "We're going to have to do something quick, or lose this concrete."

He got ahold of somebody. The concrete boss had left. He rushed out there, and in a few minutes they started dumping these barrels off, and strung them all the way up the pour, and all the scrap wood. There was always scrap wood on the forms. They built fires in all of those and warmed it up enough so that we got it finished. But that was the only concrete I've ever seen that froze here. By getting it quick, it didn't hurt it, but if it had went froze on through, why, it would have been like a bunch of dirt.

Raising the lower cofferdam, however, was not as complicated a job as the upper cofferdam had been.

WILFRED VOSS

They were putting in the lower cofferdam before the dam was ever built. That would keep the water from backing up into the damsite, you see. It was quite a structure. It was a real good little dam itself. There are no two ways about that. That was all packed in. There were mechanical devices for tapping it. There were what they called—sheep's foot was what they called them. They were big rotors with all these prongs standing up there with pads on them, and they'd drag them with tractors to compact the earth. I was down there helping build that doggone pile of mound of dirt and rock. That's what it was. That's all, because it was something to be removed. It was strictly to keep the backwash from going into the damsite.

Bob Parker remembers a story about the lower cofferdam that he uses to refute popular misconceptions that there were workers buried in the concrete of Hoover Dam.

BOB PARKER

They never left anybody buried in the dam. The only man that was ever buried down there was a big Italian. He was out there on a barge in the early days with hip boots and a lot of tools. He fell off the barge into the water and drowned. They never retrieved his body. They never found his body, 'cause it never floated; it stayed on the bottom in the mud in the river. They put the cofferdam in there, and three or four years later, when they dug the cofferdam out—the lower cofferdam below the dam—they found his remains. They knew it was him because of the hip boots that he was wearing when he went into the water. But they brought his remains out of that lower cofferdam, buried in that muck. That was the only man actually buried down there, and he was drowned and dead before the cofferdam was ever put in there.

On 12 November 1932 Herbert Hoover, returning to Washington from California after his defeat in the presidential election, paid a surprise visit to the damsite. Florence Squires Boyer and her family accompanied him.

FLORENCE BOYER

Shortly after his defeat by Franklin D. Roosevelt, President Hoover visited the dam for the first and only time.[6] He wired my father and mother to meet him, so they went to Boulder City. President Hoover had been taken to the dam by Walker Young, I believe, and he came back to the Administration

Building steps and made a little speech. Then we met him, and he asked us to ride back on the train with him.

The only recollection I have particularly is how tired he looked. I never in my life saw a man look so worn out and so completely defeated. Of course, it was a result of all the trials and tribulations of the depression and the campaign and the smearing he'd gotten, which he didn't really deserve. I can remember only how tired he looked.

DENZLE S. PEASE

I saw President Hoover in the fall of 1932 when he was here. He wasn't very high in my estimation, long about that time. The feeling that most of us had—which I now feel was erroneous—but we all blamed Hoover because of the crash.

WILLIAM D. McCULLOUGH

Hoover visited down in the mess hall. I didn't care for him at all. We was all eating in the mess hall in the big right wing by the laundry. We knew he was coming in. Whether I liked him or disliked him, I thought we should show him the courtesy of standing up. Some of the people even booed him. They wouldn't stand up. They kept on eating. People were pretty bitter about even having to come here.

On 14 November 1932—two days after Herbert Hoover paid his surprise visit to the damsite—the Colorado River was turned out of its bed through the diversion tunnels, marking the first great milestone of the Boulder Canyon Project.

STEVE CHUBBS

I remember they were really excited about taking the river out of its channel because it's quite a task. They had to have a lot of muck, and they had to have it handy, and they had to get it into the river fast, too. They worked all night. I forgot when they started, but I know by dawn the riverbed was dry.

American Legion Post #31. Cornerstone ceremonies, Boulder City, Nevada, 9 May 1932

5

A GOVERNMENT RESERVATION:
BOULDER CITY, 1932–1934

"This is Sims's town."

While construction of the diversion tunnels progressed in Black Canyon, Boulder City grew on the broad ridge above Hemenway Wash. Rows of Six Companies cottages, the government's brick houses, struggling lawns and gardens, and young families made the town more than a mere construction camp. But Boulder City was different from any town Hoover Dam workers had lived in before: federal control gave Boulder City a distinctive character. New arrivals approaching from Las Vegas had to stop at the reservation's guarded gate, where federal rangers questioned them and searched their cars. Madeline Knighten describes her first impression of Boulder City's symbol of federal influence when she arrived on Thanksgiving 1932.

MADELINE KNIGHTEN

There was a gate to come through to get into Boulder City. It was a real reservation with a fence and a guardhouse. When we got to the gate, government rangers there checked out everyone that came in. Everyone was asked their reason for coming to Boulder City. We had to state our business in Boulder City, where we expected to live, who we were going to see. Of course, I told them I was coming up to visit my husband, who had been up here several months. But we had to get out of that little bus, and everyone was checked out.

While the reservation gate was originally set up during the strike of August 1931 to control labor unrest on the Boulder Canyon Project, it soon became the government's principal tool for moral control over those who lived in Boulder City. Gambling and prostitution were absolutely forbidden on the reservation, but liquor was the greatest taboo. Even after repeal of Prohibition in 1933, the Bureau of Reclamation used the reservation's gate to keep Boulder City dry.

ELTON GARRETT

The gate pretty well controlled the question of people bringing in liquor. Of course, you can't get into every part of a car for every car, but it was a deterrent. The gate was manned day and night by federal rangers. If you had a bottle in your car, you swigged it and tossed it on the desert before you got to the gate. The far side of the gate was lined with broken glass.

BRUCE EATON

If they suspected that you had liquor, they would search your car. They didn't always do it. I don't ever remember my car being searched. But they could if they wanted to, going in or coming out.

LEO DUNBAR

The rangers knew pretty well who to search. If you were a government employee, we never had trouble, because we'd usually hold our pass out to the side of the car, and they recognized us all anyway because we all knew each other. But they really went through the cars that came in for the first time. Saturday nights they really went through the cars.

BOB PARKER

If they could smell any liquor on your breath, why, out you got, and you walked this white line they had painted there at the gate.

ERMA GODBEY

Or else you got put in the bull pen until you could walk the white line.

NADEAN VOSS

Men from Vegas or the ones with stills used to bring bootleg liquor to the men at the dormitories up Bootleg Road, up over the canyon. They'd bring it into town. They'd miss the station that way. They would come down through McKeeversville from the mountain.

BRUCE EATON

There was quite a lot of liquor in Boulder City, but it was an offense you could be removed from the reservation for. But that didn't keep it out. There was quite a bit of drunkeness in Boulder City—not near as much as there was in Vegas, but there was some. The drinkers had liquor in their homes.

ELTON GARRETT

I know of one of the top officials who got laid off the job for excessive drinking at one time. He was a good executive, but that was his failing. But they needed him. They put him back on. They made an exception for the assistant superintendent [Bernard F. "Woody" Williams]. That's why it pays to be a big shot sometimes.

WALKER R. YOUNG

Frank Crowe was the superintendent of construction for Six Companies. His assistant superintendent was a man named Woody Williams. Woody Williams got to thinking that he was pretty important on the job. He not only got to gambling, but he got to drinking. Everybody else supposedly observed the regulations about the liquor. At one of the dances, Woody [came in] with a whiskey bottle on his hip. He'd go outside and take a drink at a ranger's car.

So the next day I informed Frank Crowe, "Get rid of Williams." The rangers were instructed to get him off the reservation. The law was that anybody who did not conform to the regulations of the city would be asked to leave. So Woody Williams was thrown off the reservation for 30 days.

The next day who should I see but Frank Crowe in my office. He believed that here I was, letting this most important man in his whole crew not report in to work for 30 days. That's a hell of a note. I told him it was too bad, but Woody's off for 30 days.

But even Walker Young inadvertently contributed to the delinquency of his workers.

BOB PARKER

After the project started, there was a lot of those tents, speakeasies, between here and Vegas with home brew. However, the main source of liquor in this area when the dam first started was great big stills up the river toward Overton. Bud Bodell and his crew of rangers—police—knocked over several big stills up the river. Those people were making alcohol and whiskey. When they did that, they always confiscated several barrels of whiskey.

Walker Young was the proprietor of that whiskey when the police brought it in here to Boulder City. So what does Walker Young do? He puts it over in the paint house in the warehouse yard for the painters to use as paint thinner. I was working in the number 1 Warehouse up there. We worked on Saturday morning; we got off Saturday afternoon and Sunday. When I'd be over there on Saturday morning, just before noon a lot of the painters and the city maintenance foreman, the superintendent of maintenance, they all wound up over there at the paint house. That liquor that Walker Young designated as paint thinner kept some of those maintenance crews and painters around here pretty well supplied with liquor.

Once people made it onto the reservation, they found two law enforcement agencies: the government rangers, under the jurisdiction of the Bureau of Reclamation, and the Six Companies security force.

MADELINE KNIGHTEN

People who impressed me a lot in those first days, those first years I lived in Boulder, were the government rangers. They were, most of them, very tall men. Two of them in those early days, that first year I was up here, were called the Gold Dust Twins. They must have been well over six feet tall, and very slender men. Their uniforms were dark brown; the ranger uniform was a dark brown uniform with their various stripes and insignia and whatnot on them, and their big hats, more or less flat sombrero-type hats, or Stetsons, whatever you call them. They looked very nice in their uniforms, and everyone had a great deal of respect for the rangers.

Glen E. "Bud" Bodell, the man in charge of the government security force that broke the 1931 labor strike, went to work in 1933 for the Six Companies.

ALICE HAMILTON

I was secretary to Mr. Bodell. Bud Bodell was chief investigator and in charge of security for the Six Companies. Mr. Bodell was the only fearless man that I believe I've ever known in my life. I've never seen him afraid of anything. I can remember during the strikes at the dam, particularly one, they brought the strikers into the yard at the Six Companies office in the Big Bertha. That was one of the trucks that conveyed the workers back and forth. I can remember so well Bud Bodell taking his gun off. He always wore a gun, of course. He took his gun off and laid it on his desk and walked out in front of that bus full of men. The driver asked him what to do and what he was expected to do. The strikers had struck at the dam, and he'd brought them back to Boulder. Bud says, "Take them to the gate." That's all there was to it.

JOHN CAHLAN

Bud Bodell single-handedly prevented a strike out there. The IWW boys were talking about strike and so forth, and there was a fellow out there by the name of Red [Belmain]. But he was the leader of the outfit, and they had been in the Anderson Commissary eating breakfast, and they came out and were talking strike, and Bud told this Red, he said, "All right, you been out here talking strike, now," and he said, "[If] you can whup me, you go ahead and take your strike. If I whup you, then you get off the reservation and don't come back."

And so Red says, "It's OK with me."

So they got out there and fought for, oh, an hour or an hour and a half, and just beat the dickens out of each other. But Bud finally got him to admit that he was whipped, and he walked off the job and never came back.

ELTON GARRETT

Bud Bodell was an automobile racer turned into a law enforcement officer. He was the good, driving, dynamic chief. He got around. He had men who knew what he expected of them, and they did a policing job. A sidelight on Bud Bodell: one New Year's night, I being a bachelor not married yet, in the habit of getting around to the police and whoever was actively doing something, I was news reporting. So I wasn't bashful about getting around, day or night. Well, New Year's night. Somewhere I heard that a man had fallen to his death, and they were looking for the body. I just happened to get with Bud Bodell, the chief of police—the chief ranger. He said, "Do you want to go with me? I'm going to drive down right now." I said, "Yes." I sat alongside a speeder who got a hundred miles an hour on the winding roads down to the dam at one time. He was a good driver. We got there.

It may have seemed that Bud Bodell was in charge of law enforcement in Boulder City, but he was only an employee of the contractor, following orders. The real power on the reservation, the man in whom all legal, moral, and judicial power rested, was city manager Sims Ely. Hired by the Bureau of Reclamation to manage Boulder City for the government, Ely was founder and former editor of the Arizona Republican, *and had represented Arizona in the negotiations that culminated in the Colorado River Compact. A crusty veteran of federal commissions and Arizona state politics and a former administrative assistant in the Justice Department, the 69-year-old Ely was not about to tolerate opposition from young construction workers. Ely's influence still pervades Boulder City more than 50 years after he left.*

ELTON GARRETT

He was a very direct, effective, snappy guy who dove right into what he thought ought to be done. He didn't delay or mince words. He was very direct and honest. He incurred the wrath of some people at times by that directness and that decisiveness. Inasmuch as he was the judge and jury for a lot of these petty offenses, there were people who looked upon him with a little bit of fear and trembling.

When the rangers had someone accused of something, they took him before Sims Ely, the city manager, who as a one-man official really ran the town. He would tell the men, "Here's what your penalty is." And it might be, "You're going to leave the reservation. You've lost your job." The company didn't lose him his job—the judge did. And that was Sims Ely.

MARY EATON

I'll never forget Sims Ely. He was an ironfisted gentleman. Whatever he said, that was the law. He had unlimited power. For instance, if a man beat up his wife, he'd lose his job. Sims Ely would say, "You just get off the reservation, and don't ever come back." And he lost his job. The wife had to go too. You couldn't live here then and not have a job. Everybody had a job in Boulder City. They knew that they'd better walk the straight-and-narrow, because when anybody can take your job, that's kind of fearful. We had no fear, because we knew we were upright people. But he was the law.

BRUCE EATON

Sims Ely had full authority to govern Boulder City. To my knowledge, he didn't abuse his authority. He was a good administrator. I had lots of respect for him. He was the judge, jury, the prosecutor, and the defender. I remember one time we were contemplating buying a house and he advised us that he would not approve me for a lease for that property, because he thought I was paying too much money for it. He had that much control.

MARY ANN MERRILL

He was a hard man. I guess he was fair in a lot of ways, but he had his own ideas and he put them into practice. And you had to go by his rules. He thought of it as his town. I've heard that said so many times: "This is Sim's town."

CARL MERRILL

He was a dictator in the city. He made the rules. If you broke the rules, you went up before Sims Ely. I tangled with Sims Ely. It was my own fault. One time I was caught speeding, and the ticket said I was to see Sims Ely at a certain time. Sims Ely said, "You're barred from the reservation for one day." He didn't know what a break he was giving me, 'cause I was working seven days a week. I went in and stayed with my sister, and came back the next day and went to work.

THOMAS WILSON

It seemed to me he was a hundred years old. Wore knickers and cap, tweed suit with knickers, and a Norfolk jacket.

JOHN CAHLAN

I used to see Sims Ely, the city manager of Boulder City, maybe once a month. We would talk about what the prospects were for Boulder City and the dam. Ely was a very, very hard man. He was very hard to interview; he wouldn't talk very much. He sat up there on the throne. You couldn't get much out of him. Sims Ely was made a virtual czar. If you were caught drunk, you were brought up before him. If you could explain it to his satisfaction, he'd let you stay; if not, he'd kick you out. There was nothing that went on that he didn't handle. He had tunnel vision. If you didn't believe the way he believed, you didn't live there. I was never there for any of his decisions, but I got the decisions later, and there was no reasons that he did what he did. Some resident of Las Vegas'd go out there, and they might have forgotten to take that flask of whiskey out of their automobile. They'd find it, and he'd be barred for life. Ely controlled the community.

Erma Godbey and her husband, Tom, ran afoul of Sims Ely more than once, but the stories she remembers about Ely reflect not only the depth of his control over life in Boulder City but a little-known gentler side.

ERMA GODBEY

I didn't particularly care for him. People would write letters trying to get rid of Sims. The reason they couldn't get rid of him was that his son, Northcutt Ely, was in the Department of the Interior in Washington. Northcutt would send it back to him, so he knew who wrote the letter, and you got called up on the carpet.

Whoever got to him with their story first, they usually got preference. Some things were quite picky. If somebody went to Sims Ely and said, "My neighbor is letting all her dirty wash water from her washing machine run down on my yard and make a dirty puddle," and he liked the lady that came to him better than he liked the lady who let her wash water run, then that lady got her neck in the wringer.

If somebody came to town, they couldn't stay more than three days if they didn't have a job, unless they had somebody who would vouch for them and say they could take care of them and they wouldn't become indigents or anything. Now when my husband's younger brother came, after he'd been here three days, he had to go see Sims Ely. Of course, my husband also went to see Sims Ely and said that Everett could live with us and that we would see that he was taken care of.

Very few people know this, but my husband got a lease from the government and we got some land down below town here. We started a little ranch. We used the effluent from the disposal plant. When it becomes effluent, they had a digester at that time, and it's supposed to be free of everything. We used it for irrigation. We had some cows, and we had chickens, and eventually we had a mama pig and some baby pigs, and we had rabbits and things. We grew oats and alfalfa. Here was the funny thing. Ely didn't want us to have cows, because they'd bring flies to Boulder. One time one of our cows got clear up here to Boulder, and the rangers put it in the fence behind the ranger station. And, of course, Sims was right there in the office too, in the Municipal Building. So Sims calls Tom to get the cow. When Tom went up to get the cow, Sims comes out and he said, "Well, leave it here until after the kids go back into school—they're all having such a good time talking to it through the fence and petting it and everything. Wait until the noon hour is over." So he wasn't such a bad old guy.

But I'll tell you, he really loved to see the girls' baseball. He loved to see those girls in their shorts getting skinned up. He liked the ladies, all right.

117

DOROTHY NUNLEY

He liked women a lot better than he did the men. If a husband wanted something done and had to see Ely about it, he'd send his wife.

Ely's power may have been pervasive, but most agree Boulder needed stern control.

BOB PARKER

He was rough on anybody that they caught with liquor. Everybody thought he was a tough old fellow, but I think he meted out justice pretty well. I never had any run-ins with him as long as I knew him. I used to go up and talk to him occasionally in the office up there, and he was easy to talk to. But if he had something on his mind and he didn't want to answer, he wouldn't do it. If he wanted to talk, he'd talk your leg off. I always thought he did fairly well. He would overstep his authority occasionally.

WALKER R. YOUNG

He was a rather strict individual with respect to some of the things that people do. He established the rule that there was to be no liquor, no gambling, and no prostitutes. That rule stuck. That was one rule that I respected all my life while I was there.

MARY ANN MERRILL

Actually, rules had to be strict here. There were so many oddballs that would come in. You didn't know whether they'd been murderers or what they'd been, because there was no way of checking on them in that day and age. It wouldn't have been a decent place to live sometimes. You had to have regulations.

BRUCE EATON

To be honest with you, the people in [Boulder City] were all young construction workers. And generally speaking, the people in those days especially who followed construction work were not pansies. They were rough and tough.

LEROY BURT

In reality, you can't take anything away from him. We had a real rough class of people here in Boulder City in that day, those construction people. They'd as soon fight you as look at you.

The government's strict regulations, enforced through Sims Ely, imposed limits on commercial development. People who wanted to establish businesses in Boulder City had to qualify under a regulated permit system that fostered limited competition and diminished the extent to which Six Companies could exploit its workers through the company store and the use of company-issued scrip.

ELTON GARRETT

Knowing that a depression was affecting the whole economy, and knowing that there would be a rush of businesses if it was open for everybody, the planners did establish a permit system. There would be, for instance, two barbers allowed. If you wanted to have a third barbershop, you put in your application, but the choice is made.

Each field of activity had a number of units that could be set up in Boulder City. The number of cafés was more than some of the other types of business. Two men's clothing stores, I believe, was the limit. But the number of applicants that applied before the town was built—those were screened, those were chosen by reputation, by whether there was qualification financially, ability to handle a good business in a new town. Sims Ely, I believe, had a lot to do with that.

ERMA GODBEY

Sims Ely decided who could have a business and what kind of business it could be. He tried to fix it so there were no competing businesses.

MARY EATON

In the construction days everybody shopped at the Six Companies store.[1] It was a department [store], you might say. It was vegetables, fruit and vegetables, canned goods, meat, and clothing, just about everything that was needed, except they didn't sell whiskey. We didn't do this too much, but you could get an advance on your check with scrip from Six Companies. You could get this scrip; then they would deduct that from your paycheck when payday came around. You could get that, sort of like buying before you earned it. Some of the men, who wanted to buy the things that weren't in the department store, like, say, whiskey—there were several men in town who would trade money, real cash, for some of the scrip. They might give you like $5 and you'd give them like $7.50 worth of scrip. So they were making a profit off of you. Some people, most everything was deducted before they got their check.

ERMA GODBEY

Originally Six Companies scrip was just a little book that was stapled together. It had twenty-five [cents], fifty and dollar pages in it. It was $5. After a man had worked one day, he could do what they called "scrip up." He could get a book of scrip for his wife to get some groceries at Six Companies Store. Later they made the scrip out of metal. They were coins.

The people that worked for Six Companies, if they had a car and they needed gasoline, there wasn't any way that they could get it at Six Companies Store. So they would sell the scrip to somebody else. So people got to discounting the scrip. I knew a lot of people that would buy a five dollar book of scrip and only pay the people four bucks for it. But then they could get four bucks worth of gas, or whatever they needed for their car. We used to buy the scrip from people. I never discounted, but I do know people who discounted it when they bought it. I just never could—I wasn't built that way. I thought, well, if it buys five bucks worth of groceries for them, it would buy five bucks worth of groceries for me.

120

Among the first private businesses established in town was a café owned by Ida Browder, who became a very influential and controversial figure in Boulder City.

ELTON GARRETT

Mrs. Ida Browder was an Austrian countess before she came to America as a young woman. Ida Browder refused to go back to Austria for her heritage, stayed in America, and married an American who served in the army. She later had two children. When she lost her husband, she got a permit to build the first dining room, private dining room, in Boulder City. She lived in [a] tent while her building was being built, and she opened her café in the first year of Boulder City. She used to stash money for the boys under a mattress. That was one of the first banks in Boulder City. She quit doing it when too many of them got to saying, "Hey, keep my money, I don't want to blow it."

WILFRED VOSS

Mrs. Browder was a very refined woman. They say that she was of the nobility from either Austria or Hungary, I don't know which. She was quite a figure in town politics. You already know the town was run by the government. But she was quite a nice little dictator herself. She was just this side of being city manager.

BOB PARKER

[My father] was mixed up in politics with Mrs. Browder. They were always conniving and whatnot with [Nevada Senator Key] Pittman and a lot of these politicians. She was a good friend of Pittman and those senators, and she kept them pretty well informed of all the things in politics that were going on in this end of the state. She kind of was on the inside track as far as politics went, and she had an idea that she was the kingpin. She and Sims Ely weren't very compatible. They battled on a lot of scores.

I almost got everybody in Boulder City in trouble about the time that Sims Ely was ready to leave here. I was going down on the elevator [at Hoover Dam] one day, and I met Tom Godbey out there in the hallway. I told him that I heard that Mrs. Browder was going to be the next city manager of Boulder City and take Sims Ely's place. By 8:00 that night the American Legion, the chamber of commerce, the junior chamber of commerce, and nearly every organization in Boulder City was holding a meeting. They wound up with about a four-page telegram to Washington, to [Nevada Senator Pat] McCarran and everyone else back there that they didn't want Mrs. Browder to be their next city manager. I'll tell you, I never laughed so much in my life.

Private businesses, such as the Green Hut Café, were important in Boulder City's social life.

MADELINE KNIGHTEN

Clarence Newlin had put in the Green Hut Café. He bought food from General Foods, the very best. Everything that he sold there he wanted made out of the best materials, the best batter, and the best flour, shortening. My husband had been taught to cook by Clarence's older brother, Charles Newlin. They were all from the same hometown. My husband baked nine kinds of angel food here in the Green Hut before we ever heard of the kind of cakes we make today. He made them up in huge amounts. He had a Kitchen Aide beater that was like a big fan. It was unbelievable, the amount of dough that he could turn out.

In those early days the Green Hut was considered a first-class restaurant with its dining area and its long, long counter and stools. It had potted palms and such things in those days. When you came in the door, you were faced by a lovely potted palm. It was really quite classy for Boulder City in those days. It was really a first-class café.

HAZEL ALLEN

The Green Hut was air-conditioned. I worked from five till one. Then they put me on morning shift. My manager's daughter, Jane, and I used to get up and wrap about a hundred and eighty sandwiches for the men who worked on the Edison Power line. Then, of course, we had our regular breakfast, and our lunch. I worked a 21-stool counter. And, of course, we had a lot of the men come in at night for dinner. And families too. No special activities, just work and serve people. Try to be nice to some of the drunks that would come in. I waited on a lot of real fine people, I'll tell you, while I was here.

We had one fellow, and he was so sarcastic, you couldn't please him no matter what you done. So Christmastime came, and Jane and I went down to the grocery store. We got a lemon that was as big as an orange, and we wrapped it up. We took it down to Mrs. McCormick at the novelty shop, and she wrapped it up. We got a nice card with it. And we said, "Merry Christmas, Pickle Puss." That kind of broke the ice with him. After that it wasn't so bad. But, oh, he was terrible.

Every Sunday morning we passed the hat to get money enough to pay the fine to get our cook and his wife out of jail. One night they had been to Vegas, and they went down to the lake, and they were sitting there, and they were stark naked. Chris and Babe, his wife, and the other couple were all in there swimming. Chris, the chef, was sitting on the bank. [Boulder City ranger Fred] Parkinson came up, and he said, "What are you doing?" Chris looked at him, and he said, "By golly, I'm a-catchin' butterflies." He was so mad when he came to the café that morning. I said, "What's the matter, Parky?" He said, "I'll tell you something. You've got the worst bunch of drunks for cooks I ever saw." I said, "You're telling me? We just passed the hat to get them out of jail." But that was a ritual. Every Sunday morning. They'd get drunk on beer; we would bail them out. But, you know, we always got our money back or they didn't get their checks.

The Boulder Theatre opened on 14 May 1932. Managed by Earl Brothers, it not only provided round-the-clock entertainment for dam workers and their families but was often the stage for contests, beauty pageants, vaudeville shows, radio broadcasts, and school functions.

ALFRED BAKER

The only amusement there was was the movie house. Good Lord, they'd be four deep lined up a block long every show. They had one in the morning for graveyard or swing; then they had one in the afternoon and two at night. Boy, that was a gold mine, that little theater.

EDNA FRENCH

Mr. Brothers was so good to the children during the summers here. Our summers were terribly, terribly hot, and we didn't have any way of cooling except by fan. He had some sort of a cooling system. It was nice and cool in there. Mr. Brothers would open his theater in the afternoon and invite the children down there. They would go in and sit. They didn't run up and down the aisle like you see in theaters sometimes. That was very appreciated by the parents and everybody in town. We would enjoy too going to the Saturday-night show. That was our recreation, was to go to the picture show on Saturday night.

LILLIAN WHALEN

Mr. Brothers, who was the manager of the theater, started his shows at eleven in the morning so that the men who went to work at three in the afternoon could come in and rest and watch a movie or sleep, whichever they would rather, until the time to go to work. A great many men who lived in those little houses where they had absolutely no way of cooling and couldn't sleep during the day would spend hours down in the theater. Mr. Brothers was very happy to have them do it. He had matinees for the children, and he had little parties for the children.

ERMA GODBEY

Earl was such a jolly fellow, and everybody liked him very, very much. Everybody signed up, then they drew names, and once a month on Saturday he gave out a prize. It might be money, and it might be just tickets to the movie. Then we used to have different people just do their little act. They would hold graduation class there. The eighth-grade graduation class was there. When my daughter Ila graduated from high school, they had all of their stuff during the day at the theater for the kids that were the smartest kids.

HAZEL ALLEN

On my nights off I'd go to the picture show. I'd go to the show between times, and something funny would strike me and I'd laugh. Kids that worked on the dam would come into the [Green Hut] for breakfast and say, "Hazel, you were in the show last night, weren't you?" And I'd say, "How did you know?" "That's all right, we knew you was at the show." So one night I went and they had the Three Stooges on, and I was sitting in the back and I let out a big "Ha, ha." Harold, the fellow that worked on the dam, turned around and said, "Shut up, Hazel." So when he came in the next morning to eat, I said, "Now Harold, I know how you know that I go to the show." Those crazy Three Stooges. But that's about the only entertainment I had.

BUD BODELL

I had only one felony in the time that I policed [Boulder City] for the government for two years. Two dam workers robbed the theater owner, taped and bound his wife when he came home, and stole his car. I got them within an hour in Las Vegas. They'd see [Brothers] carrying that sack of money home every night.

The government regulated commercial development, but it did nothing at first to foster the kind of social institutions that would have made Boulder City more like a community. Government planners failed to provide for education. There were no schools, and none were planned. Private initiative, with limited help from Six Companies, provided the only education in 1931 and early 1932. Makeshift schools sprang up among the settlements at Railroad Pass, in Ragtown, in McKeeversville, and in the Railroad Wye[2] on the outskirts of Boulder City. Erma Godbey and her neighbor in the Wye, Velma Holland, remember their little one-room school.

ERMA GODBEY

The government had made no way to have a school here; they hadn't even thought about it. Neither had Six Companies. Being as nobody was paying taxes, the state and the county didn't want to do it.

[The Hollands] didn't live right in the Wye; they lived over closer to McKeeversville. Fred [Holland] was the same age as my Tommy. When we got to worrying about not having any schools, they were worried too, because it was time for their oldest boy to start to school.

Mr. Elder was camped over there too. He had a sister back in Kansas who was a teacher, and she was out of work. He said, "I'll send for my sister, and I'll build a shack, and we'll get a little school started for the kids." He did that. Different men helped him. They just used scrap lumber that they got from here, there, and everywhere. By the spring of '32, we had a school in the Wye.

My Tommy was old enough to start first grade, but he started over in the school that Mr. Elder built in the Wye. The people down in Ragtown were worried about school too. So by the first part of 1932—by January—they had built a building too and were trying to have a school for their kids the best they could.[3]

VELMA HOLLAND

It was coming closer to schooltime. Mr. Elder was a bachelor, and he lived just across the driveway from us. He said that if Six Companies would give him a load of scrap lumber, he would build a room. He had a sister that was a teacher, and he would ask her to gather up all the books she could find and come over here and teach those children in the Wye.

So he talked to Six Companies men, and one day here came a big, big load of lumber. It wasn't scrap; it was good lumber. The men around got their hammers and their saws and went over and helped him. They built this room. They put windows in and everything. They took the lumber and they built desks and benches. I can remember when I went to school, in a little country schoolhouse, that's what we had, a desk with the benches fastened onto them. Two sat at each desk. For the blackboard they just took the black roofing paper, felt paper, and nailed it up. Mrs. Bissell gathered up the books and came over, and she started the school. I think there were about 18 or 20 youngsters in there. They got ahold of a one-by-two or something and nailed it up, put the flag on it, and that was the start of the little schoolhouse out in the desert.

Elbert Edwards was teaching high school in Las Vegas at the time and remembers Boulder City's struggle to establish a school system.

ELBERT EDWARDS

The school year rolled around, and there were no schools. The federal government had made no provision for schools. They said schools are a state responsibility. Normally Boulder City would have qualified for elementary schools, except for the fact that the land on which Boulder City was built had been set up as a federal reservation. There was a question as to where the Nevada laws operated.

When people became aware of the fact that there were no schools, the people still wanted their children to get an education. There were people in the city with teaching experience, and qualified. They began holding private classes. Parents would provide the books. I think Six Companies made available two or three homes. Benches were constructed. Children went to school. Parents paid tuition—around $5 a month per student. That was the way schools got started in Boulder City. They were not recognized by the state— they were not state schools.

But the second year Six Companies Incorporated and the Bureau of Reclamation recognized that they had a problem. So they got together. The Bureau of Reclamation provided funds for the construction of a school building, which at the present time is being used as the Boulder City city hall. Six Companies made an arrangement whereby they would pay the teachers' salaries. They needed an administrator. Boulder City had a very efficient administrator in their city manager, Sims Ely. So Sims just took over and exercised his prerogative to administer the funds and hire the teachers, get a principal, and get it set up whereby it could operate. It was totally ex officio but an interesting operation.

ELTON GARRETT

There was no provision for any school in Boulder City. Uncle Sam had overlooked it, apparently feeling that it would be a man's town. But it wasn't. The women came with the kids, so they had to have a school.

In the meantime Mrs. Washington and Mrs. Hamilton each started teaching their own youngsters in their homes, Six Companies residences. The neighbors learned, "She's teaching her kid; why can't I send mine?" Pretty soon here is a classroom of 15, 20 kids sitting on benches. Here's another group over here. Mrs. Provo came and started a third one. Somebody started a kindergarten over where the Wye is.

ERMA GODBFY

Six Companies decided that they would turn over three of their houses for schools. Some of the ladies here in town who had taught school before would be the teachers. We didn't have books or anything, just whatever anybody happened to bring with them, and everyone came with very little. They had to make their own goop so that they could make copies—the gelatin stuff. You paid $1.50 for one child per week to go to school. If you had two, you paid $1 for the second one.

ELTON GARRETT

Sims Ely helped shape things up. In fact, he helped establish the school system before it became a state school unit. He helped set up the use of the school building when the I. M. Bay Company finally got it built, the building where the city hall is now. He had a lot to do with hiring the teachers, with the assistance of people like Walker Young. It happened. He helped line it up. He got Six Companies, Inc., to pay the teachers one year.

ELBERT EDWARDS

The state was willing to assume the responsibility, but they had to have the authority to collect taxes. In the first place there was very little in Boulder City that they could collect taxes on, because all the land and many of the houses were owned by the federal government. The only function they had was to collect taxes on the resources of Six Companies, Inc., which was, of course, a private company. But Six Companies, Inc., contended that they were a federal agency, and so beyond the jurisdiction of the state. The state had to fight a case through the courts and win the right to collect taxes on private property on the federal reservation before they could assume the responsibility for establishing a school district.[4] They won the case, so in 1933 the Boulder City people were eligible to establish a school district for elementary school purposes.

EDNA FRENCH

We felt like the school in Boulder City was a very good school. I tried to get in the school each year, but I couldn't get a steady job, because here in Boulder City a woman couldn't get a steady job if her husband had a job. But I did substitute. For six years I substituted before I was hired regularly. I felt like that was a real privilege, to come in and substitute.

Health care was another important aspect of Boulder City life neglected by the government. Until the Six Companies built a hospital at the townsite, workers and their families had to make their way into Las Vegas for medical attention. While there was a first-aid station at the damsite, seriously injured workers were transported 30 miles by ambulance into town. Dr. Clare Woodbury was one of the physicians on staff at the Las Vegas Hospital.

DR. CLARE WOODBURY

The Las Vegas Hospital when I came was well equipped. It had about 35 to 40 beds, and all the nurses were graduate nurses. We had modern facilities. In fact, when I arrived, I did plenty of hysterectomies, gall bladders, and removal of thyroid glands. The only ones we'd send to L.A. were the men that required specialist care. Air conditioning at that time was unknown, and we performed our surgery, in months when it was particularly hot, with a block of ice and a large fan blowing over, which made it fairly comfortable for the operating team.

When it was certain that Boulder Dam was to be constructed, [the doctors] went to Denver [Bureau of Reclamation headquarters] to try to get the [health care] contract for the laborers. They suggested to Denver that the two groups combine, which they did. At that time they had the industrial [health care contracts] for the labor in the construction of the road down to the dam. After a year that contract was taken away from [us] and given to the nephew of Mr. Kaiser [Dr. Charles Cristal (?)].

Six Companies opened the hospital in Boulder City early in 1932 but restricted its service to dam laborers, excluding even their families.

Mrs. Anna Bissell and students at the Railroad Wye School. Mrs. Bissell's brother, Charles S. Elder, ladder foreman for the Six Companies, built the school, its seats, and desks, 1932

Railroad Pass School, 1932 (*left*); Temporary schoolhouse in Boulder City provided by the Six Companies, 1932 (*below*)

MARY ANN MERRILL

The first hospital we had was up on the hill. At the time that it was built, that hospital was just for the *men* workers. There was not women allowed in the hospital as patients. No women [were] allowed for a good many years.

LILLIAN WHALEN

It was operated for the workers at the dam and was not available to the families of the dam workers, except in emergency. They [still] had to go to Las Vegas for hospital care. We did have a doctor who was not connected with the hospital: Dr. [John] McDaniel.

Many of the babies were born in the homes in Boulder City. Dr. McDaniel delivered many of them on the screen porches of the little houses, with the fans drifting around. But evidently it was a healthy thing, because he never lost a mother or a baby.

MILDRED KINE

Our first child was born on January 7, 1933, down on Seventh Street where we lived. He was born in our home. I had a nurse come in and help. It was either that or go to Las Vegas, because the hospital up here was only for workmen and they didn't want to have maternity cases up there.

Dr. Wales Haas, the physician who replaced Dr. Cristal on 15 December 1931 shortly before the Boulder City Hospital opened, was an unusual man. Bob Parker remembers Haas, with whom he developed a close friendship.

BOB PARKER

He was an awful big fellow. He was about six foot. I know he had to bend over to come in the door—six-foot-two or -three. He probably weighed over 300 pounds. He was an awful good-natured doctor. I guess he had been an army doctor in the First World War. He had a pretty good background. He was a people's doctor. In other words, the business part of it didn't bother him at all. If they hadn't had the bookkeepers up there to keep the books, he wouldn't have worried about whether they kept any books or not. He was the first master of the Boulder City Masonic Lodge Number 37. His picture hangs in the Masonic Hall.

Dr. Haas developed an appendicitis attack. They rushed him up to the hospital, and they wanted to operate right away. He said no, he didn't want them to operate until they got Dr. [R. O.] Schofield over here, who he went through the war with. They doctored together during the war, and they went through school together.[5] He wanted him to be here, so Six Companies flew him in to do the operation.

Next day—it was either the first or second day after the operation—I went up there to see Dr. Haas. He always called me Son, and he always kind of treated me like a son. I went up to see him in the hospital. He was jovial and laughing and good-natured. I said, "You look like you're about ready to get up and go home. You look like you went through it fine." He said, "I have never in all my career as a surgeon cut through that much fat." I can't remember—it was either three or five inches of fat in his abdominal section. He said, "I have never seen one survive yet." He said, "It will be a miracle if I survive." I said, "I think it will be a miracle, because I think you're going to make it." The next afternoon word went out around town that he passed away. I felt awful bad about it, because he operated on me and he treated me just like his son. I more or less fell in love with him up there in the hospital.

Dr. R. O. Schofield was the next physician in charge of the hospital.

BOB PARKER

He was the exact opposite of Dr. Haas. He was all business. Before he came in there, they didn't have anything but a lobby there. He set up an office with the girls, and a window, and an opening where you could talk through the opening. To get to the doctors, you had to go through the nurses and everybody else. To get to the doctors before, you just walked in there and walked down to the doctor's office. Not after he came in. He set it up on a business basis. From then on you went into it like a hospital in some big city. He made a big city hospital out of it in a hurry.

I don't know whether [it's] on record, but this was the first Kaiser hospital. It was the forerunner of the Kaiser hospitals as you know them today. After Henry Kaiser went out of here, he started building hospitals to take care of his enterprises all over the country, and they're still in operation. They're quite a hospital chain now, the Kaiser hospitals.

DOROTHY NUNLEY

I remember the pesthouse. It sounded like something out of the dark ages, really. If any of the single men got anything wrong with them that was contagious, they would ship them out to the pesthouse, which was a small building on the outskirts of town. The doctor would come down once a day and see them, maybe twice if it was bad. There was a scarlet fever epidemic here shortly after I came. This was when I first heard about the pesthouse. But these men, there was a lot of them that were taken with this fever. They would be put in this place, and as one would get better, he would start taking care of the others. That's the way it worked. They were kept there until they were not contagious anymore. Their meals were brought down to them.

MARION ALLEN

I was in the pesthouse with Dr. Schofield. He was the doctor. One morning I went to get out of bed. By golly, I got out, and down on the floor I went. My back was just gone. I don't know what. Boy, I'm scared. I told the wife. She goes up to my folks' place and gets them to go up to the hospital to tell them that they need a doctor. We didn't have any car. So pretty quick here come a couple of guys down. They helped me out to the car and took me up and put me in the hospital. They had me in there all day, and my back was just about to kill me. They didn't know what it was.

Old Schofield said to me, "You know, there's nothing wrong with you. You're just faking this." Boy! You know me, I'm half-Irish and -Indian. "I'm not faking, goddamn it. You wouldn't dare say that if I was on my feet." So I told the nurse, "Bring my clothes; I'm getting out of here." The nurse said, "Oh, no, you're not. You're not going anywhere." He said, "You don't have any fever." So OK, out he goes.

Next morning he comes in and walks over to the bed. He said, "Pull up your shirt." I pulled up my shirt. Here he runs out of the door. "Let me out of here! Let me out of here!" What in the hell did I do to him? I couldn't help but laugh, but what was the matter with him? So I raised up my shirt, and just red, all red. I said to the nurse finally, "What's the matter with me?" She said, "You've got scarlet fever."

I got even with old Schofield. In about a few minutes, here they come.

133

They picked me up and put me in this ambulance and took me down [to the] pesthouse. When I get down, [I see] it's the first dormitory that the Six Companies built. It had an eight-foot fence around it. They put me in there, and I was in there for 30 days. It was a nice vacation. One thing they insisted [was that] you drink all the fruit juice, which wasn't hard to take. Then they'd give you some pills. The strange thing, there was two of us in there that had scarlet fever out of this 5,000 workers and God-knows-how-many people. Then there was two or three with smallpox and one or two with diphtheria. It was all in this big dorm, but we were separated. My wife used to come up and talk to me through the fence.

Despite the government's strict supervision over their lives, Boulderites themselves transformed the town into a community. The Boulder Canyon Project provided the material security residents needed to turn their energy to establishing civic and fraternal organizations, churches, and a library and to building other social outlets few people outside the reservation had the leisure to pursue. Boulder City during construction of Hoover Dam became an island of calm in the storm of the Great Depression.

MARY EATON

Masons and Eastern Star were two of the first fraternal organizations. They wanted to form a Masonic Lodge and, of course, with the members being from all the different crafts—electricians, carpenters, plumbers, the whole thing we had right here in our town. Volunteers got together, and they built the Masonic Temple. I think they did it in about two days. It was a frame building, one story. They built it up on the hill because usually Masonic Lodges would have the Masonic Temple on the second floor, and then the basement was for socializing. We couldn't afford to have a basement, so they thought they'd put it up on the hill so they could keep their secrets.

WILFRED VOSS

The first time I went up there, I couldn't even find the road that went up there. I went up the side of the hill. Sand was about ankle-deep.

134

SAUL "RED" WIXSON

We had what they called the Stray Elks Club, I guess chartered off the Las Vegas Elks. And they had little poker games going on there, but it was clean. You didn't have much to play poker with. You hardly earned anything.

MARY EATON

A lot of people belonged to the American Legion from World War I. They always had a lot of activities, dances. The social life of Boulder City for a long time was the dances at the Legion Hall.

MADELINE KNIGHTEN

The Legion Hall was the place for socializing in Boulder City at that time. It was a huge, big, spread-out, ranch-type wooden building. It covered almost all that lot. It had a huge dance floor, a big dance floor. I didn't go to the dances, but they had the dances every Saturday night. They had good music. I could hear the music. I'd very often be down at the [Green Hut] café with my husband, and I could hear the music over there. They would pour in at intermission.

WILMA COOPER

During construction days we had dances in the American Legion building, big bands. Paul Whiteman was one of them. I tell you, everyone came from all over the country to those dances. And we had a local band made up of musicians from all over the United States. A lot of workers who came here were talented people, but they were out of work. The majority of people in Boulder City were very well educated; they just had to go where the job was.

ERMA GODBEY

When we had the Sons of the Legion dances, the boys were afraid to dance for fear that somebody'd see them, so we used to have moonlight dances.

Sims [Ely] decided we couldn't have moonlight dances, because he thought the kids were all necking. Well, they weren't. It's that the boys wouldn't even get out on the floor unless it was dark so they couldn't see their feet and see the mistakes they made. The mothers would teach the boys how to dance as much as they could, and then if we had a moonlight dance, they'd get up enough courage to ask the girls to dance. So then we just turned the lights on and let Sims see that there wasn't any necking going on. So that was all right, and he changed his mind about that.

Among Boulder City's first churches, the Grace Community Church was the most representative. Since it was nondenominational, it better represented the varied background of Boulder's residents; even construction of the church building in 1933 was a community effort, led by Parson Tom Stevenson.

BOB PARKER

The first services of the Grace Community Church was held in the mess hall by Parson Tom Stevenson. Late on Sunday evenings we would clear the back end of one of the wings, clear out the tables and set the chairs back up for Parson Tom to hold a church service. That's where he held his first church services. I think I attended the first church service that he conducted over there.

MARY EATON

People were wanting a church. They were meeting over in the mess hall, a group of people from all denominations, and they wanted to build their own church. There were seven denominations that helped with the building of Grace Community Church. They loaned us the money to do that, seven different denominations.

BOB PARKER

Six Companies helped [build] Grace Church. Grace Church was put up in a matter of two or three weeks. Six Companies had a lot of men in there working, and they put that church up practically overnight, like they did the houses here in town, the Six Companies houses.

Parson Tom took such an interest in the youth of Boulder City. That was one thing that a lot of the older people that worked down on the dam appreciated, because a lot of the elders worked most of the time and there wasn't too much else for the youth to do here in Boulder City. He spent most of his time with the youth. He took them on picnics; he took youth groups up to Charleston.

MARY EATON

He was a nice man. He was just a big ol' country boy. He was very good to work with the children. We didn't have many men in our church, because the Six Companies men had to work seven days out of the week, whereas the government workers only had to work six days. The men in our church were just the men who had government jobs, for the most part.

All of our husbands were working down at the dam, and we wanted to do something, get together. So we'd meet every Sunday. This Young Matrons class was like a branch of the Grace Community Church. There was not room for the Young Matrons to meet as a Sunday school class. Most of the space was taken up by the children. So we had our own separate building. We just did everything to make money. I don't know what we used our money for. I guess missionary projects. We put on a circus one time. We had a soup kitchen every Tuesday morning, I believe it was. The children from the elementary school would come over and have a ten-cent bowl of soup with us. And we made money with a ten-cent bowl of soup.

ROSE LAWSON

For me one of the finest things that ever happened was the Young Matrons class of the Grace Church. We had around 120 members. We had a very active membership. We gave so many parties. We gave money-making affairs. We gave a real fine circus every year. Lots of activities going on all the time. It kept many women and girls interested that would never have gone to church, never did go to church. But they belonged to that Sunday school class, and they took part in all the activities that were carried on through the Sunday school class.

EDNA FRENCH

The church was a real outlet for us. There were so many things that the church provided for us. I happened to be rather active in the church at that time, more than I have been at any other time, I believe. I taught a Sunday school class. We did many other things with the church. Our menfolk had only four days off a year—two days at Christmas and two days on the Fourth of July. So they did not enter into the church life except what was going on in the evening. But you'd be surprised to see the number of men when you'd go to church every Sunday evening. And really, it was nice.

TERESA JONES DENNING

Easter Sunday was a very special event. I never remember who came up with the idea of holding a sunrise service on what we called Cross Hill. About 500 people or more always gathered at the top of the hill for this sunrise service, and just as the first peep of the sun come over the mountain, we began the service. A little portable organ which I'm sure belonged to the [Grace] Community Church was carried to the site, and it was my honor and pleasure to play it several times. It had to be braced against rocks or held by somebody, because it was so light that when you pumped the bellows, it seemed sort of to walk away from you and you would find yourself sitting back with no organ to play. We used it to accompany the hymns and the groups while they were singing. Then always at the beginning and end of the service, Otto Littler or Tommy Nelson would give a trumpet solo, usually on the top of the hill, and quite often it was taps.

With a little government help, town boosters established the Boulder City Library.

EDNA FRENCH

We had a library started by Mrs. [La V La] Hayward. Mrs. Hayward had been a librarian at some other place where she lived, and they had a flower shop here in town. Through her past experience she was able to get books out of the library [of Congress] in Washington, D.C. She started our little library here in what was then a part of the post office.

ELTON GARRETT

Ida Browder knew some people in Washington, D.C., and so did Sims Ely. Between them and donations through students circulating around town and getting books secondhand, books from the Library of Congress and books from people's front doors together formed a sort of library that needed to be improved vastly, of course. Sims Ely had a spot in city hall [Municipal Building], a basement area set aside for use for this embryo library, which had nothing much but Library of Congress discards that had been provided by a munificent government.

CARL MERRILL

A lot of us used the library up here. I'd go up and get books. Well, all of a sudden I went to work swing shift. I had several books that I wasn't able to get back, because the library was open in the evenings when I was working. After so long a time, I had a notice to go up and see Sims Ely. It was over these books. I had to bring these books back and pay my fine to Sims Ely.

The camaraderie and mutual support Boulderites enjoyed during the early 1930s was largely among the Six Companies workers and not with the government executives and their families who lived in the shady neighborhoods surrounding the Bureau of Reclamation Administration Building. There were clear social distinctions in Boulder City.

MARY EATON

I imagine that there was probably some friction there, like the blue-collar workers and the white-collar workers. I think maybe the reason it was cliquish is because some of the people here had been together on other jobs. You might think it was cliquish, but it was because they knew each other. Maybe it really wasn't.

I think there was more feeling perhaps with the men that worked down at the dam and the people up on the hill. There was a distinction there, I think. The dam workers felt like they were doing the work, they were building the dam, and the people up on the hill weren't really doing very much, and probably getting more money. I think the men felt that they were the ones that were actually building the dam. People on the hill were needed, but I think there was a little feeling there at times. I think they just more or less stayed to themselves. They played bridge.

There were also racial divisions in Boulder City. While a few blacks, American Indians, and Hispanics were hired for work at the dam or for menial jobs in town, they were not allowed to live in Boulder City.

AGNES LOCKETTE

The people that I know usually think of Boulder as a town—it's an all-white community, most of them think it is. This is based on the fact that many [black] people have relatives who came to Boulder to seek employment in the time that the dam was being built and were turned away. Historically they think of Boulder as being an all-white community.

BUD BODELL

Right at the beginning there wasn't [any blacks], but by the time I'd been there a month, there were Negroes, 13 or 14. One was killed. I went down to the funeral, and I found out there were 14, including him, down there. All laborers.

ERMA GODBEY

There weren't hardly any Negroes in this area anyhow until they started Basic Magnesium.[6] Then they brought a lot of Negroes to work at Basic Magnesium. There were a few over in West Las Vegas, but not many. And, of course, we hadn't started all the hotels and all those things, so there wasn't any reason for them to be here.

African American laborers on Hoover Dam, 3 October 1932

Native Americans employed at Hoover Dam as high-scalers. This group includes one Yaqui, one Crow, one Navajo, and six Apaches, 5 October 1932

BOB PARKER

There were a lot of them that worked on the dam. I say a lot; I'd say a maximum probably of 50 or 100. But they all lived in Las Vegas.

Claude Dumas was a big black man. In the old days they thought that any scale or rust on reinforcing steel or concrete wouldn't cause the concrete to bond to it. So they brushed all the scale off the steel they took down there, and any rust. They had it all there in the steelyard over where the Park Service Building [warehouse] is, down through there and over below Lakeview now. They unloaded all that steel over in there. These black men, several of them, were out there brushing this steel. Black people do everything with a rhythm. Brushing steel, they'd be going this way, and the rear end would be going the other, back and forth. They developed a rhythm brushing steel, [and] they were singing hymns.

Charlie Rose had the colored crew down at the dam, the colored crew that built the parapet walls along the highway there and around the spillways, around the canyon wall there, all that rockwork. That's as beautiful a piece of rockwork as you'll see anywhere in the country. He was a white man, Charlie was. When Charlie would take a day off, they'd put someone else down there to run the colored crew, and the colored crew wouldn't work. Most of them [would] take the day off too. Charlie Rose knew how to treat them. They would work for him. Anybody else they wouldn't work for.

But there was another deal down there. We had a [Bureau of Reclamation] regional director here. I'm not going to mention any names, because I don't know whether they're all gone or not. I know that the man that put the winged figures in, and the safety island down there and all of that terrazzo work, outlined the center of the flagpole—I know that Hansen, Oskar J. W. Hansen, was the sculptor on that. He was out there one day, and one or two of the colored men asked him something about that terrazzo work there. He was explaining it to them. This project manager, he was actually—was over there and heard it. He went over there, and he really chewed Oskar Hansen out about associating with those colored men out there in the public. Of course, the tourists and everybody else heard him. Old Oskar flipped his lid. He really told that project manager off. He told him he wasn't fit to have those men working for him. He really read him off. Two weeks later that project manager was running an engineering chain gang in Redding, California, at Shasta Dam. He wasn't here a month after that happened down on top of the dam.

Clarence Newlin brought a colored cook [to work in the Green Hut Café], a black cook by the name of McKinley Sayles who cooked on the railroad diners for the Fred Harvey system. He was an awful good cook, especially a pie baker. People would come from all over to eat. They called him Red, nicknamed him Red. His pies were the best you could buy in the state of Nevada, and people came over here just to eat his pies.

142

Ralph Lowry, Bureau of Reclamation Chief Field Engineer; Sims Ely, Boulder City
Manager; Walker R. Young, Boulder Canyon Project Construction Engineer; 23
October 1935

But somebody went to Sims Ely and told him that Clarence Newlin had a black cook cooking up here and that there oughtn't to be any blacks in Boulder City. Sims Ely took it upon himself to call Clarence in and tell him he had to get rid of his black cook. Clarence said, "Mr. Ely, how much money have you got?" Mr. Ely said, "What difference does it make? What bearing does that have on the subject?" He said, "Well, I'll tell you something. If you've got $75,000, you can have that Green Hut tomorrow. You can hire who you want to or who you don't want to. But as long as that Green Hut belongs to me, you're not telling me who to hire and fire. Until you dig up the money to buy it out, don't be getting after me about my black cook." He turned around and walked out.

I guess Sims took it up with Washington and didn't get anywhere with it. Eleanor Roosevelt was very sympathetic to the colored people in Washington, so things were beginning to change right in those days about the colored people, black people.

MADELINE KNIGHTEN

I remember one time [at the Green Hut]. It could have developed into a free-for-all. In those days, you know, the Negroes weren't welcomed into any café. The Green Hut did have a very wonderful Negro cook. He was a very fine man, and he was a marvelous cook. But so far as serving was concerned, back in those days it was not common.

I was back in the kitchen visiting with my husband one of these dance evenings when we were expecting a dance crowd in any moment. The waiter rushed back to the window just all in a tizzy. He said, "There's a great big Negro out here." The waiter was a southern boy, Johnny Whittingham. He rushed back all in a tizzy and said, "There's a big Negro out here wanting to eat. What will I do with him?"

Howard, my husband, looked out and saw him. Fortunately, we had lived on the Apache reservation in Arizona and we knew the Apache people. Instantly he knew that he wasn't a Negro; he was an Apache Indian. He thought he probably was one of the high scalers. He said, "I want to talk to him anyhow." So he went out and talked to him, and he was one of the high scalers. They had at least two Apaches high scaling.

It was all eventually diverted. He ordered what he wanted to eat. They prepared it back in the kitchen, the other cooks back there. The waiter brought it out to him. My husband talked to him for a few minutes about things we knew. So he ate and left. But if he had realized that they were not ready to serve him, no telling what he might have done. He might have had a rage right there. He could have. But he didn't.

6

LAYING THE FOUNDATION: BLACK CANYON, 1932–1934

"I thought it was a Black Hole of Calcutta."

By the end of 1932, the Colorado River flowed through diversion tunnels on either side of Black Canyon, leaving the area between the upstream and downstream cofferdams dry. The Six Companies prepared the damsite for construction by excavating the riverbed for the dam's foundation and blasting away the canyon walls to anchor the dam. Of all the construction workers involved at this stage, the high scalers were the most admired. Dangling from ropes 700 feet above the canyon floor, high scalers blasted off the face of the cliff and then pried away loose rock. Tommy Nelson introduces his friend Joe Kine, whose understated description of his work as a high scaler belies the romantic legends that grew up around these daring men.

TOMMY NELSON

Joe, I've been told that a lot of these guys were pretty hungry that came to work. Some of them thought they were high scalers, and they'd come down on the job on the bus, and when they looked up where they had to work, why, they said, "It's too high for me." They weren't that hungry.

JOE KINE

But I was hungry enough. They was hiring men, and I was working down there. They just had to have men. They just took you over, and you was a

High-scalers on the Nevada wall of Black Canyon, about 1932

high scaler if you wanted it or not. I had worked in the mines, but I had never done any high scaling. It was all brand-new to me. Then it wasn't all that bad of a job once you got it going, got on to it.

My first job high scaling was over the Nevada valve house, cutting down to put the valve house in. That was the steepest canyon wall of all. We had a crew of men, and they came and went together all the time. I'd have a buddy that worked with me, and we'd be together all the time unless he took a day off or something. We tied our rope to a steel in the ground at the top of the canyon wall. We tied our safety belts and our bos'n chair on that. We had inch ropes. We had good ropes. They didn't break. That was never any worry. And then as they got frayed and unraveled out, they'd drop them down on the ground and burn them. We had an extra rope to tie the jackhammer on, and we tied our steel on, too.

We dropped ourselves over. Then we slid down to where we wanted to work, whether it was close or way down. We could move back and forth pretty good with our ropes. Then if you had to go up a little bit, you put a twist around your foot with the rope and slid up. We could sneak up pretty slow with that, but we very seldom had to go up. We used to climb out before the cableways were put up. Once the cableways got up, they'd go back and forth, and they could pick us up and move up and down and all ways. Then we had a big cable ladder too that we could go out on.

We didn't have expert powdermen. We done the whole business ourselves: drilled, loaded the holes and shot, barred down. Whatever was loose, we'd stick a bar behind it and pry it off and let it drop down. The engineers would mark it how far back we wanted to go. They'd take their transits and shoot and check it and tell you whether you had enough off or didn't have enough off. They had that all figured out. They'd mark it. Then we'd drill some more and go ahead.

There was never a dull moment on that high-scaling job. Something was going on all the time. If it wasn't one thing, it was another. One of the engineers that marked off the rock wall so we'd know where to drill slipped and fell a little bit. The story got out, and somebody wrote a big story about a man falling down through the air and a high scaler catching him and saving his life.[1] It was really out of this world, the story they had. It couldn't possibly have happened, because a man couldn't catch a man out there. It would have broke a rope or something. He'd come down too fast. He would have been too heavy. Anyway, he didn't get hurt.

But that was a good job. I got paid $5 a day to start with. Afterwards I got $5.60. I believe that was one of the safest jobs they had. I think there was less people that got hurt on high scaling than there was on lots of the other jobs. It wasn't any worse than anything else. One thing, you were sitting down all the time. It was a sitting-down job.

JAKE DIELEMAN

They hired anyone who didn't have brains enough to be scared. You was 900 feet up in the air. It took a lot of guts.

BRUCE EATON

When I first came here, there was two other fellows came with me who had been out of work quite some time. One of the fellows went to work a couple of weeks before I did. That upset Mrs. Eaton to think he got hired before I did. And he also got more pay—he was a high scaler. She wanted to know why I didn't get a job high scaling, because it paid more money. Well, after she found out what was involved, why, she wasn't quite so interested.

While Joe Kine and the other high scalers dangled overhead, other Six Companies crews excavated the riverbed, digging toward bedrock through millions of tons of sand, gravel, and boulders.

NEIL HOLMES

After the water was diverted around the damsite, we had to go in there and pump that water out, and we had to keep it pumped out. We installed pumps, pipelines, air lines, and water lines down in there. It was quite a project. There was a lot of pipe fitters. There was, I suppose, two or three hundred here at one time. I just had the one crew.

Then we moved in and started excavation for the dam itself at the damsite. That muck all had to be hauled out of there. A lot of it had to be blasted. They would shoot there. Nearly every day at noon, there would be a shot or two put off in there. We'd have pumps in there where they was excavating.

We'd have to move our pumps out, because when they shot there, it just looked like the whole side of the canyon was coming in. Everything had to be out of the way. Some of them we had to drag out with a truck or Cat, and some of them were small enough that about four men could get them out of there. We had to have electricians go in and unhook them for us first, because it was all 2,300-volt electricity and we wasn't allowed to do that. We was afraid to do that, in fact, to be honest with you. As soon as the shot was over with, we had to go in and set the pumps back so that it would be dry for the workers in there. That went on for several weeks, probably two or three months.

LEROY BURT

Whenever they moved a shovel, the shovel couldn't pull the cable. They had a group of men back there, leggers, that would pull the cables.

TOMMY NELSON

We had some Marion electric shovels down there. When I think about it today, guys dragging that 2,300-volt cable around in that water and the foreman saying, "It won't hurt you"—oh boy. It would just scare you to death.

An uninterrupted procession of trucks moved in and out of the canyon on steep roads, hauling muck. Tommy Nelson and Leroy Burt both labored on the canyon floor during the foundation excavation.

TOMMY NELSON

I was assigned to the excavation of the riverbed as a flagman. The purpose of this flagman was to keep all these trucks busy. If Joe Jones over here was in good digging, pour it on him. If this one over here is having a lot of big rocks in his dipper, just give him what he could take care of. In other words, keep the trucks busy, and the shovels busy.

There was quite a number of dump trucks down there during this excavation, hauling this debris, this rock out of there: the International, the Mack, the Boreman, the White, and the GMC. The workhorse was the old International, the corn binder. As she went up the hill with a load, she'd belch fire up the river. Many of these trucks that we had down there were hard tails. I better explain what a hard tail is, because the younger generation wouldn't know. A hard-tail truck was a truck that had hard rubber [tires] on the back, solid rubber. We had quite a few of those down there on the job. Now, a person had to be very careful where he set that truck, because if you got him

149

back in there where he was going to get mired down, you were in for a chewin'. You might have quite a job to get him out. Now this driver who piloted that truck, he was in reverse about as much as he was forward. There was a little canopy built right over the steering wheel. That would keep the rocks from falling on him.

LEROY BURT

When he started backing up, he'd step out on the side of the truck. He had a throttle there; he had it in reverse. He'd hit that throttle and back up to wherever he was going. When he got to where he wanted to stop, he'd slide back into his seat and put the brakes on.

TOMMY NELSON

Those trucks never turned their ignition off unless they were broke down. When they were hauling that debris out of the river bottom, a man coming down assigned to a certain truck might take any truck until he found his own. They would change shifts right on the run.

I recall one little incident, just to give you an idea how highball this job was. During the change of a shift—I was working a swing shift—I heard the swish of an air hose way up high there. I looked up there, and here comes a high scaler. He looks like a little ant. Apparently he got knocked off before he got tied on. He was coming all the way down. He lit very close to where I was flagging these trucks.

There was a shovel operator by the name of Red Wixson operating a shovel nearby where this fellow fell. I took a quick look to see if there were any trucks coming. I didn't think there was much I could do for this guy, but best I take a look. So I went over to him real fast. Red jumped out of his shovel. There wasn't nothing you could do for him. But there was trucks coming, and they were stacking up. Along came a hard-boiled superintendent. I won't use the language he used. But he said, "Get those blankety-blank trucks moving." I said, "Carl, there's a man killed over here." "Well, he won't hurt anybody; get 'em going."

Curley Francis worked as a truck driver hauling muck from the damsite during excavation.

Excavating the foundation for Hoover Dam in the floor of Black Canyon, 29 April 1933

Muck trucks at Hoover Dam, 15 January 1932

CURLEY FRANCIS

During the nighttime they always had their shots go off sometime around three o'clock in the morning. As we were bunched up together as truck drivers, we'd try to pan gold down in the trough a little bit. We had not excavated down to the glory hole yet. The glory hole is right down to the bottom of the dam. We were getting into gravel and sand down at the bottom. It was slow work, due to the fact that a lot of it was hand-mucking at that particular time. There was no machinery that could do that type of work. That glory hole was a beautiful sight to look at after it was completed because it was actually stripped and washed and cleaned up. Everything had to be clean as one could imagine in order to start the concrete pouring.

While crews scaled off the canyon walls and excavated the canyon floor, Six Companies erected a vast and complicated system of towers and cableways along the canyon rim. The cable system spanned Black Canyon like a steel web and solved the problem of delivering men, equipment, and concrete to any spot on the damsite. Construction workers could ride a high line called the Joe Magee, while others rode slings suspended from the cables.

HARRY HALL

They had what they called a Joe Magee, a high line that you could catch and go. They had landings on the water and also on the Arizona side. They had a cage that would transport maybe as many as 20 men perhaps. They would go into and across the canyon and also down at the same time. If you had any equipment or anything like that, you had to ride the Joe Magee.

They also finally developed a crosswalk clear across the canyon, supported on cables, that you could walk across. Just a walkway for men to get back and forth. You could walk across; no problem. Well, a little sway; everything swayed.

TEX NUNLEY

The cableway there, the government cableway, was tested for 300 tons for overweight. To ride the slings there, you just got your feet in the eyes of the sling and held on.

Construction workers occasionally took their wives or girlfriends for clandestine rides on the cableways.

DOROTHY NUNLEY

I was going with a fellow that had a friend working graveyard on the cableways. He promised me one time that he'd take me across the cableway, but we had to go after midnight because the big shots weren't around then. They didn't allow the women to go across as a rule. A few of the big people's women went, but not many.

They got me on at the end. At that time there wasn't any water underneath us. It was dry. About halfway between the canyon walls, this fellow said, "This is number 11." I said, "Oh, it is?" He said, "Yes. This is the one that's fallen so many times." Right then my heart just went. I couldn't wait to get back on solid ground again. It was very frightening.

No. 11 Cableway, known as the "Widow Maker," was responsible for one of the most spectacular accidents during Hoover Dam's construction.[2]

TEX NUNLEY

Number 11 was there to take material from down below up to the valve house on the Arizona side or Nevada side. They'd bring in lumber or anything that was supposed to go up on either side and then take it up on Number 11. Kenny Wilson, a hook tender on Number 11, hooked onto a pumpcrete gun and was going to take it up to the Nevada side.

BOB PARKER

I had gone over to visit with George Clark, the government cable operator out there with that operating shack sticking out over the canyon wall. That operator's shack has a grating in it, and you can see right down into the canyon. I was standing out there on the grating. George was operating the cableway. You weren't allowed in the shack proper when they were working a load.

They hooked up to this pumpcrete machine, and there were two men on it. This concrete machine probably weighed 25, 30 tons. The signalman had a yellow paddle with a dot on it. He gave the signal down there for them to start lifting the concrete machine out of there. It started slowly lifting, taking the slack out of the cable, and then I noticed one man jump off of the machine. He walked maybe 50, 60 feet.

TEX NUNLEY

That's what saved his life. They took the pumpcrete gun and Kenny Wilson up there.

BOB PARKER

It got about halfway up out of the canyon, and I heard that cable. It sounded like a shot. It snapped. Then it started singing like a bullet going through the air. That cable started singing. I looked down, and there went this concrete machine down for the lower cofferdam. Pretty soon it hit, and it about half-buried itself. [The] signalman didn't stay with the machine. When it got about a hundred or fifty feet from the cofferdam, he jumped. He landed 25, 30 feet from the machine. I saw him laying there, and this foreman, his boss, come running over there. I stayed out there maybe a half-hour. Doc Jensen, who then was the Six Companies first-aid man, came out there to where he was. I noticed before I left to go up where I was working that they had pulled a sheet over him. I knew then what the answer was—that he was gone.

CARL MERRILL

We didn't go to work that afternoon. They just turned around and sent us back.

Memories of other construction accidents are still clear today.

JOHN CAHLAN

They had what they called a monkey-slide, which was a sort of an open-air elevator. It went up the face of the dam when they built the thing. There were about 10 or 12 people that were on the monkey-slide, and it broke about halfway up the face of the dam and dumped them down onto a lot of steel piled on end. It just impaled three or four of these guys and bruised and injured the other people that were on the slide.

And another time down there, the scaffolding on which two men were working broke and threw them down into the river in the diversion tunnel some 50 feet below. The river was running through the diversion tunnels around the damsite at about 20 or 30 miles an hour. They rode through the tunnel on the scaffold debris and came out at the other end of the tunnel below the dam and never had a scratch on 'em!

DENZLE S. PEASE

I witnessed one death. A water boy was taking water up to a crew that was working above where I was working, and he fell. I was in a small tunnel with another man, and we were walking toward the entrance when we saw the body fall. He was partly obscured by the way the tunnel flared out. He fell and hit the edge of the tunnel, then dropped another 150 feet to the bottom of the canyon.

While high scalers were facing off the canyon walls and laborers were excavating the riverbed in 1932 and 1933, the government and Six Companies were building facilities for the production of concrete. The task required construction of an elaborate railroad network, including tunnels bored through solid rock and miles of track laid across the desert. A trestle bridge spanned the Colorado River six miles upstream to gravel deposits in Arizona that provided aggregate to manufacture concrete for Hoover Dam. Closer to the damsite the contractor built an enormous gravel screening plant. At the damsite itself a high mix plant at the top of the canyon and a low mix plant at the bottom made it possible to manufacture and deliver concrete on the spot.

WILLIAM D. McCULLOUGH

I helped build that bridge across the river to the gravel pits. We finished it in about 60 days. First they was going to build a conveyor across there, but back in them days conveyors wasn't too practical. The bridge was a pile bridge, and they thought if it washed out, they could build another one. But it never did wash out. It lasted.

You could hear [our] pile driver probably 40 miles away when we was working. I remember all the sheep and burros on the other side of the river was pretty scared at first, but later they got used to us and came down to the river to drink. One old burro, he was a pinto. He was so old he was walking on his fetlock. Poor old devil could hardly get along. He'd come down and just bray and bray when that pile driver was running.

And once we got across the river, we'd go over and find arrowheads. We'd get down around the bushes where the sand had shifted and find beautiful arrowheads sticking out of the ground.

THEODORE GARRETT

At the time I started to work, it seemed that every facet of construction was getting under way. The railroad from Las Vegas to Boulder was being completed, and the government part of the railroad [the U.S. Construction Railway] was under construction from Boulder City to the aggregate screening plant, to the gravel pits on the Arizona side of the river, to the mixing plant to be installed on the canyon wall at the upper portals, and to the mixing plant to be installed at the lower portals. This railroad operation being performed by the government was a complete railroad system on a small scale. Steam engines were used, and bottom-dump gravel cars were used to haul aggregate. The aggregate screening plant was located in the Hemenway Wash area.

TEX NUNLEY

Union Pacific wouldn't take their trains down over the railroad from the depot [in Boulder City] to the dam, because the grade was too steep for them. I guess they didn't trust their locomotives on that kind of a grade. The government had to build their own railroad from Boulder City clear on down to the dam. The government had their own locomotives. It was a gas locomotive, but later on they got a diesel electric.

156

I was a rodman with the government engineers that laid the grade out. Lewis Construction Company had the contract on the railroad. But they gave Gordon Construction Company the contract on the tunnels, for they weren't tunnelmen. But Gordon Construction was tunnelmen. There were five tunnels on the railroad. They were 18 foot square, with a 9-foot radius on the top. One tunnel was all shored up with heavy timbers. But some of the others, just where it was faulty rock, they'd timber it maybe 30 feet, or 20 feet, whatever it came to. Most of it was just opened up. The Six Companies railroad took off from Junction City all over to where they had to have railroads.

They got all their sand and gravel from over in Arizona. There were immense mountains of sand and gravel that they could use over there. They didn't find that much here in Nevada, for it was mostly mountains. They had to build a bridge across the river there for the railroad to cross to bring the sand and gravel over. They had an enormous screening plant.

At the gravel screening plant, the contractor prepared all the sand and aggregate used in Hoover Dam's concrete, washing it in clarified river water before grading and stockpiling it for transport to Black Canyon.

TEX NUNLEY

They built an enormous tank up there on an island. They had to pump water up in there to let the sediment settle down. They wanted to get clear water; they didn't want the sediment with it. That big tank is under water today. The lake came up, and it's under water.

NADEAN VOSS

For so long when the water would be lower, the tank showed up like an old skeleton. But it's certainly a long ways under now. There was talk of washing gold out of that gravel, but it had no foundation that I knew of. You often looked at the water going over those piles of gravel and wanted to say, "Well, how much gold do you suppose they're getting out of that?"

*Once the sand and gravel was washed and separated, trains hauled it
to the Nevada side of the canyon for mixing into concrete and delivery to
the damsite. But, as Tex Nunley recalls, Hoover Dam's first concrete was
not produced at the project's mixing plants.*

TEX NUNLEY

You could say the first was poured with a water bucket. It was on the lower
portal railroad. They benched off on the cliff up there to put in the track.
They had steel beams going up. They poured concrete with a water bucket
around some of those beams. When they took the beams out, the concrete
stayed. That was the first concrete that ever went into the mix. The dam was
built on up to that, so that pour was taken in. Sounds funny, but that's the
way it was.

I started down at the low mix, oiling rollers on the conveyors that took
care of the sand and gravel. Then they transferred me up to the high mix.
They had scales up there that you could set whatever you needed, for sand,
for gravel, and cement. But they took care of the water down on the batcher
floor. I was on the batcher floor there for a while. The railroad trains came
in on top of the big bins and they dumped sand in the hopper. They had
different kinds of gravel, from pea gravel clear up to nine-inch, what they
called the cobble. They dumped it in these bins. The sand, gravel, and everything like that [went] down into the mixer below, down on the mixing floor.
It was all electric, automatic.

Cement trains would come in there full [of cement], loose, in boxcars.
They would pump this cement out of these boxcars into different blending
silos. It was all mixed up in order that they got the same mix all the way
through the whole dam.

Whenever the operator down there on the mixer was ready for a batch, he
tripped the switch. So much sand would dump out, gravel, and every other
thing. Then it would come down on this belt. He added water down there,
what was supposed to go in that mix. It was a four-yard mix. I think it was
2.1 minutes that it was supposed to mix.

Below the mixer was a big hopper that held eight yards. The mixer could
dump twice into this hopper. It would hold two mixes. Then the trains came
around under the hoppers. You had lights on each mixer. You had the guy
that was dumping there. That's what I was doing for a long time. I was
dumping the concrete into these eight-yard buckets. You had to know if each
mixer was mixing the same concrete. Maybe one was mixing pea gravel,
another was inch-and-a-half, one three-inch. You had to know. The operator
up there told you what he was doing. You had to know your trains and

switch the lights according to the train. The train stopped wherever you had the lights on. If they were running fast and they would pull to the concrete a little faster than you were mixing, maybe they would pull four yards out of this mixer and four yards out of the next. They had this light on and that light. The dinky skinner—the guy that's on the train—he'd know to stop here under this hopper, get four yards, and go right on up to the next place and get four yards, and then hightail it for the high line.

Once the concrete pouring began, it proceeded at a breakneck pace. Six Companies poured the first bucket of concrete on the dam structure at 11:20A.M. on 6 June 1933 and the last on 29 May 1935. During those two years workers poured concrete 24 hours a day. Curley Francis was a dinky skinner, running locomotives back and forth between the high mix plant and the cableways.

CURLEY FRANCIS

After my dad died in 1933, I rustled around and got a job up at the high mix. I was the extra man there, running the gas locomotives and flatbed trucks. My job was to haul concrete to the cableways. I ran locomotives from the high mix mostly.

When you went into the high mix, you'd come out the outside track and come to a spring switch. Then you'd come underneath the mix, get your load.

Then you'd start out, and you'd have a red light. I worked graveyard shift. It was kind of challenging, because you'd run into a red light on the track, by golly, and you'd sit there and you'd get two or three minutes' sleep. You always kept a water bag outside the window. Whenever you didn't wake up good, you'd just put it on top of your head and shake it around.

If it was green, of course, you went around the turn. You might go on the inside; you might go on the outside. You didn't know where you was going, except when you got your assignment with the train, they'd say, "You're on Number 8 Cableway." Or Number 10 Cableway. You didn't care where they was pouring; it was just the fact that you had to go to that cableway with the bucket.

Oh, I'll tell you, that was a complicated system. The fact was that the concrete was raising in the glory hole, and that meant that it didn't take the cableways as long to get rid of their loads. Therefore we had to have more engines. At some times we had nine engines running on two tracks with two

An eight-cubic-yard bucket dumping concrete in a form on the dam structure, about 1933

The high-mix concrete plant at Black Canyon, 15 February 1934

crossovers. We had four gas engines and as many of the electric engines as we could get.

There were many times that we had to run around one engine to the other to get a specific load to a certain cableway. This was a mad confusion. All of a sudden you'd come around a turn and you'd hit another red light. Maybe another train was coming around this way and heading right for you, but he'd switch over just before you got there. Half the time when you'd be working graveyard shift, you'd be looking down the track and see another train coming right for you; then all of a sudden they'd switch him around you, and as soon as he went by, you'd go on by.

They had a switch tower up there. This young fellow, he run that switch tower for quite a while. He done it all. He had a light for every switch. They had about eight or nine air switches. They had a large whistle on the top of that switch tower, and anytime that that man hung onto that whistle, everybody stopped, because we all knew that he was confused and didn't know where everybody was at. One time all of a sudden he just pulled all the switches like that and blew the whistle and walked out. He couldn't stand it any longer. There was derailings at times, and we had a few collisions, minor ones [that] didn't amount to an awful lot. But it was a real feat to run the switch and keep all nine trains working.

You had to be quite efficient with air brakes when hauling concrete to the cableways, due to the fact that you had to stop right on the money in order to receive the empties and move the length of the bucket for the cableway to pick up the full load. We usually carried one full one, and then we received the empty one. Then we'd move up, and they'd hook onto the full one, and away they'd go. These concrete buckets, as I understand, when they were full of eight yards of cobble, they weighed 24 tons. We had train air and engine air. If you were just going to make a slow stop, you'd just use your engine air. But if you were going to make kind of an emergency stop, you'd use train air, which was all [wheels].

This small railroad, an electric train, went from Number 9 [Cableway]. The shortest railroad in the state of Nevada. You picked up your concrete right about here, and you went about 60 feet to the cable. Everybody hated it because it was back and forth, back and forth, back and forth all the time. Some places they could not get to the cableway, so they would put them on a truck and they would go on down the line somewhere.

It was kind of interesting that as the dam started to grow, the cableways became more demanding. In other words, you had to haul concrete faster all the time.

Harry Hall, who worked in the canyon as the dam rose, picks up the story from the point at which cableway operators lifted the eight-yard buckets from flatcars at the canyon rim.

161

HARRY HALL

It was picked up by the high line, and we had what they called a bell punk that was in contact with the cableway operator. The bigger cableway operated where both the tail tower and the head tower moved on tracks, so they could go upstream and downstream, and across, Arizona to Nevada, with a bucket. The signal punk would tell the cableway operator where to go, whether to go to Arizona or Nevada, upstream or downstream. When he got it down low enough, he would signal that it was in position, and then the workmen would trip the dump and discharge the concrete. Then the signal punk would have the empty bucket raised up and put back on a railroad car.

The cableway operator couldn't see the bucket, of course. There was a concrete inspector who was knocked off the form. He was sitting up on the walkway, on the railing of the walkway. The signal punk gave erroneous information to the cableway operator. The bucket swayed too much and hit him. He was seriously injured, but he was not killed.

[They used] five-foot pours on the dam. They also had keyways to key each block in with the other. They had water stops on the keyways so that no water would leak through. We moved the forms; the forms would slip up. They were fastened with she-bolts, and they would slip those up to the next form, lift the whole form up.

When they'd make a pour, they'd first brush it off with jets of water, dry that up, and then put grout on top of it to make a good bond to the concrete. They'd rinse it down first; then the inspector would call for how much grout they'd need. He would spread that around, and then put the concrete onto that, and he'd spread it around.

CARL MERRILL

A puddler is the one that pushes the concrete around with his feet. He wears hip boots. When we were doing puddling, of course, they'd bring the concrete down in buckets. Then you either opened the bottom or you had a chute that you opened. You tried to pour the concrete around to where you wanted it. Then you worked it with your feet. Of course, the concrete, when they drop it, it tends to separate. You can't have this. So you try to work this concrete in and out with your feet, just tromping up and down. Then they have agitators also. An agitator is about four or five inches in diameter, three or four feet long, and it vibrates by air. You run that in and out. That concrete's got to be thoroughly mixed after they dump it in your spot, wherever your form happens to be.

One eight-yard pour would raise the level of concrete in the form only about two feet—too little to bury a worker, despite popular stories that persist today. Bob Parker remembers one such story.

BOB PARKER

A girl wrote a few months back that her grandparents had told her that her uncle was buried in Hoover Dam in the concrete. I did find out that he was in an accident down in the slot when one of the forms gave way and concrete poured down in there. He and another man were on this scaffold down in there carrying a big plank. The concrete tore down the scaffold that they were on and dumped him and the plank down in the bottom in the wet concrete. Somehow the man that was with him hung onto the scaffold and was saved. Her uncle wound up in the bottom, and it took them a few hours to dig him out, but they got him out of that concrete. Of course, he was dead. But they never left anybody buried in the dam.

WILLIAM D. McCULLOUGH

As I remember, [Frank Crowe] was down there when the form gave way and the concrete buried the guy. [Crowe] supervised the job of taking that guy out. When they got down to his body, the concrete had set, of course, and they had pavement busters and jackhammers. When they got down to where they seen one of his hands or one of his legs, Mr. Crowe made them take and use small picks to get that body out.

Another accident buried several men, and Leroy Burt worked to retrieve their bodies.

LEROY BURT

Three of them. Three pipe fitters. You must remember that the concrete that they poured on the dam, you're talking about slump—that's the size of the gravel that goes into the concrete. On the dam all the slump was nine-inch. The rocks in there were that big around. These pipe fitters were working in

163

there when a form gave way above and maybe 8, 10, 12 yards or more of concrete poured right down on top of them. I had to go down, and we worked around the clock until we got those people out of there.

Engineers realized that if concrete were to be poured in one monolithic mass, the chemical reaction induced by the setting concrete would raise the temperature of the dam to dangerous levels. The cooling process would take 125 years, and the concrete would crack, threatening the structural integrity of the dam. A latticework of pipes laid between the five-foot pours circulated cold water through the dam, cooling it uniformly. Bruce Eaton was one of those responsible for the refrigeration system.

BRUCE EATON

I was assigned the job of operating and maintaining the cooling system which cooled the mass concrete in the dam. As you well know, when the concrete sets up, there's a chemical reaction that generates a tremendous amount of heat. And pouring concrete in the masses it was poured in it was necessary to dissipate this heat. My job was not to install the cooling pipe in the concrete itself but to connect and operate the cooling system that provided the cooling. Every five feet, vertically and horizontally, there was a one-inch-diameter cooling pipe embedded in the concrete. The dam, for all practical purposes, was poured in two sections, with a 10-foot opening left in the center to facilitate this cooling process. You can imagine the many, many miles of tubing it would take to run a one-inch-diameter tubing from the center each way to the canyon wall and back. What it amounted to was a huge radiator.

The engineering section of the Bureau of Reclamation prior to this time had calculated the temperature of each section, each of the five-foot [concrete] sections, the temperature it would be in the future when everything was normalized, considering the temperature of the water on the upstream side, the sun and its effect on the downstream side. Their idea was to cool the concrete below that calculated temperature, and while the concrete was in a contracted form, a liquid grout, a liquid cement, was pumped into the voids between each pour. That made a solid block of it. And as the temperature warmed up, the concrete would always be in compression instead of tension. Concrete is much stronger under compression than it is under tension. By virtue of these facts, it's been determined that the arch of the dam has moved upstream very slightly from its original position due to the lengthening of the arch.

Steve Chubbs was a Bureau of Reclamation technician who kept an eye on the dam's temperature.

STEVE CHUBBS

The interesting thing about the concrete was that we had two grades. We had what they called a summer grade, and then we had a winter grade. We had the different grades because for the summer we wanted the concrete to set up a little slower. If it sets too fast, that's not good for it. So we had this slow-setting cement. And the best grade came from Utah, Devil's Slide. You've probably seen concrete laboratories where they have cylinders, and they have a hydraulic machine that breaks the cylinder. Devil's Slide would break at 6,000 pounds per square inch, and the others would break at about 5,000. Of course, Devil's Slide didn't produce too much cement. It was good quality, though.

As the season grew cooler, we started to use the winter grade. We have a long summer here, though. It's called high-heat and low-heat cement. I don't know whether they use it much now or not. I'm not sure. But they used it here, I know.

All we wanted was to have the concrete cooled. We didn't care how the contractor went at it, as long as the temperature of the concrete was brought down to within reasonable limits. The concrete was cooled. They had to pump cold water through the pipes. The dam is full of pipe, or tubing. We called it tubing because it's very thin-walled. It's full of tubing to cool the concrete.

We had a great big cooling plant, just a huge outfit. That cooled the water. They used ammonia gas to cool the water. We were always being shifted around, from one place to another. I spent 30 days at the cooling plant doing some work. They have what they call operators. They were skilled men. They knew compressors. We had one that chewed tobacco. He'd walk by his instrument panel, look at the instruments; then he'd walk over to the window and spit his tobacco juice out the window. You had to watch where you walked. I guess he's long gone.

Bruce Eaton recalls one time that he was nearly caught in a scheme to defraud the government over the concrete-cooling portion of the project.

BRUCE EATON

That particular part of the construction was so unique and there was so little information available on the techniques of cooling concrete that the company was unable to submit a firm bid on that portion of construction. So they negotiated a contract with the Bureau of Reclamation on what is commonly referred to as force account or cost plus. It was a fixed percentage over the actual cost. For that reason, and me being in charge of that portion of the work, I was designated as the only one authorized to receive material and approve vouchers for payment to the Six Companies.

I was approached by some of the office personnel one day to sign a voucher for some material, and I replied, "We didn't receive this material." "Well," he said, "that's OK. Go ahead and sign it. It doesn't make any difference." I had a pretty good idea of what would follow if I had signed that. I had no intention of signing that or any other voucher for any material that we did not receive. My reply to the individual was that I would sign it under one condition, and he said, "What's that?" I said, "That I get 50 percent of everything I steal." He said, "Do you think I'm crazy?" I said, "Well, what the hell do you think *I* am? You're not paying me enough to steal for this outfit, and if I have to steal, you better get somebody else to do it."

That didn't contribute to a very good relationship between me and my department. A short time after that, I was fired—as a direct result of that, of course. The engineers in charge for the Bureau of Reclamation became concerned about why I was fired, and they paid a visit to me at my home and I explained the situation. [They] said, "We're paying your salary, you're satisfying us—you come back to work." I said, "I can't come back to work, I've been removed from the job." They said, "That'll be taken care of." The next day a representative of the Six Companies came by and told me to come back to work, which I did do, and finished the job. I was not asked to sign any more vouchers for material we didn't receive, and we got along pretty well after that.

One aspect of the concrete work impressed Bob Parker from the beginning.

BOB PARKER

Building Hoover Dam involved almost the complete production of four (and sometimes a fifth) concrete plants in the western United States. They were

166

Workers being lowered into the canyon on the overhead skip line, Cableway No. 9, 26 March 1933

bringing cement in here from all of those different cement plants. It was bound to be a different color. They overcame that color problem by building big blending silos up there at the high mix plant. They brought all that cement in in railroad boxcars. They had these huge vacuum cleaners in those boxcars. They vacuumed all that cement up and ran it down into those silos, and then they'd blend it. Otherwise you'd have had a checkerboard dam down there because of all the various colors of cement that were used to build it. They've got a beautiful structure now. That amazed a lot of people, because why would the government and Six Companies spend the amount of money that it took to make sure that dam turned out to be the same uniform color? Over the past 50 years, I don't think there's any dam in the world that's had as many beautiful pictures and been shown in as many countries and to as many people as Hoover Dam. I wondered at the time about the cost of blending that cement and making it, but I'll tell you, it really paid off as far as a beautiful dam for future generations to look at.

Construction proceeded into 1934, with railroads delivering buckets of concrete to the cableways, high lines moving workers and material, blocks of concrete rising like a chessboard in the dry gap between the cofferdams. Men, trucks, trains, and cables were in motion 24 hours a day. From the rim of Black Canyon, the activity below was awe-inspiring to some, frightening to others.

NAN BAKER

Frank took me down to the dam one evening. When I saw it, I thought it was a Black Hole of Calcutta. I said, "I'll never come down here until it's finished, if I ever do then." And I never did until the lake was full.

NADEAN VOSS

Watching the building of the dam was our big entertainment. We watched the Big Berthas unload workmen, and the men go to work on the dam, watched the buckets of concrete on the high lines as they dumped on the designated checks [forms], and we watched the monkey-slide taking men up and down the face of the dam. The trucks had no lights, but the roads were lighted by large globes shining from tublike receptacles.[3] We'd lean over, and you couldn't talk to anybody. The noise was just simply tremendous, just deafening. You couldn't make yourself heard even if you shouted. All you could do was point, then, when you got out, say, "What in the world was that going on down there?" That went on all during construction. And now it is so silent, except for a clang or so far below. It just seems so weird.

The men who worked on the dam may not have seen their job in such stark terms, but many who toiled at hard labor for low wages with no job security might have agreed with Nan Baker and Nadean Voss. Joe Kine remembers one disgruntled puddler who was outspoken about his frustration.

JOE KINE

This certain man that I'm going to tell you about was standing on the back step of the transport. As we come up going out of the lower portal, we make a hairpin curve, and whoever's standing on the back can look right back at the dam. This man had been laid off. He had been puddling concrete, and I guess he'd slacked off a little bit or something and they'd laid him off. He wasn't feeling too happy. He was standing on the back step of the transport. As we rounded the hairpin curve at the muck tunnel, he looked back at the dam, and he said, "I hope it leaks."

Dinner in the Anderson Brothers Mess Hall, 1932

7

A DAY IN THE LIFE: 1931–1935

"We could live on a dollar a day."

Although the scene in Black Canyon changed constantly during the four years of Hoover Dam construction, daily life for workers and their families settled into a pattern. With three shifts working around the clock, the rhythm of the job imposed a schedule on workers and their families that varied little but provided a sense of stability rare in Depression America.

A full stomach went a long way toward creating a feeling of security, and whether they worked day, swing, or graveyard shift, Six Companies employees began their day at the Anderson Brothers Mess Hall.[1]

TEX NUNLEY

You couldn't have any better food than what Anderson Brothers put out. A millionaire would never have had that many varieties of food on his table at any one time.

BOB PARKER

The mess hall had two wings. We called them [the] right and left wing. Each wing would seat six hundred, with a kitchen in the center, and a warehouse, and a full-size bakery with three bakers. We had a meat shop, butcher shop. We fed twelve hundred men at a meal. We had three breakfast meals. They fed family-style. By that I mean they would take hotcakes and put them on a great big platter on the table, and take sausage, and take eggs and put them

171

on a big platter and put them on the table. You could eat as long as you could eat, and they'd keep bringing it to you. That went over big with these people that had been in breadlines. It took a little while to fill up those empty bellies. Those people were really glad to get a square meal, and that's what Anderson put out.

WILFRED VOSS

I ate at the Anderson Mess Hall. The food was excellent. As a matter of fact, I have never run into anything that would compare with it—the food and the amount of food that they put out. When people came here, they hadn't had a square meal for a long time, and they certainly took the slack out of their belts. They fed, I imagine, three, four, five thousand men, pretty near. They were fed three meals a day. And they fed them fast. The family may go hungry, but I had plenty to eat. I never went hungry.

I remember one morning a man I had never seen before. He was sitting next to me at the breakfast table. There was a platter of eggs. There must have been 15 eggs anyway on that platter. I asked him to please pass the eggs. He took them up, and he scooped the whole platterful off on his plate and gave me the empty platter. I never saw anything like it.

There was always plenty of food. If you were at the far end of the line, though, where platters were passed down, chances are you'd have to wait for them to be filled up three or four times before they'd finally get some food down for you. We found that the best way that we could enjoy our meals and not squabble over what's on the table is get your share of food. The tables had either 8 or 10 men at them, 5 on each side. We had one group— we were friends. We got a table every time.

DOROTHY NUNLEY

I've eaten in there. It was very crowded as a rule. They had several different dishes, different kinds of meat and things. They didn't stick with just one thing. Fish day on Friday, that was a rough one. You could smell it all over town.

MARION ALLEN

Every holiday we'd go up to Anderson's. Thanksgiving cost a whole 75¢. The wife and I, 75¢ apiece; for the girl, it was free. So that cost us $1.50. You'd have turkey, roast beef, anything under the sun as long as you wanted.

Of course, we went in there other times too. They'd bring eight steaks out. Some of these old miners would take three of these steaks, pretty good-size steak. So then they'd bring five more. Maybe somebody cleaned those all up, why, they'd bring a couple more. They had everything under the sun. That was one thing, I guess, that Crowe was always fussy about. Two things Mr. Crowe was really fussy about: the hospital and the feeding. I guess that was where most of the holler came from.

When the men had finished breakfast and were starting off to the damsite, they lined up once more to pack their lunch boxes.

CARL MERRILL

When they'd get through with breakfast, if you start the day at breakfast, you'd line up and go through the lunch counter. They had regular lunch boxes like we know them today, about 10-by-10-by-4 inches deep.

These sandwiches were all made. They worked there 24 hours making sandwiches and setting food out, putting boxes together. They'd come in and grab a box, and then they'd start filling it with all they could put in it. Pie, cake—they baked pies there, and they baked cakes there. Of course, the fellows that worked in the lunchroom not only prepared the sandwiches; they cut the pies. They had little wax envelopes they'd drop them in. Then they wrapped the cake.

Then they had baskets. I would say the baskets were 12 inches deep, and maybe 2 feet wide, and 2½ feet long, and these were full of different types of sandwiches. Each basket had a certain type of sandwiches. Every sandwich was individually wrapped. Then the fellows would just go down the line and pick up the sandwiches they want, the fruit they want. They always had apples—and oranges occasionally, but not always.

TOMMY NELSON

That was very interesting, how these guys could get as many as 10 or 12 sandwiches into a lunch box that probably was 10 inches square by 4 inches deep. But it wasn't uncommon to see some of those guys stuff 10 or 12 sandwiches in it. They were pretty squashed up. Maybe a couple pieces of pie, an apple, and an orange. They loaded 'em up.

Fortunately, as to myself, I never carried a lunch, because I'd buddy-up with some guy on the crew who lived at the mess hall. You'd give them a carton of cigarettes for 50¢. He'd carry your lunch for you. That helped out a lot.

THEODORE GARRETT

People that lived in the dormitories had to pick up their box lunches at the mess hall. You went along the line and picked out what you wanted. Quantity was no item. You just got all you wanted to eat. Two or three kinds of sandwiches: beef, pork, ham, cheese; you name it, they had it. Fruit: oranges, apples, bananas. Pie and cake for desert. That was about it.

While the mess hall seemed like paradise to hungry workers who ate there, Carl Merrill, who was a waiter for the Anderson Brothers, recalls the backbreaking work involved in feeding hundreds of boisterous men three times a day.

CARL MERRILL

It was a lot of work, and it was hard work. We had to carry the food from the kitchen to the tables. Some of us had five tables to wait on, and some of us had four tables, according to how far from the kitchen we were. There was eight men at each table. We carried food in from the kitchen and waited on the table. A platter of meat might have 10 pork chops on it. You bring that in, set it on the table, and the men help themselves. When it runs out, you take it out and they fill it up for you and you bring it back again. You learned to carry five or six platters at a time and four to five bowls at a time.

They had huge equipment, and it was very modern equipment for that time. Right in the center of the kitchen, they had the fry station. That was about eight stoves, four back to back. In front of those stoves, they had the counters. So the fry cooks were cooking on these stoves and putting it on the plates or dishes or platters. They'd turn around and set it on the counter. You'd pick it up and carry it into the mess hall, to your station. Then they had great big pots they were making soup in. They were huge. I bet they were five feet in diameter and several feet deep. They had several of these for different purposes.

Of course, there was no tablecloths. When the men got through, you had to clear off the table, and I mean completely clear it off and wash it, take all the dishes back to the dishwasher, and you had to wash your tables. Then you go get your clean dishes and your silverware and reset them.

Then they had a huge dishwasher. This was alongside of the fry station. It was about, I would say, 15 or 16 feet long. They had a counter along down each side of it, a big horseshoe counter, and this dishwasher in the center. When you brought your dishes in, you set them on these counters. The fellow that was running the dishwasher, he would take the dirty dishes, turn them upside down, and just keep pushing them through the dishwasher on a belt. Then there would be somebody at the other end picking them up and stacking them. That's where you picked up your clean dishes to go back to your station.

We had some awful, awful duststorms in those days. Of course, there was nothing to stop the storms in those days. There were no trees or anything like that. When we had a duststorm—take an evening meal, for instance: if it started at six o'clock, we had to get there about ten minutes to six, and the tables would be covered with sand; the dishes would be covered with sand. We had to clean them up before the men came in to sit down and eat. This meant that we had to dismantle the tables completely, wipe the sand off, get clean dishes, and reset them before the men came in. These duststorms were terrible things. Of course, the windows around the mess hall had to be opened because it was warm. This meant there was nothing but screen to try and stop the sand.

Of the two Anderson brothers who ran the mess hall, H.S. (Harold Spurrier) and William, Harold was the more flamboyant; his reputation as a playboy and a ladies' man impressed the workers he fed.

BOB PARKER

Harold and Bill Anderson had furnished the commissary services for all the Hollywood movies. Bill Anderson was the older brother, and he ran the office in Hollywood. Harold came out here to run this job because it was a pretty good-size job and they figured they needed someone that knew the business. Harold Anderson originally married Senator Smoot's daughter from Utah. That was his first wife. The children were all grandchildren of Senator Smoot from Utah. Finally he [Harold Anderson] went around the world with one of the movie actresses, and that didn't set well. He and his wife were finally divorced. He was going with Janet Gaynor, but that didn't pan out.[2] He reminded me of Adolphe Menjou. He looked a lot like him, with that little dinky hairline mustache. His brother didn't have a mustache, and he wasn't near the Hollywood stars. Harold Anderson was. Harold was kind of a Hollywood dude, I'd call him.

DOROTHY NUNLEY

I knew H.S. I never was sure what the "H.S." stood for. I've heard a lot of expressions. However, he was a nice-looking man. I imagine he'd be very attractive to some women. He was quite a ladies' man too. He had a lovely little house here in town that was built for him, but it was built without a kitchen. He used to have his ladies come up and visit him there, and their meals would be delivered from the mess hall. He was going with Janet Gaynor when I was working for him. She came up and spent some time in the little house.

CARL MERRILL

Yeah, I knew H. S. Anderson. I was rushing back to the kitchen with a lot of dirty dishes one time, and I think I had 16 platters on my arm. I hit a greasy spot on the concrete floor and slipped and fell. He didn't give a damn about me, but I broke quite a few of those dishes. He came up to me and he said, "That will cost you $2 out of your salary." So he didn't fire me, anyway. I don't remember whether they actually took the $2 out of my salary or not, but that's what he said to me.

He used to come in early in the mornings all rumpled up. I don't think he ever combed his hair.

As far as being a rounder, I'll tell you, he probably was. That was the rumor. I probably would have been too, if I had his money. We didn't actually know those things. But he was married. He married one of the beauty queens. Yeah, he married a Miss America of that time. She lived here.

H. S. Anderson owned the mess hall, but the cantankerous head chef, Bob Davenport, ran the operation.

LEROY BURT

He [Davenport] sat there and he smoked Camel cigarettes, and he had emphysema so bad he could hardly breathe. You could hear him all over the place—wheezing. He was a real chef. He kept one pocket full of pepper and one pocket full of salt on his jacket. He'd go around and he'd stick his finger into whatever we were making, soup or whatever. He'd take a taste, and he'd put a little salt in it.

I think he was the orneriest person I ever met in my life. He was a real hard guy to get along with. I was hired by a fellow that was a relief chef. The first night when we came to work, naturally Bob fired me. He said, "Go get your time." So I went back and I talked to Bud Rathers, who was the timekeeper for H. S. Anderson. I said, "I came in to get my time. Bob just fired me." He said, "Don't worry about it. You go over and he'll be over there to get you to come back to work in no time at all." I went to my room in the mess hall, and it wasn't an hour and here he comes. He called me Blackie all the time. "Hey, Blackie, come on, we need you over there." So I go back to work, and I stayed there for 13 months, putting up with the stuff he used to dish out.

He came to me one morning and he said, "We're going to have scrambled eggs for breakfast. Get the eggs ready."

"How many do I get ready?"

"Six cases."

"OK." So I get myself a chair and get comfortable, and I was sitting there breaking eggs as fast as I can go. He came over and he said, "God, man, you're going to have breakfast at 9:00 tonight, the way you're going. Let me show you how to fix scrambled eggs." So he takes all these eggs, dumps them all into this huge mixing bowl, shells and all, wheels them over, puts them on the mixer, grinds it up, and turns the mixer on and whips it up. When he got them all whipped up good, then he tipped the thing over—it had wheels that you could turn it over—and he strained all these eggs through a fine screen. All you had left was eggs; you didn't have no shells. That was one lesson that I learned.

One morning I was working alongside this little fellow that was a fry cook who was cooking hotcakes. Jimmy Myers was this little fellow's name—a very nice little guy; it took a lot to agitate him. So Bob came to him and told him, "Your hotcakes are too small." So he put a little more batter on the next batch he put on. He [Bob] came by and said, "Your hotcakes are too damn big." So about this time Jimmy had had about all of this he wanted, so he just took this big batter pan and poured it all over the griddle. He looked at old Bob, and he said, "Cut 'em up to suit yourself, you so-and-so." And he walked out the door.

CARL MERRILL

Bob Davenport was a typical lumberman-type cook. I mean, he was rough and ready, that type of person, like you find in a lumber camp. Of course, he was the king. He was sitting on the dishwasher counter one day when we was getting through lunch. I was bringing dishes back in there, and he was sitting there yawning his head off. I looked down, and I said, "Sleep's good for that." He said, "Go get it, go get it." That meant you're fired. So I went back to the office, and they were about ready to send me down to the River Camp. Then he came in there and said, "Aw, let him go back to work. Be careful what you say, but let him go back to work." Everybody tried to avoid him. He was a loner. You didn't make any wisecracks to Bob. I learned.

Leroy Burt also recalls that food preparation at the mess hall was one of the few aspects of the Hoover Dam job over which Nevada law had some influence. Mess hall workers had to undergo periodic examinations for venereal disease.

LEROY BURT

Each Wednesday when we were handling food, they took us in the north wing of the mess hall, [where] we had to go through a short-arm inspection. You know what a short-arm inspection is? That's where they check your penis to see if you have any kind of venereal disease, take ahold of the penis and stretch it down to see if they had an infection. This one guy—there were quite a few in front of me, and I could hear what he said. He said to Doctor Schofield, "Doc, are you doing that for my benefit? If you are, I'd like to have you go a little faster."

Then the girls in the laundry, which was just on the north side of where we were getting this inspection—one day we looked up and there was a bunch of them outside looking through the windows while all these guys were getting the short-arm in there.

Not everyone worked for Six Companies, of course, and those who did not often took their meals in one of the small restaurants in Boulder City, where the atmosphere was less institutional than at the mess hall. Hazel Allen remembers some of the men who started their workday at the Green Hut, where she was a waitress.

HAZEL ALLEN

I'll tell you, some of those guys were just super, and some of them were. . . . But, of course, they were green. They didn't know beans when the bank was open. They just were ignorant; they didn't know. But I felt sorry for some of them, because they came out here from Oklahoma and all places back in there. Just anything, any little meager job to make a living. A lot of men came here and couldn't get a job. It was hard days. I sympathized with a lot of them. I knew one of the kids who worked on the dam; his name was Jones. He'd come to the café, and he'd always be late. I said, "What in the world is the matter with you? Can't you get up?" So he put his alarm clock in a bucket right above his bed.

I'd get up about three o'clock and come up to [the] café and wrap all these lunches for the men to take with them. We had one fellow on the construction crew that went way out to Searchlight when they were building the high line through there. You couldn't satisfy him. So when we knew that some of the men were going to be transferred out, [we] decided we'd had all of Kelly that we could take. So we made a raw liver, a raw halibut sandwich, a raw egg, and we put water in his thermos bottle instead of coffee. We gave his good lunch to Red, the boss. I said, "Red, this is what we've done. Would you take his good lunch and give it to him?" And when he opened that lunch at noon out there on that hot desert, you know what he had.

Red came in that night. He said, "Hazel, you know, it's a good thing we transferred him out of here." I said, "Why?" He said, "Well, you know, we threw his good lunch away, 'cause we was tired of him too." So we had our funny days, and we had our hard days.

I remember one time we had chocolate pudding for dessert. Jane was working the counter with me, and big Ed—I'll never forget, he was a high-line operator, always doing things. She said, "Ed, what are you going to have for dessert today?" He said, "Oh, hit me with some of that chocolate pudding." Oh, I'll tell you. Did he get it!

Getting from Boulder City to the damsite seven miles away was often a tedious adventure in uncomfortable, stripped-down transports.

Nig, about 1935 (*left*); Donkey baseball
game behind the American Legion Hall,
about 1934 (*below*)

Pool hall in the Six Companies Recreation Hall, about 1933

MARION ALLEN

I lived down on Seventh Street, [in] what they call the one-room houses. That's about a mile up here to the bus. So I'd get up in the morning. You had to be on the job at 7:30, but you had to get on this bus at about 6:30, because it was about an hour by the time you got down there and you got to the place you were working. That was one of my pet peeves, always has been, this waiting. But it wasn't too bad, especially when you could walk up there in the morning, and in the summer it was nice and cool.

THEODORE GARRETT

Everybody had to go to the garage area to catch the transport trucks. You just didn't work if you didn't catch the truck, unless you used your own transportation. Most of the transport trucks were flatbed trucks with about an 18-foot bed with planks across to hold approximately 50 men. They were all covered with canvas cloth. It wasn't that bad. Of course, everybody was 40 years younger then and didn't mind it so much.

HARRY HALL

They had large transports that would carry possibly 60 or 80 people. They had a number of them, and they'd be going to different locations. They would board those buses and be transported there. Also the bus would bring the swing shift down and pick the day shift up. They did the same thing with the graveyard shift if they were working three shifts, and they did, on a lot of the jobs.

In addition to the smaller trucks, the Six Companies built three monstrous transports especially for their work on the Boulder Canyon Project. Known as the Big Berthas, these trucks were able to carry many more workers to and from the canyon.

MARION ALLEN

When they built these Big Berthas, they had one regular engine in front. They put an engine behind, underneath, to push it, like a pusher. They built them right up here in the shop. They took 150 men. You went up in the center. Of course, the top was nicer riding. You got the air. They were divided off into sections, the top and lower, and both sides. There were three Big Berthas here by the time they finished. They paid those truck drivers $6 a day. That cut off three drivers. These rigs that took 30 men, why, they could put one driver on one of [the Big Berthas] and take 150 and save three or four men—$10 or $12 a day.

ALFRED BAKER

Our town is seven miles from the dam. Transports carried 60 men, each one. The roads were not what you would call first-class. The top deck [of the Big Bertha] went way out beyond the lower deck. One U-turn, you had to back up to make it. When you were making this turn, you were just sitting way out over the river. Believe me, it was quite a thrill on you until you got used to it. But in all the years hauling the men back and forth on three shifts, there were no accidents, which was really wonderful.

TOMMY NELSON

They were chain drive, and they made 10 miles an hour. They moved so cockeyed slow, I don't think they had time to get in an accident.

JAKE DIELEMAN

They had a hard time getting around those curves down there. They didn't have good pneumatic tires—they had hard rubber tires. Then they wasn't satisfied with the speed of the big ones coming out of the canyon, so they put two motors on and connected the two motors together with belt drives. They didn't have no fluid drive of any kind. They got quite a bit more power and a little bit more speed out of them.

SAUL "RED" WIXSON

They went a lot slower than the little trucks, and when your shift was up, everyone tried to get to the little trucks first so you'd get home quicker. No one wanted to ride the Big Berthas.

The government had its own transportation for its employees, though nothing so impressive as the Big Berthas.

TEX NUNLEY

I was finally transferred from the engineers over on the trucks. The government had five trucks as transports. That wasn't connected with the Six Companies at all. That was just government men. There were six seats across, 30 men, five across. No upholstery or anything. Thirty men, and one man rode with the driver. That made 31 men to each transport.

I had one truck. It was brand-new when they brought it in here, and they turned it over to me. I was going down the lower portal road. I had 82 miles a day, and the third day it would kick over 83. I remember that. I kept sort of track on that.

We were making five round-trips a day. The electricians went early, seven o'clock. You'd come back up at eight o'clock and pick up the other guys. You took them down, and you came back up. I was off then until 2:30 in the afternoon. I took a crew down and come back up, and picked up another crew and took them. Then I'd make a trip at midnight. I made five round-trips a day there for about six months.

Some of the most lasting memories for those who worked on the dam involve characters who enlivened the otherwise grueling hours of construction work. Many of these characters were cantankerous old veterans who taught these young greenhorns a few lessons.

MARION ALLEN

You'd get on the bus, and, of course, you'd ride with these characters, a certain bunch of characters. The bull sessions were going. Some of those were out of this world. And you didn't dare, coming back or going down, don't ask any questions, especially if you looked like a kid, like I did. I asked this one fellow who was carrying a powder stick—they had hundreds of these powder sticks down there, and they started in 20 feet long. They'd keep getting broke off. This guy was bringing one back home, about five feet. I said, "What are you going to do with that powder stick?" Just to make conversation, being curious like I always was. He said, "Well, I'll tell you. You know, I've kept one for 20 years on the back door. I knock on the front door, and I run around to the back door and grab that powder stick. You know, I've got a man every night for 20 years at that back door. And last night I laid it on too heavy and broke the powder stick." That's the kind of bull you got. I didn't ask anymore.

TOMMY NELSON

I was running a jackhammer at the side of the cliff. This was during the dam construction, after the concrete had started being poured. I was running a jackhammer in there to put an anchor bolt in. It was just shaking the daylights out of me. An old construction stiff came by, and he said, "Hey, kid. Why don't you get a Mexican to hold up that hammer?" I looked up at him, and I said, "We haven't got any Mexicans around here." "Oh," he said, "you don't know what I mean." He grabbed a piece of reinforcement steel and he came over with it, stood it up alongside the jackhammer, put a little haywire around it. "There, let it hold you up, kid." And it did. So that was a little trick, you know. You learned a lot of them. That was kind of humorous, when I think about it.

Among the characters on the project, "Dogface" Charlie Rose and "Alabam" stand out.

TOMMY NELSON

We had a lot of characters down there. I remember one particular incident. A new recruit came down, and Frank Bryant, the superintendent, said, "Take this fellow over and give him to Charlie Rose, to work in Charlie Rose's gang." Now Charlie Rose was a foreman down there, worked in the slot most of the time with his crew. So we got over there, and they were sandblasting in there. So I just pointed him out; I said, "That's Mr. Rose, there," to this fellow. Old Charlie turned around and he said, "Don't call me Mr. Rose; call me Dogface." Well, this Charlie Rose, he shaved clear up under his eyeballs. He was quite a character, Charlie Rose was.

MARION ALLEN

Alabam was known all over the country. He was probably one of the most important men on the job, next to Crowe, with his good necklace: that roll of toilet papers around his neck and on the broom. He cleaned out the chick sales and the other toilets. He kept them clean. He'd go around and make sure there was toilet paper there. He had a sack of lime in each corner of them, and he throw this lime, sweep them out. Everybody knew Alabam.

JOE KINE

"I'm the sanitary engineer," he said.

TOMMY NELSON

They put lye in them, and if you had to go, you didn't stay in there very long. I assure you, that lye was something. Jokes went around about Alabam— that he'd eat his lunch in there.

MARION ALLEN

One old construction stiff came up to use the chick sale, and there was Alabam, fishing around in the hole with a stick. "What are you doin'?" he asked, and old Alabam said, "I dropped my coat down there." Well, this guy said, "You don't want your coat after it's been down there." And Alabam said, "I don't care about the coat, but my lunch is in the pocket."

JOHN CAHLAN

There was a fellow down there by the name of "River Joe" Whitney who held the record for arrests in the city of Las Vegas. Every time that he'd get a payday, Joe'd come in and get drunk and get in a fight and wind up in jail. And I think the last time he was in jail, we counted 264 times he had been in jail during the time he was here. They'd put him in jail over the weekend, over the payday, and let him out to go back to work. There was one time that Joe was spending quite a term in the city jail. I guess it was along toward the end of his career down here. And he was incarcerated for about 30 days, and he became a trustee. He was walking by the Apache Bar, which was a bar back in the Apache Hotel, which was where the Horseshoe Club is now. And he was walking by the bar when he met a fellow by the name of Marion Zioncheck,[3] who was the congressman from the state of Washington who had been in the headlines for quite some time with rather eccentric acts that he was putting on back in the halls of Congress. He was out here for a vacation. And just as Joe was walking by, Zioncheck came out of the bar. Zioncheck stopped Joe and asked him what he was doing, and Joe told him he was a trustee in a jail, and Zioncheck wanted to know how he was getting along. "Well," he said, "fine, but we'd get along a lot better if we had some whiskey."

Zioncheck went back into the bar and brought four or five bottles of whiskey and gave them to Joe. There were about six or eight guys in there, so Joe smuggled the whiskey into the jail cell, and before anybody knew it, they were having a big wild party and everybody was getting drunk. They got in a fight, and someway Joe got his throat cut from ear to ear, but it was only a flesh wound. The jailer took him out to the county hospital and had him sewed up and brought him back. Joe recovered and went back to work out at the dam.

On my beat in the newspaper, I used to give him a good write-up every time he got put in jail, so he called me his publicity agent. I got quite well acquainted with him. The last I heard of River Joe Whitney, during World War II he was working on the Al-Can Highway. Prior to that time he was working on the dam project up by Redding, California. And I read in the paper where Joe and some of the B-girls in one of the bars got out in a town fountain and disrobed and started taking a bath in the fountain. So he made himself a bucket up in Redding too.

There was another guy by the name of "Pickpockets," or we called him Pickpockets because of the fact that his hands were as large as the ordinary man's two hands. They were so large that he couldn't get them in a pocket if he had to. He worked out at the dam also. And his demise was caused by his betting somebody at the bar that he could drink a quart of whiskey without taking it from his lips. He drank the quart of whiskey, but about 10 minutes later he dropped dead. So that was the last of Pickpockets.[4]

One of the most popular individuals on the Boulder Canyon Project didn't work for Six Companies or the government. Florence Lee Jones, the Las Vegas Evening Review-Journal *reporter who covered the project was the only woman who routinely entered the canyon during construction. John Cahlan, who married Jones in 1940, recalls his wife's remarkable career during the construction of Hoover Dam.*

JOHN CAHLAN

The first employee of the [*Review-Journal*] news department, outside of myself, was Florence Lee Jones, who was a graduate of the University of Missouri. Her father and mother, Mr. and Mrs. B. M. Jones, came here in 1931 and had a service station and tourist court. Mrs. Jones became very friendly with Mrs. Garside, whose husband, Frank Garside, was my brother's partner in the *Review-Journal*. In fact, Garside bought the newspaper in 1926 when my brother came down from Elko and became associated as a partner with him in publication of the paper. Mrs. Garside asked Frank to put Florence to work on the newspaper as a proofreader. She started in 1933 as a proofreader and later became a general reporter, feature writer, and women's editor. And after that she became my wife.

She was assigned to cover the construction of Boulder Dam. She used to make two trips a week out to Boulder City and the dam and was accepted out there by everybody who was in an executive capacity. If there were any real big accidents, she'd go out. She was the only woman who was allowed down in the canyon. It was a fetish of the construction stiffs down there that if a woman came around a construction area bad luck would follow. But [Florence] knew all the foremen down there and a lot of the workers. She was just one of the gang. She could go anywhere on the dam anytime, day or night, and would be admitted to any part of the project. She wrote all of the progress stories for the *Review-Journal* and also was the AP correspondent in Las Vegas. The *Salt Lake Tribune, Los Angeles Times*, and the *Christian Science Monitor* hired her as a stringer. So most of the stories that were published nationwide about the city of Las Vegas came right out of the *Review-Journal*.

The character most fondly remembered by Boulderites of the early 1930s, however, was a black dog named Nig, who became the project mascot.

BOB PARKER

Nig was the runt of a litter of pups born under the floor of the first police shack we had up here in Boulder City. He was a large black dog, kind of a Labrador. His tail was cropped.

Nig finally wound up as important a worker in building Hoover Dam as any of the men who worked down there. For a while men would take food down there to feed him on the dam at noon. After a while the mess hall lunchroom people fixed up Nig with sandwiches in his own sack, and he carried that sack in his mouth down to the river. He left it down there with the workmen's dinners, and then at noon he knew it was dinnertime.

He went to work every morning in the Six Companies transports. At night, he was always up there ready to get on the transport. He liked every mode of transportation at the dam: the big transports, the government bus, the station wagon with the government employees. Many times I've seen him on the railroad, coming up on the train.

He turned out to be nobody's dog and everybody's dog. Down on the dam he'd come up to you and want you to pet him, take one or two pets, and off he'd go—on to the next worker down there. He'd climb ladders, he was in the tunnels, he was everywhere.

When he was about half-grown, he was over there on the dormitory porch and one of the workmen came by and hauled off and kicked Nig. Old Bud Bodell went over there and he really cleaned up on that workman that kicked Nig.

MARION ALLEN

Harold Anderson over at the mess hall [gave] orders that "Nig comes in, give him whatever he wants. He wants a steak, give him a steak."

He caught a ride down on the bus in the morning. Nig rode down in the bus alongside of my feet a lot of times. Then some days I'd be on down in the tunnel, and here comes Nig, trotting along, just giving an inspection. He just wanted us to get it done right. He'd go down to the lower portal and usually there he caught Mr. Crowe [and rode] back in the Buick. Without a doubt, he must have been a reincarnated construction stiff, maybe a superintendent.

CARL MERRILL

If he wanted to ride one of the skips up the side of the canyon or up the side of the dam, he'd stand down at the bottom and bark until they'd come pick him up, and then they'd take him up topside.

TEX NUNLEY

He rode everything that moved. One time someone down on the dam picked Nig up in a great big black Cadillac. Nig came up out of there in the front seat with the man that was driving, and the lady was in the back. He looked over at the workmen like that and smiled. He was coming to Boulder City and he didn't have to work. Him driving a Cadillac, and they were down there having to work. That was old Nig for you.

MARY ANN MERRILL

When I worked at the Sweet Shop about 1935, some of the fellows went down in a little van-type truck. They would take a lunch down for Nig every day. If I was on shift, I would make those lunches for Nig. He'd have that little bag, and he'd go down with them in that car. He wouldn't touch that lunch until they started their lunch. Smart dog.

BOB PARKER

In the evening he'd go over to the drugstore on the corner. You'd see Nig out there with an ice cream cone, eating it out there on the sidewalk. One of the workmen had bought him an ice cream cone. They fed him candy bars. Then old Nig would get sick. Nig knew where to go when he got sick. He'd go down and see Doc Traynor. Doc would treat him; he was more of a veterinarian, I think, than he was a human doctor anyway. Finally an article came out in the local paper that said "Please do not feed me ice cream and candy bars. It makes me sick." And it was signed "Nig."[5] Doc Traynor put that in the paper. After that they were a little more careful about what they fed him.

As I remember it, it was during the summer he was killed. Nig had gotten

189

down off a truck and climbed underneath it. When [the driver] came back, he didn't see Nig under the truck. Nig didn't hear the truck start moving. The truck ran over him and killed him. They buried him right near where he was killed. And that's where he is today.

Not too long after that, the workmen down there took up a collection and they put a plaque up there by his grave in the canyon wall. A few years back some college professor from the Midwest came out here, and he took issue with that name, Nig, on the plaque.[6] The sad part of that was he was a white man, white professor. He spread propaganda in the Congress, and the Senate, and all over the United States that that was a racial slur down there at Hoover Dam. Officials at the Department of the Interior and the Bureau of Reclamation changed it. They've got a picture of Nig on a plaque down there, but they left the word *Nig* out. That's all that Nig was ever known by. He was the friend of the black men and the white men and every other kind of person that worked down there. So this professor got the plaque changed, but when the men poured the concrete, they scratched the word *Nig* in that concrete, and that's still there.

While Nig worked an open schedule, those who worked for Six Companies were locked into a relentless daily routine.

THEODORE GARRETT

The day shift started at seven o'clock in the morning. The swing shift started at about three in the afternoon. The graveyard shift started at about eleven or eleven thirty at night. Your shift at that time included your time after you got to the job.

MARION ALLEN

There were three shifts, they worked 24 hours, so there was actually no time-out. You worked for eight hours. You always took your 30 minutes to eat. But it might be one o'clock or it might be two o'clock before you got to eat. You'd work hard while there was work there; you'd work like mad. We did on these inverts, because if you didn't, they'd get hard. Oh, man, you'd suffer. You'd get them done quick, and then you'd sit down, and if there was nothing else, nobody'd argue if you sat there for an hour. But there was no question, you finished up your job and got it done.

CURLEY FRANCIS

We were making $5 a day, or $5 a shift, driving a truck. We had four days off a year. We worked seven days a week, and we had two days off at Christmas and two days off at Fourth of July. Anytime that you got sick and missed more than two days, you were out of a job. You had no seniority, no nothing. There was no guarantee that you were going to work at all.

HARRY HALL

We worked eight hours on the job. It took about 30 or 40 minutes to get down there. You wouldn't put your gear away until after your eight hours were up. So you put in nine or nine and a half hours total. We had 30 minutes for lunch, but we didn't always eat at the same time. It depended on what the workload was. We may have been checking a form or something, so we ate catch-as-catch-can.

I was better off as a government worker because actually you made as much money within $10. If you were a laborer for Six Companies, you got $120 a month and you worked 30 days in a 30-day month. If you were a government worker, you got $110 and you worked 26 days. So actually they were comparable in wages. The other thing was that you got four days off a month, which was a big advantage.

SAUL "RED" WIXSON

My wife and I worked on a budget. We were wary about the next job and a rainy day. We knew we needed $18 every two weeks to buy groceries. My allowance every two weeks was $5, and my wife's allowance every two weeks was $3—$8 every two weeks to spend whatever way we wanted to spend it.

191

HOBART BLAIR

We could live on a dollar a day, the three of us, and lived pretty good. In one year, 1932, I saved enough money to buy a brand-new 1933 four-door Chevrolet: $750. We had no overhead; we hauled our water. Electricity cost us $1.50 a month.

WILLIAM D. McCULLOUGH

I know a lot of people in Boulder City who raised a big family and educated them on $4 a day.

With wages providing barely enough to cover living expenses, money was always tight, and paydays were important events.

ALICE HAMILTON

Bud Bodell was responsible for bringing the money in from the banks in Las Vegas to pay the workers. It seems to me like they brought the payrolls out every two weeks. They just brought it in in cars, but they had four or five cars. I can remember on payday, our office was filled with guns and extra policemen to bring the money in. They used to sit in the office and clean their guns and load them. It was a great time when they brought the payroll in. There was a window that opened on to the back of the [Six Companies office] building where they could just line up outside and get their checks. I can remember they'd line up on payday. Most of the men would be stripped to the waist. The language was very coarse sometimes.

TEX NUNLEY

They'd bring it out from Vegas under guard, rangers in front of the armored car, rangers behind, rangers everywhere. They brought it into the Six Companies place where they paid off. The machine guns took over from there. There was a dorm right across the street, and they had machine guns up there on the top floor that were set up there on the door where you went in, where they kept the money. There never was a robbery.

CARL MERRILL

We were paid by check, but we could cash our check here with Six Companies. They kept what you'd probably call a bank there at that time. You'd cash them there, at the Six Companies Store, over there in the recreation room. Most of us, if we wanted to save any money, we'd go to the post office. It was just like putting it in the bank and getting a receipt for it.

ROSE LAWSON

I believe it was Christmastime in 1931 or '32, we cashed checks with gold coins. The men were paid at the Six Companies office. They usually cashed their checks right there too, because they needed the money to pay bills. Six Companies always had money to cash the checks. And this particular year they cashed all the checks for the men in gold. I remember that the man that cashed the checks for me said, "Now, that is ten dollars. Don't think it's a penny." I'm so casual with money that I hadn't thought much about it. But here this little bit of handful of gold represented all that you got.

TEX NUNLEY

In an emergency you could draw in the middle of the month, and most all of them had emergencies. I know I did.

LILLIAN WHALEN

The men could get scrip from Six Companies in advance of their paycheck, but the money had to be spent in the Six Companies Store. If people were short of money and needed an advance, they could get scrip from the office and use it in the store, because it was all a Six Companies project. Then they deducted that from their paycheck.

They got full value if they bought things in the store, but you couldn't buy things outside with the scrip. You could sell your scrip to somebody who had legal tender at a discount if you really wanted the money to spend someplace else. A lot of people did that. But you didn't have to, because you could get everything you needed from the company store. I do know that some people who were affluent enough could take advantage by buying up scrip at a discount and then doing their shopping in the store with the scrip.

JOHN CAHLAN

Six Companies were paying off in scrip. This became quite a problem for the people of the city of Las Vegas because we were looking forward to good business during the building of the dam. The fact that they had the store out there in Boulder City did a little damage to the city of Las Vegas.

Most of the top leaders in Las Vegas got ahold of their congressman and their senators in Washington and appraised them of the situation. I don't know whether a bill was passed in the Congress or whether it was a gentleman's agreement, but an agreement was made between the Bureau of Reclamation and the citizens of Las Vegas. Six Companies would not be able to pay in scrip anymore.

Unlike their husbands, wives were not a significant part of the project work force. A single woman who had to work might find a job as a secretary or as a menial waiting tables, washing clothes, or caring for other people's children.

DOROTHY NUNLEY

My first job was at the Reservation Grill. That was a restaurant that was part of the old Manix Building. I had never worked in a restaurant before. I had very seldom ever eaten in one at that time. [But] I made the mistake of telling them how experienced I was. They called me in at five o'clock rush hour, and I didn't know where I was or what I was doing. I only worked 45 minutes and I got canned. [My boss] was very nice. He told me sometime he might call me back when they weren't rushed. But he never did.

Then I went to work for a lady with seven kids. I was their baby-sitter, I guess you'd call it today—mother's helper or what have you. She worked, and I took care of the seven kids. I got $3 a week. The oldest was about 15 or 16, and the youngest one was 2. They were all pretty good kids, except the high school ones; they were kind of rough to get along with.

Then I got a job at [H. S. Anderson's] laundry, and I worked at the laundry until I got married. The laundry was just a few yards or so from the mess hall. We did all the dormitories, all their sheets. Then we did the men's laundry too, the shirts and things like that.

I worked all over the laundry [for] $16 a week. I started on the shake table, which is very hard work. If you don't know what a shake table is, it's where you pull all the wet clothes out of the big bins they bring in. Usually the sheets are all tangled up, wrapped around each other. It breaks your back to pull them out and try and get them straightened out so that they can be run through the mangle. Then I worked on the mangle, feeding the stuff through. Then I worked as a folder, and I worked as a shirt finisher, and on the presses some.

This lady that was finishing shirts—they finish shirts on a table; they don't use an ironing board; you can see their legs under the table—it happened that he [H. S. Anderson] came in one day unexpectedly and noticed that she had no stockings on. He just raised the roof. He told her that if she couldn't buy stockings on what he paid her, she didn't have to work for him. I was behind the mangle where he couldn't see my feet, and I didn't have any stockings on either. But I was so scared of losing that job, because there weren't very many jobs for women in town. Boy, that night I went out and I bought me some bobby socks right away.

MARY ANN MERRILL

I worked for quite a while at Smith's root beer stand. Root beer was 5¢. You got $1 a day for being a carhop. Big wages. But on a good night, you could probably make $5 or $6 in tips. That was usually on payday, because the day after they probably wouldn't have any money left.

But social life for Boulder City's single women made up for the grind of daily work.

DOROTHY NUNLEY

It was great. There were so many men and not very many women. You didn't have to be pretty at all to get a date. You could be very plain, and you could always get a date. We'd go to the Legion Hall dances, or we'd go to Vegas. Or we'd just go down swimming.

MARY ANN MERRILL

It was pretty nice being a single girl, because there was a lot of fellows and they'd pay a lot of attention to you because there wasn't many girls in town. I think the ratio was at least 10 to 1.

For married women the job market was all but closed, and their lives revolved around their families: raising children and taking care of their husbands.

MARY ANN MERRILL

Most who were here came with their husbands. They were housewives. They didn't have a second job. The second jobs came during World War II. Most people stayed and took care of their families. They probably were prominent in their home, but in the business world, no. If [they worked], they were a secretary, and they were very low on the scale.

EDNA FRENCH

I had been a home ec teacher, and I tried to get into the schools in Vegas. But they had a policy—which they followed in Boulder City too—that there should be only one breadwinner in the family. Since my husband had part-time work and had great anticipation of getting on at the dam, I did not get even substitute work.

PERLE GARRETT

Of course, in those days women weren't working. They just didn't work. There wasn't any such a thing as a baby-sitter. The mothers took care of their children. We'd take them with us wherever we went. We went swimming an awful lot. We went down to the river. Lorenzi's Park in Las Vegas had a very nice swimming pool. Then there was a swimming hole out in Paradise Valley that was filled with artesian water. We'd take the kids out there and swim. Then we'd go up to Mount Charleston and camp for a week or so in the summertime. Our husbands would come up on weekends. We'd pack up the kids and go up there to cool off. It was really nice.

Smith's Root Beer Stand: one job opportunity for Boulder City women. *Clockwise*: Milly Grosnick in the dark bathing suit, Mary Ann Vaughan Merrill, two unidentified men, Virginia "Teddy" Fenton, two unidentified women, about 1934

Workers coming off shift, 1932

NADEAN VOSS

I usually had three shifts going at my house: Babies on one shift, husbands on another [and] children on another. That made it kind of hard, but it was kind of fun. It was so different from anything that any of my family had ever known before.

ROSE LAWSON

The kids wandered in the desert an awful lot. Now you can be sure to step on a rattlesnake if you went out in the desert. But the kids played in the desert many an afternoon, and I don't ever remember one of them being bit by a rattlesnake. In the summertime they played under the trees. The little guys would take their little trucks and things and play for hours under the trees. I can't remember organized entertainment for the children.

LILLIAN WHALEN

Of course, with the building of the dam being the center of our lives, it was the center of the children's lives, and they built dams all over the backyard. They snitched their mothers' tablespoons and teaspoons to dig in the soft sand, so some of us had silver-plated backyards, I think. But they had fun.

Not so much fun was the arduous ritual of washing clothes. While their husbands dressed simply for the job, it was debatable who worked harder: the men in the canyon or the women over their laundry tubs.

LEROY BURT

I just wore plain ol' bib overalls. Or Levi's, whatever; it all depended. I think everybody wore the same kind of clothing except the carpenters. I've seen carpenters down there with their carpenters' overalls on.

TOMMY NELSON

Standard dress was a Six Companies hard hat. If you worked in the spillways or the dam or the diversion tunnels, hip boots was the standard dress of the day, and either a pair of overalls or a pair of Levi's, and perhaps a blue chambray shirt.

MARION ALLEN

Down in those tunnels they had a changing room right there with hot showers, but by the time you got through with the shift, the buses were about ready to leave. They always held the buses so you could take a shower, but who wanted to take a shower and then ride up in a cold bus? So you'd run home. We changed clothes. We usually pulled our diggers off because they'd stand alone. [We'd] leave them in the change room, where it was warm and dry, and they'd dry out by the time of the next shift. You'd hang them up.

TOMMY NELSON

When we came home from work down there, we didn't hang our clothes up; we stood 'em up.

MARY EATON

[My husband] worked awfully, awfully hard. He'd come home at night and his pants would just be stiff from all this mud and water that he'd been in through the day. I didn't have a washing machine, and he only had one pair of trousers to wear to work. So I'd rinse these out at night just to get all that clay and mud out of it and hang them on the line. I just had the sink. And all this silt from the Colorado. I don't know how we kept the drain open. By the next morning they were ready for him to wear again. So then he'd wear those, I don't know, several weeks. They'd wear out, and he'd get another pair.

LILLIAN WHALEN

There was a laundry for people to take their clothes, but very few people in the early days had money enough to spend on having their laundry done. I had an electric iron, and I also had a mangle that could be attached to the washing machine—drying, flatwork. We ironed [the men's work clothes]. We tried to keep them respectable-looking.

NAN BAKER

We didn't have a washing machine, but there was a man by the name of Baker that rented a machine. They called him Washing Machine Baker. He'd come and fetch it. I think it was two hours for 15¢. If he couldn't come, he wouldn't charge you. He'd do the work and he'd come on his way home.

Long hours at the dam and hard work at home made free time precious for Hoover Dam workers and their wives. Yet Boulder City offered few diversions.

THEODORE GARRETT

For the most part, there wasn't too much recreation, particularly in the earlier days. Spare time, you tried to get what sleep you could. For recreation the Six Companies had what they called the Recreation Hall, with pool tables and card games and snack bars. We spent some time in there.

CARL MERRILL

There was lots of single guys here, lots of them. I made friends with people in the mess hall, the ones I worked with. I'm still good friends with some of them. We chased around together. We'd walk up and down the streets and look in the stores. You may read. We didn't have a lot of money to spend, I'll tell you that.

BOB PARKER

Most of the entertainment was carried on in our mess hall. I think the last dinner meal that we had was at six o'clock. By seven o'clock we'd have everyone out in one wing. Then we'd pile up all the tables and chairs and we'd have these various functions. I remember on April 15, 1932, was a fight card. I remember that because I was on the card. We had Jack Johnson and Frank Moran restage their world heavyweight championship match they held in Paris, France, in 1914. That was quite a deal.

HOBART BLAIR

We had some of the famous wrestlers like Strangler Lewis and a lot of the people used to come here. Once a week wrestlers would come in here and we'd have wrestling and boxing. There was quite a few boys here in Boulder City who boxed. Bob Parker once was Golden Gloves Champion of Nevada. A bunch of us used to get together and box—Clarence Arp, myself, Harold Younger, Johnnie Sykes. We had lots of sports going on around here.

WILLIAM D. McCULLOUGH

We had a fellow by the name of Poison Smith. He was a colored guy, built like a Greek god. I think he could have whipped anybody he wanted to, but I think he had a weakness: he was a little bit scared. We had a Mexican guy from Needles, Teddy Palacio, and Ernie Duarte, another Mexican. Indian Johnny Smith—he was from Vegas. And we had a colored guy here—I can't think of his name; he was a terrible-looking guy, but God, he was a good fighter. Maxie Rosenblum was here, he was a light-heavyweight. We used to have about 13 colored people come to the prizefights all the time. Twelve of 'em sat up in the back together, and this one guy would sit down front and he was a-razzin' the fighters all the time. He had more fun. He'd scream and yell, and I think everybody come to hear him holler.

STEVE CHUBBS

You could go to watch a ball game. Behind the Legion Hall they had a ball field—dirt, no grass. They played baseball in the evenings. They sure had the energy, though. It really surprised you. They used a plain old hard baseball. They could really whack it.

SAUL "RED" WIXSON

My wife was quite an athlete in her early days back in Minnesota, and when we were out here, she organized some women into what she called the Wixson Ball Team—softball. Every once in a while, the Bald-Headed Men's Team would come out to play the women's team. Frank Crowe would come down and Charlie Shea. There was a big audience.

Then, of course, we had what we called the Donkey [Base]ball Team. A bunch of burros. That was always a great one for the Bald-Headed Men too. They'd hit the ball, then climb on the burro and try to turn around first, second, and third base without getting knocked off or pushed off or the donkey falling over.

HARRY HALL

Various organizations had their own softball teams. I played on the high mix softball team for several years. Then the Bureau of Reclamation organized a softball team, and I played on it for a number of years. But it seemed that everyone on the bureau wanted to be the manager; they weren't too congenial.

They also had a football team. They had some great football players that worked for the Six Companies, some really first-rate football players. We called it Boulder Avalanche. And they played some pretty fair football teams— college teams. Of course, they didn't have too much time to practice, but they had some fabulous talent. They were working here because they had to have a job.

THOMAS WILSON

The little Las Vegas High School used to have a time. It was difficult for them to play football against anybody. They were so isolated. And they used to have an alumni team that was really made up of former stars from Las Vegas High School. They were pretty cocky. So finally there was a pickup football team out on the dam. These guys used to finish their shifts, and they'd throw a football around and practice, and choose up sides, and play

Alabam cleaned the latrines at the
damsite, about 1933

out there. When the high school season was pretty well advanced, the Boulder Dam guys one time sent in a challenge to play the alumni team. It was going to be a massacre because the alumni team was so good—playing those dumb laborers out at the dam.

There was all kinds of talent in all kinds of positions working on Hoover Dam. It was the only job that out-of-work people could get. Any kind of a job was good! When the guys from the dam showed up, they had almost a complete backfield from Notre Dame. They had college stars from all over the country. And they called the game off. I don't know the score—60 to nothing or something like that. It was no contest.

MARY ANN MERRILL

We'd play golf. Carl and I would go down about four or five o'clock in the morning before [he] went to work. We didn't have a building, but we did have a golf pro for a while. We called it the Black Canyon Country Club. It was a nice little nine-hole course. It was all sand, and the tees were oiled sand. That was it. But we had water out there. We had three places where they'd take the water with canvas over it. You were supposed to throw a cup of water over that canvas. It had its own cooling. And that water was good and cool.

CARL MERRILL

The fairways were just ground. They just scraped off the desert and that was the fairway.

The government saw to it that whatever pastime activities Boulder City offered were simple and clean. If you were young and energetic—as most construction workers and their wives were—how could you resist the forbidden pleasures of Las Vegas just 25 miles away?

ALFRED BAKER

Everything there was wild. There were no restrictions on anything. All you had to do was go down the road, and there was everything you wanted.

8

OFF THE RESERVATION: LAS VEGAS, 1931–1935

"Everything was wide open."

Throughout the years of Hoover Dam construction, the fortunes of Las Vegas and Boulder City were linked. Small and economically depressed in the 1920s, Las Vegas boomed on money from the Boulder Canyon Project. The 25-mile road between Boulder City and Las Vegas developed from a desert track into a busy highway lined with squatters' settlements, bars, brothels, and smoky roadhouses.

Everyone looking for work on the dam passed through Las Vegas first—and usually was unimpressed.

DEAN PULSIPHER

Las Vegas was nothing. It was just a wide spot in the road. They'd get a few tourists in the cars there, half a dozen cars in a day. I remember Fremont Street. There was nothing on Fremont Street—all dirt. Not a paved road anywhere.

THEODORE GARRETT

Las Vegas was a small community railroad town prior to the influx of workmen coming in to work on Boulder Dam. There was no residential area west of the railroad tracks. Charleston Boulevard was approximately the southern boundary. Fifth Street, Las Vegas Boulevard, was approximately the eastern

Fremont Street, Las Vegas, 1935

boundary. The northern boundary was approximately the old fort, which is now a historical monument. Everything north of the old fort was desert.

At this time it was beginning to be built up with tents, cardboard shacks, and any kind of a structure that people could live in at the time they went to work. A lot of these housing areas were just composed of empty abandoned cars with a sheet of plywood over the doors to keep the weather out. On the road east into Boulder, tents, cardboard lean-tos, and what have you were set up along the road at places where there was water between Railroad Pass and Las Vegas, especially around the area which is now a part of Henderson, because of the artesian water.[1]

CARL MERRILL

I rode the bus up. We rode all night, landed in Las Vegas about four o'clock in the morning, and I thought at that time this was the dirtiest place I ever saw.

MARY ANN MERRILL

My first impression of Vegas wasn't very good. It was on the main street named Fremont where the bus stopped, and it was dusty and dirty and hot. The streets were sort of empty, except for debris along them. Thank goodness, we didn't have to stay long there; the bus just loaded some more going to Boulder City, so we didn't stay long. Later on, when my father had to take us on in to see Vegas, I found out that there was much of Vegas that was really pretty. They had trees that they'd had in there for a good many years. But your first impression at that time in the morning, probably tired, wasn't very good.

HELEN HOLMES

It took us three days to come down, three nights, on the road. The road at that time went up the side of the mountain, and it was so scary to ride on the highway up to the mesa and then on down into Las Vegas. But when we topped the hill, [we] saw this little tiny green spot in the valley, which was

Las Vegas. It is really amazing to think now when you see the huge valley that it was such a little tiny country town at that time.

BUD BODELL

Frankly, I liked it. It was open all night. The town was free and easy.

Mildred Kine's introduction to Las Vegas came when she arrived by train to meet her fiancé, Joe, to marry him and to begin their life together on the Boulder Canyon Project.

MILDRED KINE

It was the first time I'd ever ridden on a train in the first place, and I was kind of jittery. About a half a day or a day before we got to Las Vegas, an old lady sitting next to me said, "Have you got somebody meeting you?" I said, "Yes. My future husband." She said, "What if he doesn't meet you?" I said, "He will meet me." I think she had been about half-drunk. Every other word was "What if he isn't there?" I said, "I'm not worried one bit. He'll be there." I would have just done anything if I could have pitched her out. When the train stopped, she said, "Did you see him? Did you see him?" I said, "I don't see him this minute, but he is here." I don't know what she was trying to do with me.

About that time [Joe] popped up. He had everything fixed up. He had gone to the courthouse and made arrangements for us to get the license after I arrived here, [but] I didn't get here until ten o'clock in the evening and the marriage license [office] was closed. He had made arrangements for a girl to be there and let us in to get our certificate and marriage license. We went straight to the courthouse, got the license, went to a Methodist minister's home there in Las Vegas.

Joe had made arrangements for the best man and the witnesses to come, but they got stuck in the sand. So we said to the minister, "What are we going to do?" He said, "Oh, don't worry, we'll get you someone." And they did. He got his wife and the next-door neighbor.

From there we went over to a hotel. We went in very nonchalantly, like old married people, or we thought we acted like old married people, and asked for a room. She said she'd give us a nice little room. We started off to the room, and she said, "You two have just gotten married, haven't you?" I said, "How did you know?" She said, "I can tell every time." So I guess it showed anyway.

The next day we got on a bus to come out to Boulder. The roads were just like wagon wheels. My husband had to go to work on the graveyard shift. If we had been married in Boulder City, we would have been the first couple in Boulder to have been married. But since my husband worked seven days a week and didn't get to go to church or anything, he didn't know if there was a minister in Boulder. But there was a minister here. Now, since we look back, we wish [we] had known, so that we could have had that distinction.

After the 1931 strike on the Boulder Canyon Project, Six Companies hired through the federal employment office in Las Vegas. No one could enter the reservation without a job, and so Las Vegas became a temporary home to the unemployed and their families.

TEX NUNLEY

They slept on the lawns around the courthouse there at that time—on the lawns, anywhere. You practically were afraid to take your shoes off to sleep or you'd wake up the next morning, no shoes.

JAKE DIELEMAN

There was hundreds of people laying on the courthouse lawn, didn't have any money, looking for work. I felt discouraged when I saw that. The government had an employment office across from the county courthouse, and everyone would line up at the front of that window in the morning. They'd say, "We need 10 muckers and 15 drillers. . . ."

MARY EATON

The employment agency was in Las Vegas for the hiring of the dam workers. [My husband] wrote and told me that the men were quitting, about a hundred a day, because they could not stand the heat. He decided that if he stayed on long enough, they'd finally get down to where they'd need him. So every day they'd go to the employment office, and when they got all the employees they wanted, the window would come down and they'd go on and wait for another day.

BRUCE EATON

People today can't begin to conceive of the working conditions here in 1932, '33, and '34. There were literally thousands of people in Las Vegas looking for jobs, and if you didn't produce a full day's work for this $4, there was a hundred people ready to take your job.

ROSE LAWSON

Six Companies had their offices in Las Vegas, and they were hiring there. No one could come out here that did not already have their job. There was a half a block just off Fremont Street where the men waited to be called to work. That area was always full of men hustling jobs. I've driven by there several times and saw these many men sitting there, hoping that they would get sent out to work.

JOHN CAHLAN

The government employment building in Las Vegas was just a one-room shack which was operated by Leonard Blood, and all hiring had to come through that one building. And you would have lines of men a block or a block and a half long, waiting to get in for applications for employment. And people were coming from all over the United States; everybody saw Boulder Dam as a place where they could get work. And during the construction— the early days of construction of Boulder Dam—we would have Ph.D.'s working on a muck stick in the mines or in the tunnels down there and people that used to be on Wall Street driving trucks.

Interior of the U.S. Labor Department employment office in Las Vegas for the Boulder Canyon Project. Leonard Blood, Nevada Deputy Labor Commissioner, and Maxine Harrison, secretary, October 1933.

Employment agency, 1931

TI IOMAS WILSON

They used to say that every day laborer on Boulder Dam had a civil engineering degree in his hip pocket.

THEODORE GARRETT

Not being able to go to work on the jobs that were available, it was necessary that we supplement our income by working a little around the area in Las Vegas. One job was washing dishes at the old Silver Dollar Café, which was located on North Second Street at that time. Another venture was on the Union Pacific. Las Vegas was a stopover and unloading point for all the livestock being transported to the area, and they had a stockyard with a feed yard established. That was another job that we done. That paid better than dishwashing.

LILLIAN WHALEN

[My husband] came to Las Vegas in September 1932 and waited until he was called to work. Men who were looking for work waited at the employment office in Las Vegas, and from there they were given employment and sent out.

Some of the boys had tar-paper shacks, and houses made of cardboard boxes. They lived on rice, and if they had an extra nickel or dime to spend, they might get some raisins to put in the rice. They went to the markets and took the stale vegetables home that they could get for nothing.

My husband was living in Las Vegas at the time. He got acquainted with some of the young men, and he used to like to go down and play nickel craps. So the boys would go with him. If he was lucky, he took them all out to dinner. If he spent his 25¢ on nickel craps and didn't win anything, they had to live on rice until next time. He went about a month in Las Vegas before he was finally employed.

Even after they got jobs on the dam, many workers and their families had to live in Las Vegas while they waited for housing in Boulder City. Mary and Bruce Eaton lived there while they awaited the birth of their first child.

MARY EATON

Las Vegas was full of Six Companies people, people working down at the dam. So there wasn't too much housing. It was scarce. We moved over where the Ambassador Apartments were in Las Vegas [916 East Fremont Street]. They were just very small, efficiency apartments. We didn't have any furniture at all. All we had was what you could carry in a suitcase. No furniture, nothing. So we had to rent a furnished apartment. They'd be furnished with a few dishes and the necessities. [We paid] about $30 a month. That was high, because when you're making $4 a day, $30 a month is relevant.

I was starting to show. But I walked. I used to walk the full length of Las Vegas, because my husband took the car to go down to the dam. So I needed my exercise. They wanted you to walk around when you're having a baby. I'd walk the full length of Las Vegas to get my groceries. I'd go every day to the store because I could only buy what I could carry home. So I didn't want to buy too much, because I wouldn't be able to carry it. I did that every day.

I wanted to be close to the hospital. The hospital was over on Eighth Street. I think we were on about Ninth Street. I thought I should be close to the hospital if this baby started coming and my husband was at work. It didn't dawn on me I could hire a taxi or anything like that. But as it happened, the baby was born while my husband was home.

The housing shortage and desperate times were a windfall for Las Vegas property owners, many of whom rented their land out to dam workers and their families. When Tom and Erma Godbey left Ragtown for Las Vegas in July 1931, they first moved to a tent camp on the west side of the Union Pacific Railroad tracks and later pitched their tent in someone's backyard.

ERMA GODBEY

We moved into Vegas to Cowboy Bill's Camp. Cowboy Bill had a ranch. He also had a little store where you could buy breakfast foods, milk and bread, and eggs. He had made a kind of a bathhouse.

He had two artesian wells. The artesian wells were just bubbling with water, and they had streams along under trees. The people were renting spots from him to put tents. Everybody was pitching their tents under the trees and along by the streams. You only got as much space just so you could pitch your tent. They were that close together. You could just barely walk between.

So everybody knew what everybody else was doing, so if anybody spanked their kids or they had a quarrel, we all knew about it.

There were outside toilets, where they put slaked lime in. They had this big hole dug in the ground where they burned the garbage. They took their garbage and dumped it there, so the fire was going all the time. This horse fell into that hole. All this hot garbage was burning his legs and he couldn't get out. He was just whinnying and screaming. If you've ever heard a horse scream, it's just terrible. They couldn't get him out. Nobody had any pullies or anything to work with to get him out. All they could do was shoot him.

It wasn't very long after that that we moved. There was an electrician who had his wife and baby living in a house that had belonged to Murl Emery between North Las Vegas and West Las Vegas. It was out in the tules there, and they were renting that house. She was there all alone. This electrician that Tom knew said, "Well, if you guys will move over and pitch your tent in the back of that lot so that my wife won't be all alone out there, you can live there for free and not have to pay any rent." Every single thing counted, because we didn't have any more money coming in. So we moved over there after just being at Cowboy Bill's for one month.

We had tarantulas, and we had scorpions. And, of course, there were snakes too. We had opened up these cardboard boxes and laid them out to put them on the floor, on the dirt, so I wouldn't get quite so much dirt in the beds and things. I had my suitcases underneath the baby's crib, the crib that I used mostly just for keeping things off the ground. I pulled the two suitcases out one day to get some clothes, and two tarantulas came out and scared the devil out of me. I hit them with a stick, and I took them out and dropped them on the fire that I had burning garbage. Later I wasn't so afraid of tarantulas. The kids used to catch them and put them in jars.

As Boulder City became established and people found homes there, they still went shopping in Las Vegas, ate in its restaurants, drank in its bars. "Going to town" was an evening and weekend event.

HARRY HALL

After I got a job, we went to Vegas to shop. Things were cheaper in Las Vegas than they were in Boulder City. About the only store they had here was the Six Companies Store.

ROSE LAWSON

It was always fun to go to Vegas. We went to Vegas often. We all had to have passes to go to Vegas. Four miles out of the city, there was a gate. You had to have a pass to come into the reservation. Everybody carried a pass, I think from the age of 18 up. And, of course, when we got ready to go to Vegas, everybody asked everybody else, "Have you got your pass?"

PERLE GARRETT

Going to town wasn't like it is today. The road between here and Vegas was really awful. It was just an unpaved, narrow two-way lane. If we did have any rain, it would wash out. It had so many chuckholes, even from the dust. We'd have quite a time sometimes getting back and forth from town. But there were a lot of men working out here that lived in Vegas. They thought nothing about it. They'd just go sailing past us and leave us in a big cloud of dust, no trouble at all.

Las Vegas had Penney's and Ronzoni's. That was the only two stores. Things couldn't get delivered fast enough. Such a great market and not much to fill it. There were so many people [who] came in here. You couldn't get anything unless you'd be right there, unless they'd call you. After Ronzoni's got where they knew my size, Mr. Spams, who was a salesman, would call me when he'd get shoes in. "You need shoes. Now what color, what kind?" Then I'd tell him, and he'd put them away for me.

This being a government reservation, you couldn't get in without going through the gates out there. What a time those poor reservation guards used to have! You'd always have a lot of things in your car. They'd be out there in all that heat, going through every one of those packages, feeling, trying to find a bottle of liquor. We weren't allowed to have one bottle, even in your home. So after you'd show them your badge, then they'd check your groceries, then you'd be on your way.

MARY ANN MERRILL

[The Green Shack] was one of our favorite places to go for chicken. A whole bunch of us would go into town. We'd order our chicken on our way in, and go downtown in Vegas, and then come back and have our chicken. They'd have it in a big basket, and they had hot biscuits and honey. Very good.

SAUL "RED" WIXSON

Every three months they'd have a Shovelrunner's Ball at the Red Rooster in Vegas, and we'd go down there and there'd be all shovelrunners from the dam and their wives. Next month it might be carpenters, and pipe fitters after that.

MADELINE KNIGHTEN

The thing to do was to drive into Vegas and out to Lorenzi Park, the Twin Lakes park. We'd go out to Lorenzi Park and swim. They had a swimming pool and little swim lockers that you could put your clothes in and go in and swim.

We liked to go into Vegas. And, of course, Vegas—the downtown part then—was only about three blocks of business buildings. There were only two really good hotels. The Overland Hotel was all right, but it was a very old hotel. The two newer, larger hotels were the Sal Sagev up on the corner of Main [and] the Apache, which was a little newer than the Sal Sagev. They were both home-owned hotels, owned by people who had lived in Las Vegas and been businesspeople there for some time. The Apache had just about the first, I guess what you would call a cocktail restaurant, because it had Prohibition until '33. At any rate, the first time that I had eaten in the Apache Café of the Apache Hotel, they would give you cocktails if you wanted them. My husband and I weren't much to drink, even sociable cocktails. We didn't go in for it too much, but I have been in there and been offered cocktails.

Cocktails is too genteel a word for the wide-open drinking for which Las Vegas was famous even before the repeal of Prohibition in 1933. Unlike the brilliant glitz for which it is known today, Las Vegas in the 1930s was an exuberant honky-tonk. With its highway gin mills, backroom gambling, and prostitutes, Las Vegas meant escape for the young men and women living under government restriction in Boulder City.

BRUCE EATON

Probably every second or third building on Fremont street from the Union Pacific depot down to Fourth Street was a saloon or gambling hall, or both.

This was during Prohibition. They never closed them—they operated day and night. There were open saloons within a block of the police station—made no difference. It was a federal offense, not a state offense. Gambling? There was card games, slot machines, the works. Not sophisticated or fancy.

DEAN PULSIPHER

It was wild in a certain way. Of course, you got your renegades coming in there, your riffraff, naturally in a boomtown like that. And Vegas was what you would call a boomtown compared to the rest of the country.

TERESA JONES DENNING

One thing we used to do on Saturday night besides dancing was drive uptown and sit by the side of the sidewalk on Fremont Street and watch the drunks go by.

ELTON GARRETT

Bootlegging was in style in southern Nevada at that time. I shouldn't say it, but people even talked about some of the officials who might have had close contact with some of the bootleggers. The stories about those things didn't get written, but they were noised about quite a bit.

The federals knew what was happening in Vegas. They knew it was a bootlegger's paradise at that time, like a lot of other parts of the country while Prohibition was in effect. I would say they handled themselves admirably under the circumstances. No shooting match between the locals and the federals. I did not attend any of the raids, but I wrote news stories about them.

At Railroad Pass, where people were driving in from Las Vegas, there had been a settlement called Alunite, and there were a few tents out there where people were living temporarily. They were bootlegging. One of the tents was larger than most of the others. Claude Williams gave me a story about finding an old pair of shoes while he was scouting around, worn on the bottom like a shovel would wear the soles of shoes. He said, "That made me suspicious. I talked to the owner, told him I wanted to check around a bit. I found underground inside his tent was where the liquor was stored, in a container where it could be brought out. The shovel had told me someone had done some digging. What was the digging for? It was to bury a container for liquor." He said they quit right then.

HARRY HALL

All round the place was bootleggers and tents, selling home brew and whiskey and hiding out under the rocks someplace. They just grew like Topsy. This guy Tony that was the oiler on the shovel, he had a tent out here. He was selling the home brew for 25¢ a bottle. It was a regular-size beer bottle.

Joe Keate was the sheriff. He'd come out and give them the word when the federal marshals were going to show up. The federal marshal could have jurisdiction, but Joe Keate apparently knew when they were going to pull off a raid, so he warned everybody.

The only trouble was, the bootleggers—there were so many, they almost had to wear badges to keep from selling booze to each other. There were 21 bootlegging joints between Railroad Pass and Las Vegas, by actual count. Just tents.

When you'd get into Las Vegas, you'd have a little better type of establishment. But everything was wide open in Las Vegas. You could buy a drink anyplace in Las Vegas. This was during Prohibition. We could buy a gallon of whiskey for $4, and it was pretty fair stuff. In East Las Vegas they made home brew down there, and bootleggers bought it for a dollar and a half a case. Of course, they had ice tubs that cooled it off a little bit, so they had a little [expense] there.

LEROY BURT

You could always find booze in Las Vegas; you could find bootleg whiskey most anyplace you wanted to go. About as good as you could get in those days. I went to the Nevada Bar on Second Street, and that was just a block up from Block 16, where all the prostitutes were. You'd go around the side and knock on the door, they'd sell you a pitcher of beer for 50¢. This was homemade beer. Of course, they had liquor there too. You could get all that stuff in Las Vegas.

JOE KINE

Now you know that Nevada never went dry, so Nevada never bothered the bootleggers. It was the federal men that bothered them. The Nevada men didn't bother them; I think the Nevada men were on their side. They'd be selling booze, and then they'd call them up and say, "The federal men's here." I heard that story. I don't know whether it's true or not.

THEODORE GARRETT

One of the interesting parts in Las Vegas at that time too—of course, it was during Prohibition period. All of these saloons in Las Vegas, the front door was locked and you had to go around the back of them to get in. There was just double doors in every one of them. There weren't signs, but everybody knew without signs. It wasn't in the law. It was such a situation where "You pay me and I'll keep quiet."

BUD BODELL

The [police] commissioner at that time didn't levy any fines for bootlegging. Everything down on this side of town, First Street, were either cathouses or bootleggers. Whiskey was flowing all the time like there was no tomorrow— they could get anything they wanted. But there were some who were paying off and others who were not. Whoever [was sheriff] at that time would have a Collection Day. On Collection Day they'd go into the spots and say, "Well, it's payday." They'd pay off a percentage of whatever the fine would be, depending on the business.

ELTON GARRETT

You asked about the roadhouses. They existed. When the Cornero brothers built the Meadows, that was a plush place. All the big shots in Las Vegas went to see it dedicated. From that to the little Four Mile shabby ones. All kinds.

They obeyed the regulations and the mores or they didn't. If they didn't, they'd get dinged. If they paid their dues—call them fines, call them whatever

Liberty's Last Stand, Block 16, 1932

Bootlegging operation near Railroad Pass raided by prohibition agents, 1931

you want. I wouldn't use the word *bribes*. So long as they obeyed the mores of the area. That's letting them go a long ways in those days. They operated, and when a dam worker was off, nobody was in charge of his itinerary—put it that way.

BUD BODELL

The average men were hard workers. Hell, they liked to go in to drink. Sometimes they'd send me in to get some of our key men, like skiptenders, engineers, even the hard-rock miners and powdermen. I'd take a truck in, pick them up, and take them back to work. I'd find them in every saloon in town, too sick to go to work, or forgot to go to work.

HARRY HALL

Each place had their own girls. The Purple Sage, three or four places which would be in the vicinity, before you got into Las Vegas. Things were a little bit rough and tough. Some of these people working on the job were pretty rough people.

They had another place over at Texas Acres, where the railroad track went by. They had a little music, a little dancing. It was just entertainment. They had a bar; they had girls. The only one I remember over there was Barrelhouse Betty. She was shaped like a large Coca-Cola bottle. We called her Barrelhouse Betty.

CARL MERRILL

Texas Acres was over the hill up on the left going toward Vegas. To drive in there, you drove under the railroad tracks. It was an awful rough, rough place. It had an awful reputation. And there was hookers over there. The only time I was ever out there, I went out there with one other fellow, and his name was Althouse. [We were] working at the mess hall at that time. We went out there in the middle of the afternoon. I couldn't wait to get away from the place. You was scared to death every minute you was there, you know. Afraid somebody was going to cut your throat or slit your arm or do something. It had an awful reputation.

ELTON GARRETT

Texas Acres was beyond the pass. As you head toward Vegas, it was on the left, on the far side of the railroad track. It was a temporary roadhouse structure.

I was in school administration after I quit newspaper editing. I was in Vegas late one evening. I don't remember why, but on the way back—it was closer to midnight than eight o'clock—I thought, "Well, I wonder what Texas Acres is doing?" I had never been there.

I parked where I could look into the entrance. It surprised the daylights out of me to see one of my ninth-grade students pulling a slot machine in the entranceway of Texas Acres. I don't remember whether I got out of the car or not, but after seeing that and learning what had been going on a little bit, I wrote an editorial in which I mentioned that a student was seen late at night pulling a slot machine lever.[2] Within a couple or three weeks, the place was gone.

DEAN PULSIPHER

They had liquor joints there. There was one coming in toward Boulder City they called the Four Mile. That was the one that was four miles out of Vegas. It was clear out of town, and you'd go out there for a Saturday-night celebration.

They had home brew. They didn't make beer like they do now. It was good stuff. Twenty-five cents for a quart of beer. You'd drink a quart of that home brew, and I'll tell you, you'd go away talking to yourself. They had home brew, and, of course, they had other whiskey. They had bootleggers around there that kept the places going.

JOE KINE

We had one about halfway down; they called it Joe's Bar. It was just a building down there, and they served liquor. I had heard that they had girls down there too, but I didn't know for sure.

TOMMY NELSON

Not that I was ever in there, but the guy that ran that bar, his name was Joe Reddle. One day a guy came in and he said, "Give me a bottle of squirrel whiskey." And he [Joe] said, "Well, I haven't got any squirrel whiskey, but here's some Old Crow." And he says, "Well, I don't want to fly; I just want to jump around a little."

BUD BODELL

I raided the still back in around the Three Kids Mine. Stinkingest thing I ever saw: damn water was full of rats and snakes. They were drinking that stuff, supplying all the whiskey on Boulder Dam and to all those joints along the [highway] for $2.25 a gallon.

LEON ROCKWELL

One of the pretty big bootleggers was out at one of the ranches out here. They used to bring a little truck with eight kegs of about eight gallons of moonshine. They brought it down in back of our home, which was on Third Street—just off of Fremont. Right across the alley was an empty cabin, and they stored the stuff in there. They used to come up there with a load of this whiskey, and they'd look both ways, and finally they'd unlock the back of that truck and the man driving would take it on his shoulders and put it in this building and leave it. And I had been told—how true it was, I don't know—that there was a machine gun in that truck.

We did have some trouble with the prohis [Bureau of Prohibition agents] and their raids and so forth in Las Vegas, but the police were all bought off. In fact, the head of one of the unions started a place (I went and wired his place, see), and he said, "You know, the prohis can't do anything with this, because this agent, he has a stake in this place." I know it, because the man told me himself. "They couldn't do anything anyway," he said. "This is funny stuff. It's made so they test it and it don't show any alcohol, but after they drink it, it turns to alcohol." Well, that's silly—I think that's old witchcraft. He opened that place up, and boy, he did a wonderful business. And they never did catch him.

223

But sometimes they did get caught. Elbert Edwards remembers an elaborate sting operation conducted by the U.S. Department of Justice in 1931 to rid Las Vegas of its bootleggers.

ELBERT EDWARDS

There was a federal undercover agent came to town, and he got next to a businessman—his name was R. A. Kelly—who enjoyed the confidence of everyone, offered him a job with the federal government in San Francisco if he would use his influence as an undercover man for the Bureau of Internal Revenue.

He went along with them, and under their direction he opened up a speakeasy or saloon under the name of Liberty's Last Stand. He went along with the federal agents in bugging the place and also working bugs into other places. Of course, he became a purchaser of moonshine from the moonshiners around—and there were plenty of them. He got their confidence, and after they were pretty well settled, the federal boys came in and set the trap.

They had him order from every moonshiner in the county for delivery at such-and-such a time, the times for delivery staggered so no one would be aware of the trap. Then they brought in an army of federal men. (There was quite a story. In fact, there was a book published called *Liberty's Last Stand*.) Anyway, the day the trap was to be sprung, he had these moonshiners coming in with their deliveries. They would come in at a certain time, and the federal men would take them in, place them under arrest, place them in the back room, and get ready for the next one. The next one would come in, and they would take him in. In the meantime there were other federal men hitting every known speakeasy in the area. They just cleared the valley of moonshiners, of bootleggers, saloon keepers, everything.

In connection with the story, this fellow that went along with the prohis went to San Francisco to get his job. Nobody knew him or had ever heard of him. He told his story; they had no authority for that, sorry.

BUD BODELL

One time the [Nevada] attorney general ordered me to raid all those places along there. There was about 50 places, tents and shacks, all bootlegging. And some of them had tents in the back where their wives were working. At least down on the line, they visited the doctor every week. Out on the highway they had nothing.

We took two busloads in, shook them down. The judge fined them all $15 apiece, and before long they were back out there, going strong as ever. We raided them all a second time, took two more busloads in, escort car in front, one in the back, shook them all down for whiskey. This time the judge fined them all $25 or $50 apiece—and they went right back to work again.

We raided them again—only this time we burned their shacks, too.

John Cahlan remembers that the road between Boulder City and Las Vegas, crowded with bars and bootleggers' shacks, became a deathtrap and was known locally as Shambles Alley.

JOHN CAHLAN

[In 1931] there was no paved highway between Las Vegas and Boulder City. It was a dirt road and was nothing more than just a place cleared out so the cars could drive. But in 1932 the highway department put in a two-lane paved road which generally follows the same road that is there today. That road was the beginning of one of the worst eras of carnage that has happened here, because the dam workers would come to Las Vegas, visit the bootlegging joints, and start back to Boulder City. Often they would wind up underneath an automobile someplace out on the desert. Numerous people were killed on the highway out there.

To the consternation of federal officials, the most popular roadhouse in southern Nevada stood just a quarter-mile beyond the reservation gate. Railroad Pass Casino, behind which ran the Union Pacific's branch line to Boulder City, opened on 1 August 1931. It is the only one of all the Boulder Highway roadhouses left, and it has grown into a substantial resort where Boulderites still gather.

BOB PARKER

I did a survey on the railroad in 1937 and recapped all the railroad shipments into Boulder City for the dam. Most people down here won't believe it, but the first carload of lumber that was delivered on the Union Pacific Railroad was for Railroad Pass Casino. That's the first carload of lumber that came over that railroad. I couldn't believe it when I did the survey, but that was the first. Freight bill number 1 covered a carload of lumber.

MARION ALLEN

As I recall, Railroad Pass was one big room. The bar was against the back, and they had a dance hall in the front. That was always about the first place we'd stop to get a drink when we went to Las Vegas on an evening out. They had pretty big glasses, and they'd fill them full of ice and put a very little bit of whiskey in them—whatever you drank, gin or whatever it was. This one lady, as I remember, said, "I hate to drink all this whiskey to get that ice."

ALFRED BAKER

They had a pool table in front of the Pass, and when you got too drunk, they would take you out and lay you on the pool table until you cooled off.

HARRY HALL

It was a very small place. The Pass was just one room, actually. They had a three-piece orchestra. There was a little dance floor. They had a bar. I don't recall if they had any gambling—if so, very little. Railroad Pass made their own brandy. They'd buy five-gallon cans of alcohol, which was 200 proof. They'd cut it to at least 50 percent, probably more, and they'd put flavoring in. If you wanted blackberry brandy, why, they made blackberry brandy. They just put flavoring in.

ELTON GARRETT

There would be fights out at Railroad Pass sometimes, instigated by a truck driver who resented the other organization. There were two organizations that would help people at Railroad Pass Casino at times, the parties when they were off. The truck drivers and the [shovel] operators sometimes would square off a little bit. Sometimes it was a peaceful contention, competition.

But a few times it got to fisticuffs. But not much. There were arrests, but I have no recollection of it being important.

CARL MERRILL

I've seen Railroad Pass when it was pretty rough. They had the High Scalers' Ball out there one time, and boy, a fight every 10 seconds. They called it the High Scalers' Ball. They should have called it the High Scalers' Brawl.

LILLIAN WHALEN

I wouldn't say it was wild. They went out there to let off steam. When men worked in such dangerous and such unpleasant surroundings, as a lot of the work at the dam was, you couldn't blame a lot of the fellows for sort of letting their hair down. They were having fun. They didn't bother people who didn't want to be bothered. If you went out there with your own crowd and wanted to just have fun with them, I'm sure you could.

There was certainly a lot of drinking and noise, but I have never heard of any big problems out there. I don't think the police ever had very much of a problem keeping things under control. There was a lot of fun.

TEX NUNLEY

A cop used to be out there. He wore gloves all the time, but he had knuckles in there. Two guys got in a fight there one night, and he stopped it. Everybody settled. A few minutes later they were arguing again. He finally said, "OK. You guys want to fight? Come on out here and fight." Everyone around there rushed out. He said, "Form a ring." They're all holding hands. These two guys got in the middle there. They just fought and fought, like two old roosters, just sort of pecking at each other. On the windup they were both whipped, and he finally said, "Have you guys had enough?" One of them said, "Yeah, I think so." The other one said, "Yes." He [the cop] said, "Come on. Go and wash up and I'll buy you a drink." They went back in, washed up, came back, and sat at the bar there drinking. He bought their drinks.

ALICE HAMILTON

That was the closest place you could get a drink or gamble. Legally. We would go out to Railroad Pass and dance. It was the honky-tonk of Boulder City. That's the best way I can describe it.

HELEN MANIX

You see, when Boulder City was built, there was no gambling, no liquor of any kind allowed in the city. Whoever wanted something like that had to go outside the city limits. So the first place they could find was Railroad Pass. It was quite a casino, restaurant, dance floor. Many of the men used to spend their whole paycheck at Railroad Pass. Many a time my husband and I went out there and danced, had dinner. Lots of people from Boulder City did. And one thing—Tommy Nelson played the most beautiful music. He was a real musician.

TOMMY NELSON

That trumpet opened a lot of gates for me. I played many dances. It was a big diversion to come off that job down there all sweaty and everything and get cleaned up and go up and perform a nice job. All the townspeople from Boulder City and Las Vegas, they'd come up to the Pass and dance. Now you of the younger generation must bear in mind we had no television or anything like that then. Dancing—that was something people liked to do. During the construction of the dam, if there was a layoff coming or something, why, the word would get around, "Don't lay this guy off; transfer him because we want to dance."

I recall one cute little thing I want to tell about Railroad Pass. A little bitty woman came up there, and she put a nickel up on the bandstand. She said, "Would you boys please play 'Tiger Rag'?" Now a nickel, that was really an insult, but it wasn't an insult, so I said, "Your tip really isn't necessary; we'll play it for you." Now "Tiger Rag," you know, is break-the-neck speed. People were dancing to music on the pretty side; they were romancing. So I stalled her off a little. I said, "We have a number of requests, but I'll get it pretty quick." So she came in pretty quick and said, "I'm ready for that 'Tiger Rag'; I'm gonna dance." So we talked it over a little bit—we hadn't played "Tiger Rag" for a while, and as to the key that we were going to play in. So I made an announcement that we were going to raise the tempo a little bit and play a special request. Now all you guys have probably been around a railroad yard when you were kids or something. You saw a lone engine pushing a caboose, or maybe a caboose pushing an engine while switching. Well, she got ahold of this little bitty guy, and she went around that floor 60 miles an hour. She was just pushing him all the way. That was so funny. Now after that I can assure you that she didn't have to ask me to play "Tiger Rag." I asked her, "Are you ready to dance 'Tiger Rag'?" Then I would alert some of the people along the tables, "Hey, keep an eye on her, you're going to get a floor show."

HAZEL ALLEN

Jane and I went out there one afternoon. I think it was on the Fourth of July, if I'm not mistaken; it was some holiday. I was working nights, and we went out in the afternoon.

We had a fellow that washed dishes, a little bit of a fellow. He was about 75 at that time. His wife wouldn't move up here from Los Angeles. Jane and I said, "Oh, come on, Shorty, go out there with us." I said, "I don't care if you're busy, come on." And he sat there and played that piano, the most beautiful music I ever heard. I'll tell you, it was simply beautiful. But the funny part of it was they had a lot of murals on the wall and the ceiling. He sat there and he looked at those naked murals. We said, "Why, Shorty!" But, oh my, did he play that piano. Golly, he was good.

But I never did go up to the dances. I never did go out to the dances, 'cause it was gobs of prostitutes.

BOB PARKER

They had several girls up there. They kept Railroad Pass decent up there. People here took their families out there. The girls didn't intermingle with them. They kept their place, and they knew where their place was. The people that ran Railroad Pass kept the girls out of circulation, or sight, you might say. They didn't cause any trouble. The only fights out there at the Pass was when these big muckers and laborers down there would get drunk.

MARION ALLEN

We were down there one time. And, of course, the girls, there were a few girls there, but they were very low profile, so the women never had to stay [out]. They always went in. They had a few cabins, a few buildings out in back where they entertained their male guests.

TOMMY NELSON

I think I could write a book on Railroad Pass. However, if I told it all like I saw it, I'm quite certain some of it would be censored. They had the girls out there. I recall one night I was playing a big dance out at Railroad Pass with Chip White and his Dam Band. We took a brief intermission. A pretty good-looking woman came up to me. I should have known what she was right then, but I didn't catch on. She said, "Honey, what do you play?" So I thought I'd feed her a little line of baloney. I told her I played trumpet, and a little bit of anything in the band. She said, "Do you really? Come back and show me." So I asked for that.

Harold Wadman had a very different encounter with the Railroad Pass prostitutes. In 1932, when he was just 14 years old, he ran away from home and headed for the Boulder Canyon Project.

HAROLD WADMAN

I got disenchanted with school. So I eventually started playing hooky and slept instead of going to school. My grades were falling. Then when Christmas vacation come along, I didn't return to school.

I stayed around home for about a week after Christmas vacation. Then I packed my suitcase and took off. I had an old J. C. Penney kind of cardboard suitcase, and that was all. Two bottles of Mom's cherries and 10¢. That's all I took.

I intended to go someplace where it was warm. I wanted to get out of the snow. I'd heard so many stories, I was scared to ride the railroad. My dad was a railroad engineer. He told stories about the hobos and stuff like that. So I just hitchhiked. I got short-hop rides. There was a lot of people on the run, out doing the same thing I was doing. It took me, I think, three days to get down. It was just after the first of the year.

I didn't even stay overnight in Las Vegas. I just came through. It was dark when I left Las Vegas, and I got a ride out towards Railroad Pass.

It was nighttime when I got up there. Cold—I was freezing to death. They had outside johns there, and I stayed out in the john. Finally I was so cold sitting in there I had to get up and walk around. When I got up to walk around, these hookers came out. They had little cabins out in back. They took me over. I slept on the floor of one of their cabins. It must have been midnight or so when they did that. And then they laughed and gave me $5 [and] then I walked on into Boulder City.

At the other end of the Boulder Highway stood Las Vegas's most popular nightspot, the Meadows. Opened on 2 May 1931 by the Cornero Brothers—Tony, Frank, and Louis—the Meadows catered to the Vegas hoi polloi.

JOHN CAHLAN

It was out where the present Montgomery Ward store is. There was a little nest of nightclubs out there, and the Corneros decided that that would be a good place for a hotel, because it was on the way to the dam. They would get tourists going to and coming from the dam.

The story that went around the city of Las Vegas at the time [the Corneros] came up here was that the then powers-that-be in the city of Las Vegas promised them that if they would come up and build the nightclub here in Las Vegas, they could have exclusive rights to the prostitution. The city of Las Vegas would close down prostitution on Block 16, move it up to their hotel, and then they could set up gambling out there. At that time gambling was not legal. But they could set up gambling out there and run gambling, liquor, and prostitution exclusively in this area. There was a leading legal firm here in Las Vegas, which I will not name, who made [that] promise, but the city commissioners backed off from closing off Block 16 and closing all the bootlegging joints downtown. So these powers-that-be, so-called, had to back off from their promise, if any, to the Corneros. For a time there was quite a little fear among those people in the legal firm, because [Tony] Cornero was a hood and knew how to use a revolver.

Almost overnight one of the members of the law firm disappeared. Nobody knew what happened until he popped out as a district judge in another county of the state of Nevada. This attorney who disappeared was a scapegoat for the other people who made these promises. When they couldn't pull [the] deal off, why, they just said, "You'd better leave town. And we'll see that you're taken care of where you go." And the Corneros had to be satisfied because they had their place about three-quarters completed and couldn't pull out.

The Meadows was quite an establishment. As you walked in the front door, there was a big room on the north side of the building and another room on the south side of the building, which were divided by the hallway. They had the gaming casino in the south wing of the room, and around the walls they had little parapets behind which sat guys with 30–30 rifles. They had about four of them up there, so that if anybody ever came in and started to heist the joint, they were ready to take care of 'em. One guard always sat there, all during the time that the gambling was going on. There was a bar right off the gambling casino, and the dining room was across the lobby from the gambling casino, to the north. And this was the popular place for Las Vegas to go for as long as the place was open. It became the social center for the city of Las Vegas. Locals would patronize it. Anytime they wanted a party— a birthday party or anything—they'd go to the Meadows.

When they had the opening night, Tony wasn't here. But Frankie and Louis were there in their tuxedos, and Mrs. Cornero, their mother, was there too. Incidentally, their names were Stralla; that was their right names, and their aliases were Cornero. And everybody who went to the opening that night had to wear a tux. Now this was in 1929, and there were very few people outside the members of the Las Vegas Elks Lodge who had tuxes. So there was a grand scurrying to get the tuxes in for the opening. And that is the opening that set the stage for all future openings in the city of Las Vegas by the resort hotels.

Everyone was wondering why the dickens Tony didn't use chips. He used silver dollars. Nobody could figure out why. The reason he used silver dollars is that if anybody tried to heist them, they couldn't get away with very much money, because a bag of silver dollars weighs a lot of pounds. They couldn't run very fast with a bag of silver dollars. In the start of the gambling on the Strip, they used silver dollars.

THOMAS WILSON

Tony and Louis and Frank Cornero were the [liquor] wholesalers with gangster connections in Los Angeles. And they brought the liquor into the Las Vegas area which supplied to the retail outlets, which were various bootleg saloons.

I used to go to the Meadows and take a date when we had the money to buy a couple of drinks. And [the Corneros] were very pleasant. And, of course, people from the newspapers particularly got along well with 'em.

The Cornero boys sent me an invitation to come out to their New Year's Eve party! And this was black-tie. And there were other people in Las Vegas who were invited. But it was a private party of their own. And when I got out there, the youngest Cornero boy, who was Louis, introduced me to his other guests, and his brothers, and some of the gals in the chorus, and some of his friends who came up from Los Angeles.

And then he said, "I gotta identify you, right?" We had starched white tux shirts in those days, and they were stiff. And he drew with a pencil a U.S. shield like a badge on my shirtfront. And put "U.S. Prohi" lettered on the shield. And gee, they thought that was just funnier than hell! And from there on everybody was just as nice as could be. I had a wonderful time—all the scotch in the world, all the champagne in the world—all these crazy characters that were having a wonderful time. It was sort of like being on the set of a grade B gangster movie.

One night out at the Meadows, when legal gambling was new,[3] [Nevada] Senator Key Pittman and his wife were there. And Mrs. Pittman came over to Key (I was standing next to him) and she said, in a very low voice, "I just won $200! What do I do with it?"

And Senator Pittman whispers, "Give it to the Red Cross!"

The famous Meadows nightclub finally met an ignominious end on September 7, 1931.

FLORENCE BOYER

The place caught fire, and the city fire department dashed out as far as the city limits and wouldn't go any further. They had been fighting a lot of fires outside of town, and the city commission had decided that they would have to limit their activities to inside the town. There was no county fire department, so the Cornero brothers had to watch their place burn. They were disgusted then and left.

There was a nest of night spots out there near the Meadows which provided restaurant service and bars and some gambling, maybe a table of craps or twenty-one. They were nightclubs that were visited by most of the people who were in this area. There was the Green Shack, which still is in existence. The Cactus Garden probably was the fanciest of the clubs that were out there.

233

The Cactus Garden was owned by Paul Warner, who later became an assemblyman and served a couple or three terms. There was the Red Barn, the Black Cat, the Cave—which was built into a regular cave. It wasn't a very large place, but it was attended. And there was the L.A. Beer Parlor, the Bull Pen, the Red Mill. Those were the night spots that the people of Las Vegas and the people in Boulder City and along the way in visited as their entertainment.

Las Vegas had its share of bootlegging establishments. Probably the most famous was the Golden Camel, which was located on the alley between Fremont Street and Ogden Street on First Street. It was operated by Fred Rump, who came here from Colorado. This was the gathering place for the entire community on a Saturday night. Every Saturday night the Golden Camel used to provide the women with orchids, which was the forerunner of the various giveaways which the gambling casinos and hotels went in for in a later date.

There also was the Nevada Club, which was run by Sammy and Dave Stearns, across the street and a little north of the Golden Camel. And across the street again from the Nevada Club was the Tivoli Bar and the La Salle Club. There was a place on Fremont Street, between Main and First Street, that was known as the Barrel House. This was owned by Art Schriver and Wes Westmoreland. Then Joe Morgan had his Silver Club on First Street, right off of Fremont Street.

For Boulderites, Dave and Sammy Stearns' Nevada Club, known also as the Nevada Bar, was the most popular watering hole in Vegas.

TEX NUNLEY

Sammy Stearns' was on First Street there, about two-thirds of the block in from Fremont. We'd go around the bars there and gamble a little—just nickels, then. Poker, you know, nickel cards, then two bits for drinks. You'd buy one drink and they'd give you two. Something like that.

DOROTHY NUNLEY

You'd get something for a nickel, then. A lot of Boulder City people went around the Nevada Bar. If you were stuck in Vegas, which I used to get that way every once in a while—I'd ride in with somebody and come home with somebody else—you could always find somebody from Boulder City in Sammy Stearn's bar.

MARY ANN MERRILL

It was a favorite place of people from Boulder City. On Saturday nights you'd find a lot of your friends in there. You'd buy one drink, all except Saturday night, if you bought a drink in there, the second one was free. That was there. All of the bars were doing that, but on Saturday night they didn't.

Marion Allen recalls one memorable evening when he started out at Railroad Pass and ended up at the Nevada Bar.

MARION ALLEN

We were down there [at Railroad Pass], and there were a couple of young Indians here. We called one of them "Chief," and I don't know what they called [the other]. They were all "chiefs." These young Indian boys worked around us, real nice guys.

They'd get to hitting the firewater pretty hard. This one kept talking. He still had his belt on, and his hat. He'd just come from work, and he hadn't stopped to clean up. He was arguing or something. There was a little old boy there who was bouncer. I don't think he was over five-foot-six, and he weighed 125 pounds. This pretty good-size Indian there talked a little loud.

See, there was a funny thing. Construction stiffs are rugged and all, but foul language, especially in front of a woman, was just something that wasn't done. This boy used a few bad words, and this little bouncer said something to him. I guess he said something back. So he just started to stand there watching him. This little guy just bounced up and hit him right under the chin. So down he went. He [the bouncer] grabbed him by the one leg, goes right out across the dance floor, right out to the front of the building. Out in the front—it was just sand out there. He just pulled him out in the sand there. This kid lay there. Some of them said [the bouncer] shouldn't have done that. "Oh, I didn't hurt him," he said, this little guy. You didn't argue with that little guy, or not many of us was going to.

So we were finishing our drink, and looked out there, and this boy raised his head up and looked at the guy. So the Indian boy came back in and stood at the bar, but he was quiet now; his noise was all gone.

The strange thing about it—we went right on downtown, and after a little while here's this boy, all cleaned up, shirt and new pants and all. It was the Nevada Bar, which was kind of a meeting place, right around on one of the streets off of Fremont. This boy meets us there. "How do you do, how do you do." "Oh, my jaw is a little sore. But I got to buy you a drink." Oh well, OK, so he bought us a drink. "Well, we'll have to buy you a drink." We shouldn't have done [it], because he'd already had one too many, or enough.

We just walk out of the bar and down the street, and this is a big parking lot along the back of the bar. The boy goes around and gets in his car. Instead of getting it in reverse to back out, he got it in the go-ahead hole, and he goes right into the bar. Oh my God, we're walking down the street. We didn't go back. We went on down someplace else. I saw him on the job, and I said, "What in the world did they do to you?" He said, "Oh, well, it wasn't too bad. I couldn't help it. I broke about a hundred dollars worth of whiskey and something, but they said it's probably good advertising. I don't think I'll have to pay for it."

CURLEY FRANCIS

There were many, many bars in Las Vegas at that particular time. But you had to be careful because Prohibition was still in force. [You] had to show a little card when you knocked at the door to get into a bar. They'd slide open a little drawer and you'd show them your card, and then they'd let you in. Believe me, I thought I was real important, but I found out later that I wasn't so important about that. Money and gambling and the booze and the girls— that's all they really cared about.

> *At least one person cared about something else: evangelist Minnie Kennedy, known as Ma, was Aimee Semple McPherson's mother. In 1931 she visited Las Vegas with her young lover, Guy Edward "Whataman" Hudson, and held revivals at local clubs. The two were married on the edge of Black Canyon on 19 September.*

FLORENCE BOYER

Hudson had been around here for a while. The folks here didn't know his name, but he used to come into the newspaper office every few days to get exchanges from other parts of the country. One day Frank Ryan, who was justice of the peace then, invited my parents to be witnesses at a wedding they were going to have out on the rim of the canyon. It was just when they were starting construction of the dam.

They stopped and picked up the bride; she was at the Ryan house, but Mother didn't get her name when she was introduced. Mother said she looked so much older than the groom—she looked old enough to be his mother or his grandmother. When they got out to the dam and had the service—Judge Ryan performed the marriage service—they found out then that it was Ma Kennedy, Aimee Semple McPherson's mother. They came back to town just a little bit chagrined that they had been shenaniganed into attending this thing.

THOMAS WILSON

She gave a sermon at the Pair O'Dice, which was a speakeasy out on the Los Angeles road where the Strip is now. She stood on a crap table and gave a sermon at the top of her lungs on a Sunday morning. We whipped up a congregation for her, and we got stories on all this nonsense.

ERMA GODBEY

She was preaching [on 23–30 August 1931] at what was called the Labor Temple, which was in the old Boulder Club. That's at Second and Fremont. One of my girlfriends hunted me up, and she said to me, "Erma, I hear that Aimee Semple McPherson's mother is holding church in the Boulder Club. What do you say we go and listen to her?" So she and I went to hear Ma Kennedy preach. Upstairs above the Boulder Club was where all the unions had their union meetings. She had it set up there, and she was preaching. It was Four Square stuff, just like Aimee had down in California. [Aimee] used to have all these gals dressed like angels that would come swooping down. Ma Kennedy didn't have that much. She just had Whataman to sing. He would sing different hymns. He was a wonderful tenor.

All these poor men who were trying to get work, who were sleeping on

View of the Boulder Club in Las Vegas advertising Ma Kennedy's revival, 23–30
August 1931

Marriage of Ma Kennedy and Whataman Hudson on the edge of Black Canyon, 19
September 1931

the Union Pacific lawn and the courthouse lawn and hadn't maybe had a meal in three days, went to hear Ma Kennedy preach. My friend and I happened to be the only women in the whole congregation that night with all these poor guys. Ma kind of ran a soup kitchen along with this, but the men had to come and listen to Mother preach and Whataman sing before they got any food. She took up a collection. Of course, hardly any of these guys could give them even a penny. She asked if anybody wanted to come to God. If they would walk up and kneel down, she would pat them on the head and pray with them. Then she'd kiss them on the head and give them a little slip of paper which entitled them to a free meal. Of course, they had a lot of converts because there were a lot of hungry men. We went and we listened to her and we didn't come to God. We got out of there just about as quick as we could afterwards.

While Ma Kennedy and Whataman Hudson were saving souls on Fremont Street, around the corner the prostitutes of Block 16, Las Vegas's red-light district, were saving libidos.

DEAN PULSIPHER

Block 16 was where the girls were. That's on North Third Street. They had a whole block of them there, all on one side of the street, two blocks off of Fremont Street. They'd sit out in front in the summertime and the spring of the year, and you'd drive by. People would come into Vegas just to go to Block 16. My relatives and friends would come in and say, "Listen, I want you to take me down to Block 16." So we'd drive by, and the girls would wave at you and holler, "Take your wife home and come on back."

TEX NUNLEY

Block 16 was where the white girls worked, and the next block, Block 17, that was the colored girls.

MARY ANN MERRILL

When I first arrived here, one of the first things my father told me when we went to Vegas was that "That's out of bounds, that's out of bounds." So those were places that they still had the house of prostitution.

Block 16 was one block long, one side of the street. They had big houses there. They were licensed there. It was legal.

My uncle worked on the dam. He wanted to see it. The first time that we went in, my uncle took Mother and I. He told us he was going to take us to a fashion show. My brother was in the car too.

So we went down on the opposite side of the street. I saw these women, and they had long dresses on, like formal dresses, sitting out in front of the buildings. Didn't think anything about it. They didn't say anything. My uncle told George, "Go over to one of those and buy a pack of cigarettes." Immediately when George went on over there, one of these girls hollered out, "Move on, we're working this block."

TEX NUNLEY

The girls in Vegas there, they'd take [scrip] as a discount. They'd get so much of it and then they'd come out [to Boulder City] to the drugstore and buy perfume, this and that, whatever a woman uses. They'd use the scrip, take it as a discount. It didn't go full value with them.

MARION ALLEN

This was a whole block there, 16. They had two or three gals standing around in the front of these little cabarets. They usually had a bar to sell you a couple of drinks before. The back rooms were back behind. Everybody talked about Block 16.

I can tell you a story. I don't think it would hurt to get into it. I had a couple of sisters and a brother-in-law. He'd come down, and he had never seen anything like that. He was a character and a half. I might say he wasn't too smart. He drove them around there. This sister was telling all of us about a wonderful cabaret where these girls were standing out in front to get the guests to come in. She didn't find out until about a year afterwards, and then she was so embarrassed.

Quite early on the project, a gal came up here with a whole box full of [work] badges. They used these badges. It cost you 50¢ if you lost one. That was before my time, because when I came, if you lost a badge it was $2. The regular union scale down at Block 16 was $2. This gal came up there, and she told the Six Companies that she brought these badges back that the fellows had left down there, and [the workers] said that they were worth $2 and that they couldn't get their checks without these badges, so they would come back and get them. Well, [the Six Companies workers] all went and got a 50¢ badge and went on and got their check. This I had on pretty good authority. Mr. Crowe said, "There isn't much I can do for you. I think you've been had, but I'll fix it. Those badges are going to cost $2 apiece from now on." And they sure did cost $2 apiece after that. So it was part of the help of the building of the dam. Of course, I think Anderson Mess Hall and Block 16 probably contributed more to the building of the dam than anything.

THOMAS WILSON

The dam workers would all come down on payday evenings to Block 16, which was the line, and take over. And I remember one payday night goin' down there to see what the action was, and the whole street was just full—sidewalk to sidewalk, just a mass of humanity. There were some old cotton-wood tree stumps maybe a couple of feet high. I stood up on top of one of those, and I could look out over the top of the crowd, and I could see a ripple here and a ripple there. Well, those were fights goin' on in different places. And then every once in a while you'd hear a helluva crash—some bouncer had thrown some drunk out of one of the houses—and they'd thrown him right through the screen door, usually. And they'd land out in the street.

One time a police car came. In those days the police used open touring cars, top down, "squad cars," they were called. And there were two policemen in the front seat, two in the back seat. They came in, and they had the siren going slowly and making a low growl. And the crowd opened up, and they came down the street, and they got in about a third of a block, the crowd filling in behind 'em. And some guy yelled, "Hey, it's the cops!"

And somebody yelled, "What'll we do with them?"

And somebody shouted, "Let's hang 'em!"

Well, there were 3,000 drunks, irresponsible, ready for anything. The police just turned white. You could just—they might shoot their way out of part of it, but they were completely engulfed. They backed slowly out with their siren goin' just the same, low growl, crowd opened up, backed up. They got out of that without any incident at all and never came back. And from then on, there really wasn't any kind of law down at Block 16 that you could speak of, except bouncers in the joints.

JOHN CAHLAN

There was one gal down there by the name of Vera, who was in the Arizona Club. She was queen of the block, and whatever she said went. She kept it under pretty good control, and no problems. If anything went wrong, the police'd go down and tell Vera about it and she'd correct it.

As popular as the prostitutes may have been among the Hoover Dam workers, they were nevertheless social outcasts and targets of exploitation.

THOMAS WILSON

They had a health examination done by the city health officer. And I think it was a weekly checkup. One of these gals told [*Las Vegas Age* reporter Shelby] Calkins, "I just don't feel the same way I do when I've had the shot. I'm not sure what's going on, but somethin's wrong." Seems to me that the medicine given in those days was arsphenamine for syphilis. And the theory was that a person who used it, who was under treatment, was not infectious. And if they were on treatment, they could still have a ticket. So the city health officer would give 'em a shot, charge 'em ten bucks, and clear their ticket for them. And the city health officer was a very close buddy of our publisher [Charles P. Squires].

One of the gals told Calkins that she didn't think they were getting the medicine they were supposed to get. Calkins had a very close friend who was a very fine doctor in town. Calkins went to him and told him about the prostitute's tests. And so he said, "Well, I will examine this woman, give her blood tests after each inoculation. But I will have to give my findings to the medical association." (I doubt if they had a county medical society there at that time. So it must have been the state association.)

Anyway, he did. And these gals were gettin' a shot of distilled water and charged ten bucks. So Calkins came back [to the *Age*], but he made one mistake. He told the boss. And the public health doctor, of course, was the boss's best friend. The gal disappeared overnight and was no longer in Las Vegas. And she was the witness and it was the end of the case. Calkins was told to forget it.

Dave and Sammy Stearns's Nevada Bar, 1937

FLORENCE BOYER

There was one girl from what we called "down the line" who died. She had been very well liked. The people on Block 16 decided they wanted a real funeral service. They went to the Methodist minister, and [he] said he wouldn't have a service for her. They went to the Episcopal minister, Percival Smythe, and he said certainly, he would give her a Christian burial.

In those early days I used to sing at practically every funeral there was. Sometimes we would have a quartet of my mother and myself and Mrs. May Corkhill and often Carrie Heaton. That day we managed to get a little quartet together. The funeral parlor was down on Fremont Street between Second and Third, just a big store building. The funeral was supposed to be in the morning when the train came in, because they had ordered flowers from Los Angeles for the occasion. As it happened, the train was about an hour late, so we sat around waiting. I am sure that every prostitute and every gambler in Las Vegas was there at that funeral service. They were all so grateful for the fact that so-called respectable people would take time to do something for them. It was rather touching—the fact that they were so pleased.

BOB PARKER

Theoretically you could say Block 16 built Hoover Dam. Block 16 was a full-fledged prostitution area. The morality people in this country can argue until they're black-and-blue in the face about whether prostitution is something we need in this country. I'll say this: prostitution helped build Boulder City, because those workmen would head in there, get a few drinks, and down to Block 16 they'd go.

Those girls were pretty well taken care of. Their doctors checked them either once a week or once a month. Some say once a month, but if we had to be inspected up here in the mess halls once a week, I'd sooner think that the county inspected them once a week. But anyway, there weren't as much venereal diseases and we didn't have any AIDS in those days; we didn't have a lot of things that you got today. I don't know if there was near as many murders or near as many cases of venereal diseases as there are now. It's six of one and half a dozen of the other. I'm kind of on the fence. Morally I think it's wrong, but socially I think maybe it has its point. I don't know. It didn't do any harm to building the dam, I know that.

9

TOWERS, PENSTOCKS, AND SPILLWAYS: BLACK CANYON, 1934

"You didn't stop and have a coffee break."

While the main structure of Hoover Dam rose in Black Canyon, work proceeded simultaneously on the dam's ancillary structures: intake towers, penstocks, and the spillways designed to carry water around the dam in times of flood. Water to generate electricity passes from Lake Mead through the cylinder gates in the four 395-foot intake towers, through the penstocks, to the generators in the powerhouses below the dam. The system is simple, but building it was complicated and required construction innovations unique to Hoover Dam.

NEIL HOLMES

There are four intake towers above the dam. They sit on a 900-foot elevation, [but] the dam was started at a 600-foot elevation, so they're 300 foot above the elevation of the dam. Your water goes into them intake towers and goes down through a penstock to the units in the powerhouse [where the water] turns the waterwheel that turns the rotors that generates the power.

HARRY HALL

I was a rodman. That's a lower form [of] animal life on the survey party. You do whatever. You hold the rods; you set points for the instrument man. We

Intake towers and the Hoover Dam structure under construction, 17 August 1934

were working on the intake towers, trying to establish an elevation. You held the rod; you gave them turning points. You'd give the instrument man a shot on the bench, what's called the bench of known elevation. He would read the rod at a given number—HI, heighth of instrument. Then you'd give him a turn at some solid point, and keep doing that until he ascertained the elevation at the point that he wanted. You'd give him a shot on the bench, and then you'd move to another point and he would establish. He'd get an HI, and then he'd read the rod and then transfer an elevation through that point. We checked the [concrete] forms from those points to ascertain that they were plumb and that the brass guides would be plumb.

The intake towers were constructed in lifts. They had a stiff-legged crane on each side that was mounted permanently. They swung them out to pick up the concrete from the flatcars pulled by the dinky engine from the upper high mix [plant], and then it was lowered into the forms. They picked up the eight-yard bucket and placed the concrete in the forms on the intake tower.

We had one transman there. His name was Glen Bird. He was a little bit scared of high places. We had a monkey-slide that was pulled by an air tugger that was used for an elevator to go up the intake towers. He dropped just about three feet, and Bird said, "She's deep enough for me; I'm getting out of here." So he transferred down to the tunnels, where he wouldn't have to put up with that.

LEROY BURT

I spent most of my time on the intake towers. The intake towers were built like a wagonwheel, with the center around and the spokes that came out. In between these spokes there's a trash rack. They'd pour the concrete, and one pour would come up 10 feet each time on the intake towers. Each bucket would probably bring it up about 2 feet. They'd just keep working all even; when they'd get one spoke finished, they'd move around to the next one. In an eight-hour period, we'd pour maybe half of the circle of the intake tower.

We'd work it with our feet with boots on and puddle it—that's puddling concrete. They'd keep pouring it, and you'd keep coming up. The concrete was getting harder. Then we had to spade around the edges so you'd have no rock pockets when they moved the forms. There's a lot of concrete in there. I don't know how many cubic yards each one of those pours would hold, but it was a terrific lot of concrete.

My last job before I left down there was putting the trash racks down the intake tower. They only did this on day shift. I was running the hoist and I had a fellow on what they called a bicycle deal up on top, so they could go around and pick these things up and come back. The hoist went up through this, and a fellow by the name of Manning was my hub tender. Called him Paddle Foot Manning. We put every trash rack down in every intake tower.

We were down there one Sunday, just looking around, my wife and I and my little girl. I was showing them around where I was working. The guy that ran the hoist was a very good friend of mine, lived in the auto court with us. His name was Miller, Art Miller. My wife was young and full of the devil, and she said, "I'd like to ride that bucket down there." I said, "No, you don't want to ride that bucket." She said, "Yes, I do." So she got in there, and Art just took the brake off, and down she went, 375 feet to the bottom gate. You could hear her screaming all the way down.

JOE KINE

We put the machinery in [the intake towers]. They have some big long shafts that go down from the top, and they have a winch on top to raise and lower those [cylinder] gates. I helped to put all of those in, and the big gates down at the bottom, the 30-foot-diameter gates. They come in sections of steel. They had them put together with fitted bolts. I worked on all of those too.

One time they were lowering down one of those pieces of steel. The hoistman let it come pretty fast. When he went to stop, he stopped pretty quickly. It broke loose and knocked the scaffold off. They lost a man there.

WILFRED VOSS

When they were building the intake towers, I worked on the rigging crew. They were probably 50 percent complete when I got up there. I was foreman for a crew. I worked there on the intake towers, moving forms, putting concrete chutes in, the placement of reinforcement steel, and one thing and another for the intake towers.

That's when I was hurt. I fell. I didn't fall off the intake tower; if I had fallen off the intake tower, I wouldn't be here today. They were up probably 150 feet when I took a tumble. I just broke a leg all to pieces. They told me I'd never walk again, but they found out they were wrong.

That was just one of those things. A lot of us got hurt. We had our work. I had personal insurance, besides the state insurance that the Industrial Commission paid. As a matter of fact, I made more money off the job than I did on.

The Babcock & Wilcox Company won the contract to fabricate, transport, and install the steel penstock pipes required to carry water from the intake towers to the generators. The pipes were 30 feet in diameter and 13 feet in diameter—larger than needed for any previous dam. It was impossible to manufacture pipe of this size at Babcock & Wilcox's Pennsylvania plant and transport it to the damsite—no railroads or highways could carry anything that big. Instead, the company built a steel fabricating plant and annealing furnace near the edge of Black Canyon.

DEAN PULSIPHER

I went to work for Babcock & Wilcox. They were pipe fitters out of Pittsburgh, Pennsylvania. They brought cars in all loaded down with flatiron, slabs of steel. Some of that was two, two-and-a-half inches thick, and I don't know what the pieces weighed. They brought it out in flatcars because they couldn't possibly fabricate it back there. They built a fabricating building big enough to put these 30-foot penstocks in there. They'd take it in and start to roll it.

HARRY HALL

They had to roll this plate. They had an immense roller in a large tin metal building. That was a tremendous job. It was in three segments. They made 30-foot sections, [and] it was all electric welded. The welding was all inspected by X-ray.

DEAN PULSIPHER

They had a lot of people in there operating machines and welding. They had a big cooking oven that operated with bottled gas. After doing all the welding—they'd inspect them pretty close. They put them in and cooked them up to a certain degree so it would stand stress—expansion and contraction—from the temperature of the water coming down through the intake towers. They'd leave them in [the furnace] roughly 24 hours. It would cool down pretty fast, especially in wintertime. Summertime was different.

HARRY HALL

They had stiffeners, or spiders, in there to keep [the pipe] in its position.[1] It was a series of long one-inch rods that would hold it, probably six or eight struts on each end [that] kept it from warping. It was machined on each end.

They had a cableway inside the warehouse of the Babcock & Wilcox plant. They would load [the pipe section] on a lowboy, and they had a D-7 tractor on each end. To back it out of there, one would back up and the other would push to get it out.

DEAN PULSIPHER

My job, with the crew that I was working for, was to move them penstocks out from the plant, and store them up and down the corridor there.

They had railroad tracks going back and forth, and they had a big steam engine on this railroad. Every time you'd move a pipe, you'd have to build a railroad line. They have two railroad ties about two foot apart. I was helping moving these rails.

You'd have to jack [the pipe] up, and they'd have two big timbers underneath each 30-foot penstock. They had them sitting on the ramp. They had these timbers to handle the weight. Then on each corner we had a skip [and] two men on each corner. We had eight five-pound bores about two or three inches in diameter [to help roll the pipe section]. You had about six or eight of them on each corner. You had to keep them under that corner. If you missed one just a fraction—just a second—too late, we'd have to stop because they're so heavy. You'd have to jack the pipe up, and put one under there.

I worked them cars by myself many a time, because guys would come out there to go to work; they'd work there maybe half a day, or a day, or two days; then they wouldn't show up the next day. I'd work them corners by myself. I'd reach back and get [the bores] and put them under by myself many a time. You'd have one on the front end, and as soon as you'd go down and get one underneath, you'd roll that one off, reach back and get another one, put it up there. That's the way you'd work it. You just moved them just a few inches at a time.

The only break you got was at lunchtime and at four o'clock. You had your head down, and your rear end up. You put in eight hours of work down there, I'll tell you.

After Babcock & Wilcox built, annealed, braced, and stored each section of the pipe, Six Companies had to haul each section on a flatbed trailer

down the narrow road, around a hazardous hairpin curve, into the canyon.
Curley Francis was one of the men given this dangerous job.

CURLEY FRANCIS

Our job was to haul the penstock pipe, which was 30 foot in diameter, from Babcock & Wilcox fabrication plant down to the cableways. I got into that job because I was doing Cat skinning work. All of a sudden there was an opening. I told the foreman of that job I wasn't particularly enthusiastic about it, but after I got started with it, I could see it was a real challenge.

I went to work at two o'clock in the afternoon, and you never knew when you was going to get back. You just never knew. If there was a pipe ready to go down at the end of your eight hours, you'd just pick it up. Sometimes we'd get two or three. And then sometimes we wouldn't haul them for sometimes two or three days. This was because of the demand for the pipe. Otherwise if they wanted the pipe down the hill and they didn't have it ready up at Babcock & Wilcox, they'd just have to wait until it was ready. There were times when we thought we were going to get a pipe on one shift, and they wouldn't get [it] until the next shift. And there was no such thing as time-and-a-half or anything like that. They'd just add hours on to your paycheck.

These pipes ranged from 86 tons to 210 tons, which would include the spiders, which were to keep the pipe round. They'd put a spider inside and then tighten all these jacks so when they picked it up with the cableway, it wouldn't make it egg-shaped. We would receive these pipes up at B&W. We had panels on the trailer contoured to the pipe itself. We had no way of clamping it down. It just sat down on the trailer on these panels. The trailer was a 200-ton trailer. Every wheel on it steered. They had a little motor, and it helped with the hydraulic steering and with the hydraulic brakes.

When we started hauling this pipe, all the engineering aides, both for Six Companies and the government, were there, because I think this was a new type of transportation. The hydraulic steering trailers [were] new in the construction game at that particular time. We had air brakes on the trucks; air brakes were nothing to be alarmed about, but the steering—they were more concerned.

Frank T. Crowe was right there most of the time until after we got down into a routine of hauling pipes. That was where I became acquainted with him. He was a man that didn't talk very much, but nothing, I don't think, ever missed his observation and understanding. I think he understood every aspect of construction: concrete and rigging and hydraulics and the works.

It took two Cats to start the load. We always started this load with two

Cats, and as we made the turn towards the road, the front Cat would drop off and go to the back end and hook onto the back end of the trailer. All the time this trailer was moving. We'd unhook this Cat on the run. I'd go in the back, and we'd hook it on the back end on the run so we would never stop. If we stopped again, it would take two Cats to start it again.

The idea of this back Cat was to give the trailer a stable ride down the hill. Hopefully you had a good brake job on this trailer, and this Cat in the back would stabilize the speed. If it started to slow down too much, then he'd let off the brakes and let it start to run a little bit. So the result was you were pulling with the Cat here and holding back with a Cat here. That stabilized the speed going down the hill. Some of the trips down, that load would get to rolling too fast and it would take some time for the brakes to take hold. We lost quite a few bearings out of the back Cat from pulling it on compression. It wasn't built for that; it was built for pushing. We had quite a bit of difficulty with that.

We did have a mechanical failure. One of the brake linings went out on a rig wheel and locked real tight. We couldn't move the trailer whatsoever. So we had to repair it. We had several 100-ton jacks underneath it. Our biggest problem was trying to get the wheel and the brake assembly off [because] the brake lining had folded over. I believe we worked about 18 hours on that. After we got the wheel off, got the brake shoes out, and put the wheel back on, we continued on down to the dam.

We also had a little trouble with hydraulic fluid. We had leakage with different pipes now and then, but we were able to overcome this situation by using heavy-duty pipes. We didn't care too much about having the steering fail, but when our braking system failed, we were all concerned.

The leg [from the plant] was a dirt road at that particular time. It was not hard-top or anything. Our job between pipes was to keep this road absolutely level. You couldn't stand any tipping of any kind as far as the trailer was concerned and the pipe was concerned. There was no tipping of the road, even though it did make a hairpin turn towards the dam.

It was an outstanding event for everybody when we'd come down the hill with a pipe. I don't know whether people just enjoyed seeing it go down the hill or [were] looking for something to happen someday. It was quite a job. In fact, it had never been hauled. It could scare you to death to haul a 150-ton trailer, but as you can see, they could haul better than 200 tons.

We had two traffic guards. We had two policemen that would usually come down. One would stop traffic down at the dam, and then the other would follow us down and try to get all of the vehicles off the road. We did have some problems once in a while, but we got real efficient at moving cars that were in our road. We would use coat hangers and wires of all kinds, and we'd open up a car and hook onto it and drag it off to someplace and get it out of the road.

252

Changing shifts on the structure, 2 January 1934

Thirty-foot steel penstock sections ready to be moved into the canyon, 10 December 1933

Then when we arrived at the cableway, it would take two Cats to push this large pipe into place so the cableway could pick it up, and that meant making a real right turn. On this trailer every wheel had a steerer, both the back and the front. It was all hydraulic, and it had air brakes. It was a real piece of machinery for that particular time. When we got there, we would have to put the rigging on. We had to hook up the moonbeams[2] and the cables, and the cross cables to balance the load.

We'd bring it down, and then we'd have to rig it, pick it up, and set it down. After it got up off the trailer, we didn't care. We'd ride this thing down in the canyon. Then when we set it down, we'd take these cables off. But Frank T. Crowe came down one day and said, "This is the last time you'll ride the rope."

The 30-foot penstock pipes extended from the bottom of the intake towers. Crews connected them to other sections laid into the old diversion tunnels closest to the river. From the 30-foot penstocks a series of 13-foot pipes branched off to deliver water down into the Nevada and Arizona power plants. Dean Pulsipher moved from the Babcock & Wilcox fabrication plant to the dam, where he helped install the penstocks.

DEAN PULSIPHER

They had rails inside of tunnels on the Arizona and Nevada side. They'd run [the pipe] in on rails. They'd pull them up [with] air tuggers, and maybe some of these big 13-and 30-foot penstocks had several air tuggers on 'em to get them up in place. It took a lot of rigging, I'll tell you. They had to have lights in there too.

Those first three or four penstocks up there, they had a terrible time. They'd take a long time. It might take a week to get that first one in up there. It all depends on how far you are going. When they first started, it took a week to get them into the tunnel, pulled up in place so we could fit it together.

Now the 30-foot penstocks, they had a hard time getting them to fit. They cut them to the thousandths of an inch, but naturally when you put anything together for the first time, you have problems fitting it. They'd use dry ice on one side and heat on the other to expand and contract the pipe to fit.

We walked up steel ladders [inside the tunnels] all the way up to the top. There's about a 300-foot climb up there. And when you start up, you see a spud wrench coming by your head, or a nut or a bolt, something coming down. You could hear them hitting the tunnels coming down, and all you could do was just hang on and say, "Well, hope it misses me."

When we had been working there quite a while, we were lowering this one 13-foot penstock. A cable broke, and there was three guys riding this 13-foot penstock down to the bottom. It broke right after they started, and it's quite a ways down there from the top of the upper penstock to the bottom. It killed all three of them. It happened on swing. They just got it cleaned up when half a dozen of us working in there at the time came to work there on graveyard shift.

After they had the 30-foot and the 13-foot penstocks all set in place, they had a crew come in and rivet them. These big steel rivets are a pretty good size. They put a man on the bottom. The rivets went in from the bottom inside of the tunnel, inside of the penstock. Then they'd pound them; they'd ping them, flatten them out on the outside. They had a groove, they had a seat in there that they fit into, and that's where they kept them from leaking.

Carl Merrill helped install support cradles in the tunnels for the penstock pipes.

CARL MERRILL

I was always looking for more money, I guess, [so] I got a job with the steel crew. I didn't know how to tie steel. They taught us. They taught us everything we had to know down there. The first job with the steel crew was getting the steel into the place where it had to be used. On the powerhouse it wasn't too bad. They could let it down with the high line, and all you had to do was spread it out. The journeymen would go ahead and tie it in position. That was fine. First they'd tie so much steel; then they'd pour a floor. When that was finished and set up, they'd go on to the next floor and wall, to get that much higher. That wasn't too bad.

But when they started putting that steel back into the tunnels, that got to be work. They had a cradle every so often under that steel penstock pipe that went through there. That steel was about inch-and-a-quarter by inch-and-a-quarter square and about 20 feet long, in a curved form. We carried that steel back through what are today these small observation tunnels. We carried steel, 20-foot long pieces with a curve in them so it would fit the curve of the penstock. We pushed it back through those tunnels by hand.

When I went to work for the steel crew, I went from four, four-and-a-half, to five dollars a day. During that time they taught me how to tie steel. Finally when I learned to tie steel and could fairly well keep up with the journeymen, they gave me $5.60 a day. The journeymen were getting $6.00. We were all doing the same work, the journeymen, the laborers, and everything else. I thought I should be getting as much as a journeyman, [so] I asked the boss for a raise. He says, "I pay men for what they know, not for being a mule." I've never forgotten that to this day. I didn't get the raise. No, sir.

Bureau of Reclamation inspectors and technicians kept a meticulous eye on construction. They not only had to ensure that Six Companies maintained quality construction but had to determine whether all systems were operating as they had been designed. Was the concrete cooling uniformly? Were there any signs of movement in the structure? Was water seeping through any fissures in the concrete—or in the cliffs abutting the dam?

STEVE CHUBBS

As soon as they started actually pouring the concrete, then I got a job as a technician. I'd had experience using Wheatstone bridges, and the instruments used Wheatstone bridges.[3] So they put me on as a senior laborer.

I think there were 8 or 10 of us. It was all mapped out for us. We worked in shifts measuring stress and strain, the temperature of the concrete. [We] put in strain meters and thermometers in the concrete according to the specifications. Then after they were in, we had to read them every eight hours for two or three weeks, so it kept us pretty busy.

HARRY HALL

The strain meters and joint meters had leads connected to a series of boxes. There were maybe 80 in a box. They were read to ascertain what the temperature of the concrete was and whether there was any movement. They would be put across the joints, and ascertain if there was any movement in the joint, any contraction or expansion. We didn't find any appreciable movement at that point. Very minute. It could have been an error in the readings.

[We also] measured deformation of the dam. They had three triangulation stations on the Nevada side and three triangulation stations on the Arizona side. They had a broken base line on Number 10 [Cableway] tail tower and also a broken base line on top of the dam.

There was a five-man chain crew. The head chainman had a 15KG measuring device. The rear chainman had a stick that he could hold it with. The rear contact man set it on the point. The front contact man used the millimeter scale. He read the scale to a tenth of a millimeter. He measured each broken base line. Then we computed the distance between the Nevada base and the Arizona base.

We embedded 60 brass points on the downstream face of the dam at different elevations. We painted the Maltese cross on each one with white paint so we could see it. We had to [read] at night because you couldn't keep the instruments level if there was any sun. If you smoked a cigarette, you couldn't keep it level. We used a big searchlight on the closest station to the dam, which was the end one on the Nevada side and the end one on the Arizona side.

We'd measure the elevation of each intermediate station twice each direction with two tapes. We'd compute the side, the temperature correction, the pull, [the] deformation of the dam. It would move slightly, maybe three-eighths of an inch, between low water and high water.

Leakage was a major concern throughout construction. Not only did the dam itself have to be sealed, but the canyon walls had to be grouted to keep water from seeping around the dam.

NEIL HOLMES

They went in and drilled from tunnels in the dam down into the rock, and they grouted that to stop leakage. [Grout] is just fine cement without any sand or gravel or anything in it. Of course, the dam had to be leak-proof when it was through. There had to be grout piped in between every form, pumped in there at high pressure. Wherever there's a crack, that cement will find it, and it will stop all the leaks.

The biggest block [of concrete in the dam] was about 50 foot or 55 foot square. They tapered down on the lower end to about 25 foot square. Of course, they had to have grout pipe in there too. After the dam was poured and it shrunk a little bit, these seams all had to be grouted. That went on from the bottom clear to the top. There were no leaks through the dam at all when it was finished.

Ordinarily water flows from Lake Mead through the intake towers and generators into the Colorado River below Hoover Dam. Engineers knew the notorious record of Colorado River flooding before dam construction, however, and planned for emergencies when the river's flow might exceed the capacity of the towers and penstocks. They designed spillways on either side of the dam that could be opened to divert floodwaters through the canyon walls.

HARRY HALL

The spillway has drum gates on the lake side, and as the lake rises, it floats the drum gates up in position. Drum gates are 16 feet high. If the lake gets up to the elevation of the top of the drum gates, then it will go over the spillway. Or if they want to test the spillway, they can lower the drum gates and let the water go over the spillway down through the incline tunnel to the diversion tunnel and on out through the diversion tunnel. It's designed for a flow of 200,000 acre-feet.

They tried a test, I believe in 1941, on the Nevada side.[4] It was passing perhaps 40,000 to 60,000 cubic feet a second. The cavitation was tremendous. Cavitation means that the concrete was eroded possibly 60 feet deep, the width of the tunnel, and 300 feet long. Just the test carved that much out of it.

They have what they call a stilling well on the spillway. It's at the bottom of the spillway and about 50, 60 feet deep before it starts going down the raise. That forms a cushion before it goes down the raise. I think they thought that cavitation might occur as it came over the spillway if it didn't have a stilling basin. The stilling well really doesn't protect the flow of the water through the raise; it just protects the water coming over the spillway itself from the lake. What happens is they set up turbulence at the point where the horizontal diversion tunnel meets the slope, the raise, and that's where the cavitation takes place. So if they ever have a flood to the extent of 200,000 feet on each side, it's really going to be pitiful.

Joe Kine worked on the riveting crew for the drum gates on the spillway.

258

JOE KINE

I went to the Arizona spillway to put up construction steel. That was really an endurance test there, on that hot steel, driving rivets. You had to wear four or five thicknesses of burlap sack to keep from risking your eye when you leaned against iron to drive rivets. Inside of the drum gates was really, truly an endurance test. You had the heat from the natural heat outside, and you had a forge going in there heating rivets, and then you had the hot rivets and everything. And you didn't stop and have coffee breaks like you do now. You worked right straight through. Nowadays they put in fixed fans and move the air out and make it a little more comfortable. But not in those days.

Leroy Burt had an accident while stripping forms in the spillway.

LEROY BURT

I had a stupid accident. My foreman got a new big coil of rope. [We would] hook onto the rope and go over the wall. During lunchtime one night I was working off this coil, and he told me not to cut it, just to use my tail line and fasten onto this rope that he had tied off on a big jumbo that went up and down in the raise. During lunch hour he moved the skip up, or the jumbo, because we needed to get up a little farther for the forms we were stripping. He didn't tell me that he had untied my line. So after lunch we'd just go up and tie our line on, and jump off the jumbo and go to work.

Well, I jumped off, but I wasn't fastened. I kept on going right down the raise. At this time the Colorado River was going underneath through the diversion tunnels. Luckily, this railroad track that this jumbo went up and down on was anchored in cables into the concrete. It set up on a pedestal about two, three and a half, four feet—big square timbers. Luckily, as I rolled down the raise, one of these cables hit me right across the back and stopped me. That's the only thing that saved my life, because I would have went right into the Colorado.

As work proceeded on its related structures, Hoover Dam rose in Black Canyon. Marion Allen was one of the concrete finishers working on the face of the dam.

MARION ALLEN

About three of us did all the faces of [that] dam. I liked the job too. You had a comfortable bos'n's chair. It was a board about so wide [gestures], and it had four ropes come up out of the corner, [which] hooked on your rope or your block or your single rope. I always used a block, because it was always going up and down. Most of the high scalers would go down, and if you had to climb, you had to climb out. Well, I always had a bunch of tools, and it's pretty hard to carry out with a bucket of tools.

The upstream face was a bearcat because you had to swing in under and get yourself anchored. Charlie Hughes and Dave Mudiman were finishers. They all worked on those chairs, and also the intake towers, as we'd come up on those. Some of them had a staging underneath where you could catch some of the work. But you still had to drop down 100 feet down below there.

At that time height never bothered me. All these slopes of the dam, downstream. But at that time I worked on those ropes all over the downstream face.

There were two men [who fell]. One was working on swing shift, and he apparently went to get out of his chair or something and fell on top of the powerhouse. They found him the next day on top of the powerhouse. We never did know what happened to one of them. In fact, we never did know what happened to the other, except one got hit with something over the top.

I always had a helper up above. He guarded me there for years because

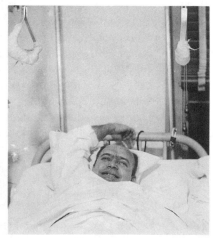

Injured worker being loaded into an ambulance for a trip to the Six Companies Hospital in Boulder City, about 1933 (*left*); Injured worker at the Six Companies Hospital, Boulder City, 1933 (*right*)

they'd be throwing stuff off the dam or something, and somebody wouldn't look. If you ran out of ice, he'd send you down some ice. Water bag—you never got away from your water bag, never.

JOHN GIECK

Down in the canyon they pumped that water right out of the river into tanks on the side of the hill and let the silt settle out. Then they put it in 20-gallon cream cars and carried those over the job, and guys'd pour it in their water bags. You'd hand [the water bags] up and they'd cool off a little bit. But it still had silt in it.

By 1934 compensation laws in Nevada and Arizona for workers injured on the Boulder Canyon Project had been settled—although Arizona was more generous than Nevada. In time workers learned to take advantage of these laws.

LEROY BURT

State compensation was much higher in Arizona, so they always said if you got hurt in Nevada, get someone to drag you over to the Arizona side so you'd get more money.

TOMMY NELSON

As I recall, Nevada paid after seven days, depending on the seriousness of the injury. If he had a broken leg or something, get him over into Arizona, because he's going to be off longer than 15 days.

When a fellow got killed over in Arizona, a coroner had to come from Chloride or Kingman, way over there. You can imagine what kind of roads, and he was traveling in a Model A Ford. He had to go up above the dam a couple of miles to Cashman's Ferry and come across that way to come around into Nevada to make the coroner's inquest. I recall a time or two seeing the guy lay there for several hours with a canvas draped over him, waiting for a coroner. But as I recall, a mutual agreement was made later on between Nevada and Arizona where Nevada did make the inquest for Arizona.

TEX NUNLEY

Arizona paid a lot more compensation than Nevada did. If you got killed in Arizona just across the line, you got more in compensation than you did in Nevada. There was one man who got killed there where they were mucking out the center part of the dam. He got crushed and killed. They didn't know whether it was Arizona or Nevada. It was so close it had to be measured.

An engineer gave me a 300-foot reel of tape. He held the dead end of the tape and gave me the full reel. I could call anything there, but he said, "Tex, make it Arizona." What they should have done [was have] someone go with me for evidence to read the tape. I took the tape and went to the Nevada side, read the tape, come back, went to the Arizona side, read the tape, come back, and told him the measurements. It was Arizona, but there wasn't anyone there to disqualify me.

CURLEY FRANCIS

They had a catwalk across from the Arizona to the Nevada side. One night we were working in the upper penstock tunnels, and one of the fellows got hurt pretty bad. We knew at that particular time that a man received more money compensation wise when he got hurt on the Arizona side. So we made a litter out of a couple of two-by-twelves and a two-by-four, and four of us fellows loaded him on that makeshift stretcher and took him across the catwalk to the Arizona side, and there we called first aid. Bob Dressen was with Six Companies, and he was on 24 hours a day. He moved from place to place, and he had a first-aid kit, a truck. Any time of night, any time of day, you could call him and he'd be right there. He usually had a thermos bottle with him when he came along, and usually if you weren't hurt too bad and so forth and so on, he'd have you drink out of this thermos bottle, and that made everything rosy.

Night view of construction progress, 18 October 1934

LEROY BURT

I'd like to tell you one little incident that happened down there, and I discovered in later years that this accident didn't happen on the job at all. The fellow that I worked for on the intake towers was named Denny Greenwood. Denny came down there one time with a cast on his leg when we were working swing shift. He was my foreman. I had been off a night or something; I can't remember exactly. I asked him what happened. He said, "Well, I was over in Arizona, and I fell and broke my leg."

Denny is since then deceased. So a couple of years ago his brother Dillard came to the Thirty-Oners.[5] I got to talking to him—I didn't know Denny was gone. "Oh, yeah, he's been dead for several years." I said I remember he lived out at Railroad Pass in a little tent. I used to take him into the doctor at Las Vegas Hospital because he didn't have an automobile and I did. His brother told me, "I have to tell you something about that accident he had down there. He got that in his tent out there, because he and I were wrestling on the bed and he got tangled up in the covers and fell off the bed and broke his leg. We took him down to Arizona, and that's where he was supposed to have broken his leg."

Injuries, deaths, and working conditions were still a source of complaints, but fear of losing their jobs and recollections of the forceful suppression of the 1931 strike kept workers from seriously attempting another walkout. In 1934, however, the IWW attempted to stage another strike.

MARION ALLEN

They say the one in '34 was the last IWW strike. The IWW was the International [Industrial] Workers of the World. They organized a lot of stuff, changed a lot of conditions, which did a lot of good. But they were a lot of working men, and most all employees hated them.

There were two or three organizers here that we knew. They wanted pay from the time they got on the bus to report, which the unions actually got afterward. We spent about an hour going down and an hour coming back, which was on our own time.

We just began to get the wrinkles out a little bit. It's a pretty good job, and they're not pushing us too hard, and this guy pulled this strike. He was an organizer that came in here from San Francisco or northern California.

We sat on the buses down here in front of the recreation hall where they were loading up. One of the fellows here went to run up the recreation [hall] steps. There was about six or seven steps up to the recreation hall. He was all excited. "Come on, boys. Get off of the truck here and we'll make this a real job. Come on, boys." Well, all these boys, like me, they're sitting there, saying, "Do you think I'm crazy?"

He run up these steps, and the poor guy hooked his toe, and down he went and hit his face right on the top step. It hurt, you know. It hurt me, sitting there. Blood running down his shirt. He climbs up there, and he comes running around a little, lays on the other side of the truck, and he says, "Look what they did to me, boys, look what they did to me! Come on, get off here and help me." Most of us had seen it from the other side. That's what made it so funny.

It never amounted to anything.

Hoover Dam power houses under construction, 24 June 1935

10

COMPLETION: HOOVER DAM AND BOULDER CITY, 1935 AND AFTER

"That dam was a part of us."

By the start of 1935, the main structure of Hoover Dam was nearly complete. On 1 February 1935 workers diverted the Colorado River out of Diversion Tunnel No. 4, through which it ran unobstructed, into Diversion Tunnel No. 1 on the Nevada side of the canyon, which was equipped with a bulkhead gate. When workers lowered this gate, the reservoir began filling. Years of dreaming, planning, and building came to a close. As Lake Mead rose, the Bureau of Reclamation studied its effects on the dam.

LEO DUNBAR

There was quite a bit of water coming in around the dam area. After February 1935, when they closed the gates and started raising the reservoir, we began to have trickles down the canyon, everywhere below the dam. [Water] was going around what grouting they had done as they poured the dam. The only explanation for that was that as the water raised in the reservoir, it was finding voids [in the rock]. As the water raised, it would get into one of those [voids] and the sides of [the canyon] would begin to slide in or tumble in. The same thing was happening in the river here. After storage began, there were great walls of sandstone, loose stuff that would fall into the river. We had great times having those big shelvings falling off the sides of walls into the river.

A lot of people worried about it. I think geologists could answer the

267

question of what was happening there. Shocks occurred. Some of them were large enough to rattle dishes on the shelves, and you could hear it down in the canyon—you'd really get a vibration of it. Seismographs would pick it up readily. I don't have any idea how many. I do remember that there was a report came out that in one 24 hour period, when the reservoir was partially filled, the seismograph had picked up 85 separate tremors.

HARRY HALL

The filling of the lake and the tremendous amount of weight from the water caused the crust of the earth to change position. We had a tremendous number of earthquakes—not fatal ones, but you could see the dust fly, you could hear, you could feel some of them.

In 1940 they decided to build a seismograph station in Overton. So I went over there and located the place and made a concrete seismograph building there with a central pier (it was isolated from everything else) that the seismograph would be placed on. We also built a seismograph building at Pierce's Ferry and also a generator house with a small gasoline generator to furnish power to the seismograph building. We also had a seismograph placed in the Administration Building basement [in Boulder City].

The people that took care of placing the seismographs was the Coast and Geodetic Survey. From triangulation from the three stations, they could ascertain the epicenter of the earthquake. After the lake filled, the seismic activity ceased.

MADELINE KNIGHTEN

There was a series of earthquakes in Boulder City in May [4–7] 1939.[1] When that earthquake hit, it tumbled our chimneys. It was a pretty powerful earthquake. There were differing thoughts about it. Some claimed it was because of the immense weight of the water that was just filled up behind the dam, and others said that no, it wouldn't make any difference.

As the lake rose, the government initiated studies to determine characteristics of the reservoir that would affect performance of the dam and its capacity to generate electricity.

LEO DUNBAR

When those gates finally were closed and the reservoir started to raise, the Bureau of Reclamation engineering offices decided that they should have studies made on this job that had never been made on any other project, and had never been required. [One was] what the evaporation of the lake itself would amount to. How many horsepower was the loss to the power plant through water that went off in evaporation? I had no idea how to go about [this], but since I was associated with most of the water situation here, it was kind of dumped on my shoulders.

In connection with the evaporation, I first went to the weather bureau. They had a pan for evaporation. They had good hook gauges that you could measure accurately the top of the surface of the water on these pans and so forth. They were willing to help us with that in any way possible.

We made lots of mistakes. The first three or four small areas, we had barges with these pans mounted. I did change the normal size of the pans that the weather bureau used. I made mine 10 inches deep, a galvanized pan, and 6 feet in diameter. These pans were anchored in small barges. But we found out that that wasn't going to work at all, because with practically no wind here, you still had a pretty good wave rolling down in Lake Mead. After a lot of unfortunate attempts at devising some way to get a pan floating on Lake Mead, we finally found a method that worked very fine.

I conceived the idea [of] a great big float out there made of timbers. We bought a 120-horsepower diesel 42-inch tugboat. It was called the *St. Thomas*, after the town that was submerged under the lake. We used it to tow our enormous floats around. In the center of that, you had a small platform or a small section of lighter material, and then right in the center of that was our pan. You could set the hook gauge plates on the edge and read that to a thousandth of a foot.

When we finally wound up, on the basis of just a little over three years that we made those tests, that evaporation from the surface of the lake was just a very slight amount less than seven feet per year.

ELTON GARRETT

[Leo Dunbar] was handling the evaporation measuring system for the Bureau of Reclamation. I got from him a story about how much water evaporates from that lake in a day. I translated that into horsepower if it went through the machinery at the dam: here's how much horsepower we are losing by evaporation every day. I even had a little illustration of a horse flying through the air, [representing] the horsepower that was lost. The Bureau of Reclamation man got in touch because I published this story, which made it seem the Bureau of Reclamation was inefficient in letting all this water evaporate. My ears were red, but I didn't get fired. It settled down after a while.

By the summer of 1935, the dam structure was nearly complete. The last section to be filled was the slot, where the concrete-cooling apparatus had been installed.

NEIL HOLMES

That dam was many months being completed. There was a slot in the center that all of these pipes, this refrigerated water, was taken into. This slot, as they called it, was eight foot [wide] in the center. It had to be poured later on.

All this cooling pipe couldn't be taken out. There was miles and miles and miles of that pipe left in there. They had to plug that up. Then they could pour this slot up so far. They started in on one and pumped it [full of grout] until it started coming out the return pipe.

HARRY HALL

The slot was in the center of the dam. That's where the control for the valves for the headers for the cooling water piping was controlled from. As they raised the placement of concrete, the cooling pipe was also raised. Consequently the slot was the last to be concreted in. The width of it was not quite the width of the dam, but it had access to all the blocks. So it could be almost 50 feet from either edge. As the dam comes up, it has a slope on it, so it would be hidden more and more as it increased in elevation. It was not completed when [the dam] was dedicated by Franklin Roosevelt. Part of it was still open. It wasn't very wide—10 or 12 feet.

Shortly before the slot was finally filled in, Alfred Baker's brother was one of the first three men to cross the dam.

ALFRED BAKER

My brother was carpenter foreman on the dam. He built this form, which was quite complicated, and it was used from the powerhouse roof to the top of the dam, which saved the company thousands of dollars. He was a wonderful mechanic.

The dam was finished, but there was what we called the slot. It was six foot wide, and it went from the bottom, from the foundation to the top, in order to give sides expansion and contraction until they got a certain temperature. Then it could be filled. So the dam was built to the top, the roadway. My gang laid timbers across the slot so that these three men could ride in a pickup across the dam. They were Mr. Crowe, Woody Williams, and B. H. Baker.

As work on the dam wound down in 1935, Six Companies began laying off workers. By summer the work force was small enough for the company to eliminate an entire shift. But officials handled the change poorly, and between 12 and 26 July 1935, workers staged a final strike.

MARION ALLEN

The strike was in 1935. This fellow Malden was a company man out of San Francisco. Nobody knew who he was. He wasn't a regular construction stiff. He could have been with Kahn and MacDonald, or he was with some of these deals anyway. This Malden was the kind which caused the strong organization of the union; he was one of that type. A man wasn't very important, you know. He was in charge while Crowe was gone. Crowe was planning jobs ahead all the time, and figuring jobs for the company, so he was gone quite a bit. Woody Williams was gone by that time. And Frank Bryant, [who] was next to Woody, was a superintendent. But they were all gone; these old-timers were all gone. They'd taken on other jobs.

I'd got a week off and went down to Los Angeles. We'd just come back from a vacation. I went to work on the dam. I got down there. There were only a few people, a couple of dozen people working on the dam. "What's going on?"

"Well, there's a strike. Didn't you know there's a strike on?"

No, I didn't know. So I came back up and got off of the bus, and here's all these guys coming around [asking me], "What the hell you doing down there working?"

"Why didn't you let me know? I got in last night."

"We're on strike."

"What's it about?"

We'd work from 7:30 to 3:30, which was your eight hours. They took the graveyard shift off. This guy decided there's only two shifts, there's no excuse, so they got to work another half-hour. Anyhow, this Malden wasn't very well liked to start with. He was the one that took this half-hour away. That's what all this '35 strike was about, that half-hour's time.

But here's the whole crew, and it was about the most successful strike I've ever seen in my life. I think everybody kind of enjoyed a vacation. The lake was up. We went swimming every day. That was one of the things that made it nice. So we weren't a bit anxious to go back to work, or I wasn't.

Crowe was gone for about a week. So while we were off on strike, he came back, and oh, man. "What are you boys doing?"

"We're out on strike."

He had to talk to a bunch of us. "You know we're about through here. We'll be through here in a short time. No use of you losing all this work now."

We decided we want this. Then they decided they wanted a dollar for a carpenter or a skilled worker, a dollar an hour—electricians and so on. They finally decided: "We'll settle up," he says. I forget who they picked anyhow, but I know that Crowe represented the company, and we picked Parson Tom down here, which was the parson of the [Grace] Community Church. They picked somebody else. Now who the third member was, I couldn't tell you. They went to work. The first thing they set up [was] a dollar an hour for skilled labor.

"That's all right," Crowe says. "That's fine. On the next project, it will be a dollar an hour."

So that's about all you could do. We've only got a few weeks left. It turned out about a year by the time we got six months. That was what they decided on that. Crowe says, "We'll go back to the seven and a half hours, same as always. We'll put that back." He did that immediately when he got here. He didn't even wait for that.

So that was the strike. When they decided this a dollar an hour and took this off, why, we went back to work. But when this six months appointment came up in the Bureau of Reclamation the following year, we got the a dollar an hour. So we gained.

Six Companies had good reason to reach a quick settlement. Formal dedication of the dam was scheduled for 30 September, just two months after the end of the strike, and ceremonies were to include an address by President Franklin D. Roosevelt.

WALKER R. YOUNG

The celebration was set; all the arrangements were made that Franklin D. Roosevelt and his staff were coming out to dedicate the dam September 30, 1935. We were told that the ceremonies would be held at the top of the dam at two o'clock in the [afternoon]. Platforms had been built, and parking areas were scarce down there. We were preparing for, we thought, an estimated 20,000 people. They came by train in those days. I received the telegram from Harold Ickes, who was secretary of the interior and the official bringing this party out here. He was, of course, charged with [making] all those arrangements. He told me to meet him on the train in Las Vegas, which I did.[2]

The interesting part was that a political situation arose. There was Nevada senator Key Pittman, there was the governor, there were senators from other states, all of them claiming to have a great deal to do with the appropriation of money for the construction of the dam. They didn't know who it was they were going to pick to ride with [the president who was so] politically popular—nobody! So [the secretary who] took care of all the details of Mr. and Mrs. Roosevelt's traveling finally came to me and asked me if I would ride with President Roosevelt and Mrs. Roosevelt to the site and back in their car. The party started out. Mr. and Mrs. Roosevelt, their chauffer, [Harold Ickes,] and a Secret Service man, and I were in the car. I sat between President and Mrs. Roosevelt.

On the way out [Ickes] told me the ceremony would be at eleven o'clock. I'd been planning the whole thing with the idea of starting at two o'clock. What happened [is that] back in Washington they had forgotten the three-hour differential between Eastern time and our time, so it upset everything. At least 20,000 people would be there on the top of the damsite, which would cause confusion. Harold says, "We don't care about the 20,000 people; we're talking about the 20 million who are going to listen to us on radio."

A lot of people didn't get there at all. They were still on the way to Boulder City.

HAZEL ALLEN

President Roosevelt came through in an open-air car, and, of course, we [waitresses] all rushed to the window to look at him. He was waving his hat. It was really something.

Dedication day crowds at Boulder Dam, 30 September 1935

Franklin Roosevelt dedicating Boulder Dam, 30 September 1935. Note the support frame at the president's hips.

MARY ANN MERRILL

I saw part of [the dedication]. That was the day that I quit working at the root beer stand, because I'd had promised to have that day off and they said, "No, you have to work." I said, "No, I don't have to work. I quit."

DOROTHY NUNLEY

I had to work that day and didn't take time off to go down. But Mrs. Roosevelt took a tour of the mess hall, and she came through the laundry and looked it over too. She spoke to everybody before she went on down to the dam.

MADELINE KNIGHTEN

We walked up to the park up here, the one that goes around in front of the Administration Building. The car came up the curb and stopped there. We got up there in time to be in a good spot close to the curb. Close by us was some very old little old lady, a tiny little frail thing. You could see she simply worshiped the president. You could see that she was just absolutely overwhelmed. She started out toward him with her hands up. These huge, big Secret Service men swarmed down off the sides of that car. Cars in those days had runningboards. They simply swarmed down off. They just enveloped her. They carried her back, and put her back. They didn't let anyone, of course, get near. But that little old lady, she only wanted to say something to the president.

Mrs. Roosevelt was there too, in the car, and Mr. Harold Ickes. He was not afraid of anybody by any means whatever. They started on down to the dam. We ran back and got in our car and started down to the dam.

LEO DUNBAR

I got involved a little bit when he came through Boulder City because we knew that the president was going to stop in front of the Administration Building. All government employees had been assigned parking places down in the dam area. I said, "I know where my parking place is, so we'll drive my car to the end of Denver Street and we'll leave it right on the corner there."

I figured we'd pick up as the crowd started coming down [to the dam]; we'd get in line someplace.

Here was the Secret Service coming with their cars, and the president. Every limousine in town at least was in use and probably a lot from around the country. After the presidential party passed, they stopped everybody from pulling in behind him. Not knowing, I pulled in behind all those black limousines with my old Chrysler 70, and we headed down for the dam. Hundreds of people had lined the road. Cars were parked on both sides of the road for at least a mile this side of the dam. I tried two or three places; I wanted to pull off. Officials on the highway wouldn't let me—they made me go right on.

MADELINE KNIGHTEN

Going down to the dam, the highway between Boulder City and the dam was bumper to bumper with cars, all the way across. It was supposed to be a two-lane highway, but I think the cars were three across going down. Everyone from all over the country who could get to Boulder had come to that dedication because the president was going to be here. Then we went on down to the dedication of the dam.

WALKER R. YOUNG

There was great confusion, because all our rangers and two or 300 soldiers [were] down there to guide the traffic. We finally got [Roosevelt] down there the best we could. We pointed out the reservoir, which was a beautiful sight looking down from the top of Hemenway Wash—beautiful blue water. With the mountains it was a beautiful sight, and Mrs. Roosevelt was quite impressed with that.

CURLEY FRANCIS

All of us truck drivers and everything were federal marshals. They gave us a certificate and a badge and they wanted you to wear a pistol. I said, "No way. I'm not going to do anything like that." Most of us directed traffic.

LEROY BURT

They drove him in a touring car. And they had a pipe from the big 30-foot penstock pipes out there, and they had a ramp up, and they drove him through this pipe in his big car and then on down to the dam.

DEAN PULSIPHER

I helped put that pipe up on the road so Roosevelt could drive through it. We worked a week to get this big penstock out there. We just pulled it out for him to drive through it and to take some pictures. I never got a picture of him going through it. I was standing there watching him at the time too. I was right there when it happened. And it took us a week to get [the pipe] back in after we got through with it.

Everybody was excited, and there was a lot of activity there. My wife's uncle, Ron Perry, was driving a big Cadillac for Roosevelt. Of course, we had two thrills: my wife's uncle driving the car and Roosevelt sitting in there smoking that long holder for the cigarettes.

The situation at the dam was pandemonium.

MARION ALLEN

We pulled down and parked off on the side somewhere. It was jammed there. We went down there and stood. My daughter is a pretty husky gal. I tell her my arm still hurts from holding her up so [she] could see Roosevelt. Of course, he was next to God to me. My father never did like him. That's like so many people getting mad if you mention Roosevelt or Hoover, either one.

I think about it today. Here he came down this road in this open car, Mrs. Roosevelt and him a-wavin' to everybody. They had dozens of kids out here, a whole row of kids. I had three kids with me and a neighbor's kids. This lady swears that Roosevelt shook her hand. But I can't remember if he did. But he was a-wavin', and we were about five or six feet from him. [There were] two Secret Service men walking along each side of the car, standing on the runningboard. Think about now, there'd be an army out there!

TEX NUNLEY

They built a platform down there for the president to be on to dedicate the dam. It was people, people, people, and then some more people. It was just a big, big crowd.

MADELINE KNIGHTEN

They had a big wooden platform built out where the observation point is, just a little bit across from where the winged figures are now. The president and his entourage were there on the platform. They had a little podium for him to stand by. And, of course, the poor man had to lock his braces in order to stand at all. He stood up, and then his braces were locked, and he placed himself before this podium and talked. Of course, they had loudspeakers to carry the sound all around. We were not too far. They had lots of chairs put out, and people stood where they couldn't get a seat. But we were fortunate enough to have a good place to stand. Harold Ickes sat there in his chair behind the president and jingled his change, dropped it on that wooden floor. Oh, I wanted to choke that man. Oh, I would liked to have poked his head with my thimble. To sit there and drop his change on the floor while the president was trying to make his dedication speech.

TOMMY NELSON

I was real proud to have been part of that ceremony. I happened to be sitting up on top of that dam, playing in a band. There was Bill Dunn, Leonard Atkison, myself, and the late Otto Littler, a drummer by the name of Lou James who cut meat for Manix Department Store. We were playing in this band, and my mother sang a duet with the late Serene Ziemer, [whose husband] was a [Bureau of] Reclamation ranger back through the years. So that was really something. To hear Franklin Delano Roosevelt stand there and say, "In fifty years, this will be paid for with interest."[3] And he said all the wheel pits down there would be full of generators. It was just wonderful, everything he had to say. And how true it had all been. That baby is the father of all the dams, and it's paid its way all the way through.

DEAN PULSIPHER

That was quite impressive, hearing him dedicate that dam. After that we went right back to work, moving that pipe again.

When Roosevelt headed back to Las Vegas after dedicating the dam, several Las Vegas business leaders and politicians wanted him to see a road the government had built on Mount Charleston at the northwest end of the Las Vegas Valley. The poorly planned side trip was nearly disastrous.

HUGH SHAMBERGER

The WPA had built a road off the [Lee] Canyon road up in the Charleston Mountains, along the side of the mountain. Some way or another they enticed President Roosevelt to inspect this road. Jim Cashman furnished an open Buick touring car and Archie Grant a Lincoln. I remember seeing the party starting out from Las Vegas with the president; Jim was driving. This road that the WPA boys built was a narrow road and ended up butting right against a mountain wall. In other words, they could go only so far, and then they stopped.

JOHN CAHLAN

Senator Key Pittman, the senior senator from Nevada and a powerful figure in Washington, insisted that the president must see what the WPA had accomplished in Nevada. So nothing would do but that the president should go. I don't know that he wanted to go up, but the people wanted to take him up to see it. And he was not averse to going, because he had a couple of hours to waste before his train left.

They ducked [the president's Secret] Service protection outfit and took off in a motor caravan to Lee Canyon. They drove to the end of the road, and there was no way to turn the automobile around. They were stuck up in the mountains. Mrs. Roosevelt didn't know where [the president] was; the Secret Service people didn't know where he was. So for about an hour and a half, the United States didn't have any president.

Finally the chauffer of the automobile said, "If you'll get the president out of the automobile, I'll get it turned around." Because of the president's handicap, this was an embarrassment to everyone. They got him out, sat him on one of the big rocks out there. This driver that they had jackassed that [car] around until he finally got it turned around and headed in the right direction.

Well, the Secret Service people who were waiting in Las Vegas (while others went with Roosevelt to the mountains) were just sweating themselves out real good. They didn't know whether Roosevelt was at the bottom of a canyon in the mountains up there or what the dickens had happened, and there was no telephone or way to find out. After about an hour and a half of waiting, a couple of them started out toward the canyon. But they met the caravan coming down from the mountains about 10 miles out, so they turned around and came back and loaded Roosevelt aboard the train and sent him on his way.

All the reporters from around the country naturally were speculating on what a real big headline it would be if Roosevelt were killed in a car crash up in the mountains of Lee Canyon, where he should not have been. The Secret Service had been in the area for many days to check for security on the president's every move, but nobody checked Lee Canyon, where it never was intended he would go. It was a great relief to everyone when that train pulled out of the Las Vegas station with the president safely aboard.

Work on the powerhouses, the switchyards, and the transmission lines continued in the year following Roosevelt's visit. Power was first generated at Hoover Dam on 11 September 1936, nearly a year after the dedication. Los Angeles received its first electricity from the dam on 9 October 1936. Both Carl Merrill and Dean Pulsipher were involved in construction of the power-generating facilities.

CARL MERRILL

When you had the walls of the powerhouse up and started to put the roof on—and I think I'm right on this, if my memory serves me—the roof is in three layers. The first layer is a layer of concrete with two curtains of steel in it. It's about 10 to 12 inches thick. On top of this there's a layer of 3-inch rock. It must be 12 inches thick or so. I'm just guessing at these figures. Then you had another layer of concrete with steel in it, two curtains of steel. This must be 6 or 8 inches thick. On top of this you had a layer of inch-and-a-half rock about 6 inches thick. Then to top the whole thing off, they had another layer of concrete about 3 or 3½ inches thick. On top of this there's a layer of sand, and on top of this there's a layer of tar. They were bomb-proofing it so that bombs wouldn't penetrate the powerhouses.

DEAN PULSIPHER

When they built the dam, they had a mass of copper, just massed in there about every foot apart, for grounding all the generators, all the high lines. It's buried down there in the concrete at the base of the dam. Later on I helped build all them switchyards down there. Almost every one of them—the city of Los Angeles, the Metropolitan Water District switchyard, the Edison Company. When I got [to be] a journeyman, I started to work at $12 a day. That was more money than I had ever made in my life, and that was a lot of money in them days. The Bureau of Reclamation built the switchyards up there, put the towers in. Ben Fleury was a foreman down there for the switchyards, over the iron workers.

When I got through at the switchyards, the first line that we put above the dam was a 138,000-volt line, and that was the first one. We would take a boat across the lake. The lake was pretty well started to fill then. We'd go across the lake, and we'd take a hemp line—that was regular rope, about three-quarter-inch rope. We'd take that across, and we had a big Cat over on the opposite side. We'd put this rope on to that Cat, and we'd bring the hard line over, the half-inch hard line. Then we'd bring the electric circuits over. That's the way we got it over there. We worked on that line there for several months, to get that first line above there.

The city of Los Angeles and the Edison Company was putting their lines in—mostly the city of Los Angeles. They would bring them into the switch-yard, and the Bureau of Reclamation would take them from there down to the units. We did all the work on the units. At that time they were doing the contract work, installing the units, installing all the equipment on the roof and the towers and everything.

The city of Los Angeles had three lines going from Boulder Dam down to Los Angeles. That copper in there is what they call tongue-and-groove copper. It's about an inch and an eighth in diameter. It's tongue-and-groove, just like you see [in] the old flooring. The tongue-and-grooving is round, and the harder you pull on that, the harder it pulls together.

The final details completed on the dam were its decorative features: the plaques, bas-reliefs, the Winged Figures of the Republic, and a terrazzo star map.

281

HARRY HALL

Oskar J. [W.] Hansen was a world-renowned artist. He cast all the winged figures and designed the base for the winged figures. Over each elevator tower there are also some figures there. All those are his. He was a very hard man to get along with. Oskar, just like so many artists, had an artistic temperament. He didn't want anybody standing around watching what he was doing. He'd run 'em off pretty fast.

NADEAN VOSS

The thing I quite often remember, Oskar Hansen, who did the statues down at the dam, told Dave[4] that he could have used him for the model of the figure that stands above the dial indicating by stars the time the dam was [dedicated] on the Nevada end of the dam. That always stayed in my mind, all the years that Oskar was here.

HARRY HALL

Leland Robinson ran the instruments for [Hansen] to locate the stars and the constellations on the star map. He had drawings that showed the declination and the angle between each one. Leland would turn the angles where he'd measure the distance. They would be set, and then the terrazzo was placed to conform with the star map.

However, in years later the temperature and the terrazzo didn't get along too well. So the terrazzo began to crack and had to be removed. Oskar J. Hansen was right back on the job. He didn't want anybody else fooling around with his star map. So they put another surface around there. There was a different mix. So far it's worked out OK.

With the end of the Hoover Dam project approaching, workers and Six Companies officials alike looked to the future. Six Companies bid for the contract to build the next major Bureau of Reclamation project, Grand Coulee Dam on the Columbia River in Washington. The stakes were high, for a successful bid would have provided jobs for many Hoover Dam workers.

ALICE HAMILTON

I helped with the bids for Grand Coulee. All of the office help was called out to help with the bids. We worked all night. I can remember the sun coming up as we left the office after completing the bids for Grand Coulee. Six Companies lost. They had failed in their bid for Grand Coulee. Their bid was simply too high. They were very much disappointed. And, of course, the employees were terribly disappointed too, because we would have gone with the companies. As far as I can remember, that was the end of the Six Companies as a unity.

Six Companies continued issuing pink slips as the company completed its work. Workers seldom knew from one day to the next how long they would have work, and an atmosphere of uncertainty pervaded the final months of the project.

MARY EATON

A lot of people were moving, going to other projects where they were building a dam or whatever. It was kind of a sad time, because many of your friends were leaving. You didn't know, of course, how long you were going to be there yourself, [or] if you were going to work tomorrow. My husband would come home from work, and he'd say, "Well, I worked today. I don't know about tomorrow." So there was insecurity.

ERMA GODBEY

Even before our dam was finished, they were beginning to build other dams. There was Parker Dam, and there was the All-American Canal. There was Shasta Dam. Lots of people left here and went to Parker or to Shasta, or the All-American Canal, and then on up to Grand Coulee, and worked on all these other dams.

HAZEL ALLEN

From here I went to Vancouver. They were building Grand Coulee Dam. I had [a] job waiting, and I thought, well, I better go. So I went to Grand Coulee. They had a café in Mason City across the river, and I worked there for quite a while. Then after that I went to Shasta Dam. I saw Shasta Dam from about the first bucket of concrete to the last one.

TEX NUNLEY

The old-timers, they were leaving. It was sort of like breaking up your own family.

On 1 March 1936 Six Companies turned Hoover Dam over to the Bureau of Reclamation. Some workers were able to get jobs with the government, and a few fortunate employees never missed a day of work.

JOE KINE

When they made the change, when Six Companies stepped down for the government to take over, I was working on the intake tower putting up those cylinder gates and putting the things on to raise it and lower it. The [government] inspector over that job was E. H. Dana. He took over the whole business as a foreman; he finally became superintendent of operations and maintenance. So he just took us all right over. I never missed a day; I never missed even one day.

LEROY BURT

When Six Companies finished, I thought I was going to leave here. I didn't want to stay in this desert. I wanted to get out of here. So I sent my wife to Salt Lake City, where we came from, and I stayed behind to sell the trailer house and I was going to join her later.

In the meantime the fellow that was in charge of the electrical department came down and said, "I understand that you know something about refrigeration."

I said, "Yeah, I served an apprenticeship on refrigeration."

He said, "How would you like to come to work for the Bureau of Reclamation?"

I said, "Fine."

So he said, "I'll find out for sure, so you come up to my house and talk to me tomorrow night."

His name was Wolf. So when I went up there, I knocked on the door and I said, "Is Mr. Fox here?"

And he said, "Just call me Lobo." He had worked in Guatemala several years, and he could speak Spic pretty good. So anyway, I went to work for the Bureau of Reclamation as a helper, an electrician's helper, and I took care of the air conditioning in the Ad[ministration] Building and in the government houses. I took care of all the refrigerators and stuff that was in there.

While some of the guys stayed on the dam, I came uptown. I was out maybe three weeks before I went back to work again. I worked up here on power distribution for 25 years. I didn't go back down to Hoover Dam until after the city was incorporated [4 January 1960].

TOMMY NELSON

The contractor, Six Companies, Inc., [was] obligated to tear down some of the transmission lines and remove some of that material. So I was driving a truck for a lineman by the name of Ted Hoppes. I stayed with Six Companies until March; they were all through after that.

Then I moved over with the United States government. Fortunately, I got into the electrical end down there. We had no such thing as an apprenticeship back in those days. You could have been a helper down there for 11 years and maybe never been elevated. Some of these old journeymen were pretty jealous of their trade. If they had something a little intricate to do, they'd run you off to get a breast pump or some crazy thing, and when you'd come back, they'd have it all finished. So you learned catch-as-catch-can.

Marion Allen got a job with the government, but it lasted for only a short time. Then, like many others before him, he moved on, looking for a new line of work.

MARION ALLEN

I was laid off from the company. I was coming up after we got our slip on the dam, and a guy was standing there to meet me, a fellow by the name of Charlie Hughes. He said, "I want you down on graveyard on the powerhouse in the morning." "Well, don't I get a day off?" So I went right to work. I worked on the terrazzo down in the powerhouse and the tile in the [visitor's] galleries.

I didn't want to leave, but in the meantime I got to selling insurance to make a little butter on the bread. The Occidental Life agent came up here, and he talked me into going to San Bernardino. I had been doing pretty good selling to construction stiffs, and out to the mines out at Jean and Blue Diamond. I could talk to construction stiffs and sell insurance. He said, "There's only 40,000 people in the whole state of Nevada." He said, "There's 40,000 people there in San Bernardino County and in Riverside County right close to you. Just think how much money you'll make." That was another one of those fairy tales. I got down there, and there was 10,000 agents too! And no money. The money was all up here on the construction jobs.

As workers left and the population of Boulder City dwindled, people wondered whether the town would survive. The government intended the town to be merely a temporary construction camp, and the contract under which Six Companies built the dam required that houses erected for construction workers, as well as the dormitories, the offices, the mess hall, the recreation hall, and the company store, be dismantled at the end of the project.

ELTON GARRETT

We had a population of around 7,000 in this town while dam construction was going on. When the dam was finished, the population shrank to about 2,500.

JOE KINE

When the Six Companies took the contract, they were supposed to take all of these houses down and leave it just like it was—a desert. That was the contract. They didn't expect these houses to last more than five years. They were going to tear them down.

MADELINE KNIGHTEN

The Six Companies' part of the dam was supposed to take eight years. In their contract with the government, they were required to tear everything out to the ground and leave no trace of their buildings here. Of course, all their big dormitories and the big mess hall, all that sort of thing was taken down and completely obliterated. They started tearing the Six Companies houses out way out at the end of town.

DOROTHY NUNLEY

It was supposed to have been just a skeleton crew left here. The brick homes that had been built for the government workers were supposed to be permanent. But the frame ones were all going to be torn down. I think the [Los Angeles] Department of Water and Power was going to have a crew here also, but they thought it was going to be just a very small place.

WILLIAM FRENCH

In the very beginning they only intended that the houses on Denver Street would be occupied, and that one or two buildings were left for management. Everything would go automatic on the dam; they wouldn't have such large maintenance groups as we have now. They were going to cut it down, make all operations push-button.

MARY EATON

The government had really planned that there was only going to be about 100 men, and maybe that included some of the families. Only a few people were to stay here and run the powerhouse and the dam. These one-room and two-room houses, most of those were torn down and moved away. It had been planned that even the three-room houses would be torn down.

But there was so much need for housing that they finally relented and let the people buy them. Everybody was wanting to buy a house, especially those who had gone to work for the government in the meantime.

WILMA COOPER

The houses all up on the hill was for the bosses. But for us peons there wasn't anywhere to live.

MADELINE KNIGHTEN

People were crying to the government to allow them to buy the houses so they could have a place to live. So the government made arrangements with the Six Companies to sell the houses to people. Houses sold for $250. That was if they were in good condition. If they had been kicked around too much by the people who lived in them, then they sold even down to $75.

THEODORE GARRETT

The Six Companies housing was put up for sale. There were three types of houses, with three prices. A one-room house was $100; a two-room house, $200; a three-room house was $300. They moved out pretty rapidly. Everything south of New Mexico Street was removed, either torn down or moved out.[5] The houses in the other areas, people bought those and some of them are still being used after being brought up to certain minimum specifications.

MARY EATON

[We] paid cash—$250. We lived there about a year or two and put linoleum on the floor. But we didn't do any remodeling or anything while we were in there, because my husband was wanting to get a government house. In the meantime he had gone to work for the government. When the dam construction ended, he wanted to stay here and work for the government if it was at all possible. He thought if he were in a government house, he'd be more assured that he had a job.

The Eatons finally got the government house they had waited for.

MARY EATON

He worked for the government by this time. They had a list. There were no strings attached. You could just rent a government house if your name came up. [It had] a Pullman-type kitchen, a living room, one bedroom with bath, and a sleeping porch.

It was a frame house. They'd build a brick house, and then a frame house, in between two brick houses. The plan was that when Boulder City no longer needed all these houses, they'd take down those frame houses. But they've never torn one down. We felt more secure in our job.

JOE KINE

When the government took over and the Six Companies moved out in 1936, we bought this house that we're living in now on Avenue C. Paid the whole sum of $250 for it. Of course, we've remodeled and we needed to pay more than that for our electrical box that we put on the outside of the house—we had to pay $265 for our electrical box. That really made me wake up to the fact that things are really much, much higher now, and, of course, who would think that you could buy a house for $250?

The decision to sell Six Companies houses did not guarantee the survival of Boulder City, and for several years few believed the town would last.

ALICE HAMILTON

We were going to buy one of the Six Companies houses. We had one picked out, and we were going to pay $250 for it. One of the engineers came to me and told me I was very, very foolish to buy one of the houses, because [Boulder City] would be nothing but a ghost town in three or four months. Of course, the ones that did buy were the lucky ones. I can remember I just filled in a paper and specified which house I wanted, and that was it.

TOMMY NELSON

Upon completion of the dam, my brother, who was a secretary for Mr. Ely, asked Mr. Ely about buying a couple of these houses. You know what Mr. Ely told my brother? He said no, that would be a bad investment. He said, "You may be forced to remove them from the property. This is not going to be a town." How wrong he was. It is a town.

MARY EATON

I remember when we built our house in 1940, they said, "What do you mean, building a home? Don't you know this is going to be a ghost town?" Everybody said that. They were talking even then that Boulder City would be a ghost town, because I remember people asking me that. They never dreamed of all this that was to follow, that there would be the lake and all the activity around the lake. Evidently there were more jobs at the dam than they realized there would be, and the [National] Park Service and the Bureau of Mines. But people just flocked here. They loved it.

As Boulder City struggled to survive, residents found ways to supplement their uncertain incomes.

LEROY BURT

There's a bunch of us people that worked for the Bureau [of Reclamation] at the time that Six Companies was selling all these houses, and they were tearing out a lot of the houses further out to the east. Marlis Toney, myself, Emmett Randall, and my brother Elmo took the contract to take all these [electric] poles down for the material and the hardware that was on there. All the poles were dry-rotted, and the wires were still on them. We'd hook a truck onto the first pole and start going, and a lot of those poles would just snap off. All you had to do was just take the hardware off them. We got the wire, the copper—we got all that stuff. Between the four of us, after we took all those poles and all the hardware, we sold them to the Nevada Power Company and we made $400 apiece. That was a good chunk of money.

EDNA FRENCH

I must tell you how we, as housewives, were able to get a little extra money. There were only two motels in town. Many people would come to visit the dam, and they didn't have no place to stay. Someone thought of the idea that maybe the housewives would like to double up a little bit and rent out a room. So many of us did that. It was a means of making a little extra money that many of us appreciated. We could get $3 a night for our bedrooms. There was people that would come and rent rooms out of the homes. The way you would get these visitors, Mr. Meisner [owner of the Lake Auto Court] would phone and ask, "Do you have a room? Would you like to have someone tonight? Because I'm full."

I did that for several years. We made some very, very nice friends that way. People came in, and you would feel like they were your guests. In several cases the friendships continued on for several years for some of us, which was really very nice. We took care of many, many people that came to town that would have had to have slept out in their cars because Vegas was full, and there was no place else to go except someone's home.

Tourism soon became an important part of the Boulder City economy.

ELTON GARRETT

The newspaper in Salt Lake had a headline when the dam was finished: "Boulder City Being Razed."

Paul Webb, called Jim Webb, got into building activity, organized the Boulder City Development Company to build homes and duplexes. I got him and Earl Brothers to a breakfast one time, and I said, "Hey, we should publicize the fact this town is not going to die." I said, "Why don't I get out a little weekly publication that says Boulder City's going to live in spite of what the Salt Lake paper says about us about to die as a town?" They said yes, they would support it.

We got excited about it and started to yell to the world that Boulder City is not going to quit; we're going to start growing again. Every week for half a year, I put out a little one-page bulletin like publication called the *Boulder Dam Challenge* with short items telling how Boulder City was doing things, was going to live and go on and on. The Bureau of Mines was going to set up here. In 1936 I had a short story that Uncle Sam was going to start this research center for metallurgy.[6] Also the National Park Service was scheduled to start a recreation area.[7] I had a little item about that. These little items, every week, went for half a year to a mailing list of 1200 businesses around the Pacific Southwest. There were about 800 that I had printed that we passed around to businesses in Boulder City. This was one activity that pointed ahead to the fact that this town, with tourism, with the guide service, had the impulses to go ahead.

It gradually grew, and tourism did become important. The tours of the dam and the tours on the lake both enhanced the business community enough that the town gave promise of being able to survive, and increasingly, gradually, it built up.

Boulder City survived and flourished. Hoover Dam not only provided electricity to surrounding states but became one of the Southwest's major tourist attractions. Hoover Dam power was important for America's wartime industry. For the people who built the dam and Boulder City, the construction years provide nostalgic memories.

EDNA FRENCH

It was really the friendliest place that we had ever lived. The people were so considerate of each other. If they knew that they could help in any way, or if they had anything that they could bring to you, they were just more than glad to do so.

PERLE GARRETT

With all these hardships Boulder City was a very happy town in those days. The people were so friendly, and being so much younger than we old-timers are now made for a wonderful time.

TOMMY NELSON

I was making a repair one day on one of the parapet lights up on top on the Arizona side [of the dam]. Two fellows were there, one fellow giving the other fellow a big snow job about the beautiful rockwork that faces the

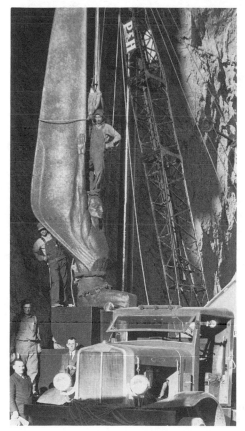

Tourists at Lake Mead View Point overlooking the future bed of Lake Mead, about 1933 (*above*); Hoisting the Winged Figures of the Republic onto their diorite bases on the crest of Hoover Dam, 8 November 1937 (*left*)

highway coming down on the canyon wall. He was telling this fellow, "Indians put that in."

I knew he was far wrong. I said to myself, "I've got to correct him, but I'll do it in a diplomatic manner." So I walked over to the drinking fountain in a few minutes and I faked a drink of water, and I said, "Sir, I heard you make a statement to your friend here about Indians putting in that rockwork." I said, "First of all, I must agree with you"—before I put the stiletto to him, you know—"it definitely has an Indian look. However, sir, for the correct information, that rockwork was put in by people from the Czechoslovakian countries, most of them."

So he says, "Sure looks Indian, doesn't it?"

JOE KINE

I was in the Seabees. When I was working at Camp Perry, out in the swamps, getting rid of the mosquitoes, we sat down to take five, and one boy got some of these younger kids around him and he told them about working on the dam. He told them, "I used to back the mules and the carts over, and when they'd fall down, I'd just go and get me another mule and another cart." Then he said, "They buried men in that cement; they don't know how many people they got buried in that cement, they poured it so fast."

He never had been out here. So when he got all through and everything, I said, "I worked out there from the very beginning to the end. They never had a mule down there."

LEROY BURT

When people come, when I have friends come, and they want to see it, I take them down. I don't take them down for their benefit; mainly it's for mine. I have a lot of memories of all the places I worked on and everything I did down there. It was a beautiful place to work after it was finished. There was nobody rushing you, and you had all the time you wanted.

DOROTHY NUNLEY

In the old days it was depression times. Everybody was in the same boat. We were all looking for our next meal, practically, when we came here. It made

Dinky skinners, about 1933

a different feeling amongst people. They were friendlier and closer, and they'd do for each other. Now it just seems like it's more like a city, where people don't even know their neighbors half the time. There's not very many old ones left.

TEX NUNLEY

I don't know my neighbors right across the street there. I go to Safeway down there. Once in a while I'll see someone there that I know, but most of the time I go, I don't see anyone. I used to. Everyone. "Hi, there," across the street and all. It's no more like that. I don't imagine there's over 50 old-timers that were here in '31 that's still here in Boulder City. You go to the reunion there [the Thirty-Oners' annual reunion], I don't hardly know anyone. I [might] just as well be down in L.A. to some doings.

TOMMY NELSON

But you know, condensing it down to a few quick words, there's lots of nostalgia down there. That dam was a part of us. We were just young fellows, and look at us now.

Conclusion

President Roosevelt's dedication address in September 1935 (see appendix B) was a milestone but did not mark the end of the project. Work remained on the powerhouses, the dam itself needed finishing touches, and the reservoir had just begun filling. In February 1936 the Bureau of Reclamation named the reservoir Lake Mead in honor of Commissioner Elwood Mead, who had died a week earlier. Secretary of the Interior Harold Ickes officially accepted the dam and the nearly completed power plant on behalf of the United States on 1 March 1936, thereby terminating the contract with Six Companies. In August the Bureau of Reclamation relinquished control of most of the reservation lands to the National Park Service, retaining only the dam and Boulder City. The former reservation became the Lake Mead National Recreation Area.

While Boulder City's population dropped from a high of more than 7,000 at the peak of dam construction in 1934 to less than 4,000 in the years preceding World War II, it never became the mere maintenance community the Bureau of Reclamation planned it to be. The government and the private power companies that operated Hoover Dam remained an important presence in Boulder City. In September 1935 the Civilian Conservation Corps set up two companies in Boulder City in dormitories that had housed Six Companies workers. In July 1936 the U.S. Bureau of Mines established a pilot plant in buildings it bought from Six Companies to conduct electrometallurgical experiments with Hoover Dam power. The National Park Service moved its headquarters to town to administer the new recreation area. The Bureau of Power and Light of the city of Los Angeles and the Southern California Edison Company brought hundreds of employees to Boulder City as the dam's generators were installed and went on-line. They built dozens of houses and occupied buildings abandoned by the Six Companies and the Babcock & Wilcox Company.

World War II brought a boom to Boulder City, as the developing war industries in southern California increased demands for Hoover Dam power. In 1941 the government's Defense Plants Corporation built Basic Magne-

Hoover Dam completed, Gene Segerblom, about 1940

sium, the world's largest magnesium refining plant, northwest of Railroad Pass because Hoover Dam power was available and water could be drawn from Lake Mead. The government built two hundred new houses and twenty-six apartments in Boulder City in 1941 and 1942 to accommodate new workers at the dam and Basic Magnesium.

The war also posed security problems, since the government feared that the dam might be an inviting target for Japan. Camp Williston, built early in 1941 on the outskirts of Boulder City as an encampment for military police, now housed soldiers assigned to guard the dam. Residents remember being herded across the dam in convoys, and today they still point to an abandoned machine gun emplacement on the Arizona canyon wall high above the dam.

The government did not begin to give serious consideration to relinquishing control of Boulder City until after the war. As far as the town was concerned, the Boulder Canyon Project was unfinished so long as Boulder City remained under federal jurisdiction. The Bureau of Reclamation had intended to let go of Boulder City as soon as dam construction ended, but local business leaders and other residents persuaded the bureau to remain. World War II further postponed Boulder's freedom.

Wartime growth forced officials to ask who should bear the cost of running Boulder City. Whereas expenses had been covered through the sale of Hoover Dam power and congressional appropriations, costs rose as the town grew, and the power companies complained that Boulder City was draining their profits. Boulder City businesses also complained now that government ownership restricted growth and cut them out of the postwar boom going on in Las Vegas and the rest of the country. The Bureau of Reclamation no longer relished its administrative responsibilities in Boulder City and welcomed the opportunity to shed them. By the mid-1940s the bureau took steps to push Boulder City out of the nest.

But plans to incorporate the city met fierce resistance from Boulder citizens. Most of these people had come as dam workers and stayed to work for the government. Uncle Sam to them was a paternal figure, and even though the reservation gate was long gone, for most Boulderites the world was still divided between federally protected safety inside and chaos and uncertainty outside. When Congressman Berkeley Bunker introduced the first Boulder City bill before Congress in 1946, the outcry against it was so great that the bill never made it out of committee.

"We felt that if we voiced our grievances strong enough," remembers Mary Eaton, "maybe the government would relent and keep us. We liked it like it was and didn't know what would be in the future if they turned us loose. We weren't like other Nevada towns, and we liked that."

"Boulder City was a delightful place to live," says Alice Hamilton. "We were well protected and it was a beautiful little city under government control. Most of the old-timers liked it that way."

The debate over incorporation was as contentious an issue in the 1940s and 1950s as the Boulder Canyon Project Act had been in the 1920s, and its ramifications were equally far-reaching. Boulder City incorporation created legal, economic, and social problems no one had foreseen. What were the government's legal and moral obligations to the city it had created and nourished? If Boulder City were released from federal control, how would it fund self-government? There was no industry, no tax base: the government had always provided whatever the town needed. How could democratic self-rule be established in a modern American city where there had never been democracy? Boulder City became a test case for self-determination just as construction of Hoover Dam had set precedents.

In 1949 the Bureau of Reclamation hired University of Southern California public administration professor Henry J. Reining to conduct public hearings in Boulder City about incorporation and to produce a report detailing how the government might divest itself of Boulder City in the least painful way. "I had done other consulting work," Reining says, "to do with city charters and matters of local self-government. I was asked if I'd be interested in this, and I was fascinated by the idea. The challenge of Boulder City was uniquely different. One of the calls I made in Washington was to the Budget Bureau. I expected that they would be able to tell me about experiences in other places of the country where this same kind of problem was in existence. Instead, they told me they had no such policies. They weren't aware of any such studies. They were watching my study with great interest. So I think I can say with great confidence that this study was a pilot; it was a model."

The *Reining Report*[1] suggested that the government go slow with divestiture and that self-rule be introduced in steps before the final release and incorporation of Boulder City under the laws of Nevada. On 27 July 1951 Secretary of the Interior Oscar Chapman issued an order officially separating Boulder City and its administration from the Boulder Canyon Project as the first step in weaning the town from government control.

At that point Boulder City divided into two factions. Local businesses joined the Bureau of Reclamation and the power companies in promoting incorporation. The antiseparatists opposing them included residents of Boulder City who believed they had little to gain and much to lose by breaking away from federal control. Many valued government prohibitions against alcohol, gambling, and prostitution as giving Boulder City a more wholesome environment than that of Las Vegas, and federal control of land prevented uncontrolled growth.

"Government people," says Reining, "were not happy about the change, and positively not about the idea of incorporation. They didn't want the status quo changed. . . . They weren't too much impressed by the democratic value of self-government."

Elton Garrett and Bruce Eaton played key roles on opposite sides of the incorporation debate. Garrett's experience in business, newspaper work, and real estate led him to advocate separation as the key to Boulder City's growth. Eaton represented antiseparatists on the newly elected Advisory Council formed to implement the separation plan Reining suggested. A majority of the popularly elected council members opposed incorporation, and for 10 years the fate of Boulder City was caught in this division.

By the mid-1950s there was still no resolution and the fight had become bitter. Boulder City residents voted three to one against incorporation in a nonbinding referendum in November 1956. The government nevertheless was determined to divest itself of Boulder City. When Congress once again considered the Boulder City bill in the spring of 1958, Elton Garrett and a group representing proincorporation interests went to Washington to lobby; Bruce Eaton went alone on behalf of those opposed. But influence of the antiseparatists had waned in Washington, and Eaton was rebuffed. "When I got back to Washington," he says, "I found myself isolated. . . . It didn't take me long to figure out that the cards were stacked against me." He was able to press for some modifications, including prohibitions against liquor and gambling unless approved by local referendum.

Congress passed the Boulder City bill on 19 August 1958, and two weeks later, on 2 September, President Eisenhower signed it into law. Finally, after Boulder City wrote its city charter, the Bureau of Reclamation signed over control of its property and 33 square miles of surrounding land to the city's leaders in incorporation ceremonies on 4 January 1960. After spending 30 years as part of the Boulder Canyon Project, Boulder City at last was on its own.[2]

Since being separated, Hoover Dam and Boulder City have followed their own courses and wrestled with their own problems. Boulder City has tried to maintain a life-style as close as possible to what it enjoyed under government rule. Gambling is still illegal in Boulder—the only Nevada town where this is so—but the sale of hard liquor was legalized in 1969. In 1979 the city passed a controlled-growth ordinance designed to limit development and to avoid the sort of uncontrolled population boom and urban sprawl that has afflicted the Las Vegas metropolitan area. When Las Vegas's population was growing during the late 1980s by as much as 5,000 new residents a month, Boulder City's population increased only slightly. Aside from keeping the town relatively small and easily managed, the controlled-growth ordinance has made real estate in the one-time construction camp the most expensive in Nevada.

Meanwhile, seven miles away in Black Canyon, Hoover Dam has changed considerably. The last generator was installed on the Nevada side in 1962. In 1986 the Bureau of Reclamation began a $126.9 million program to upgrade the dam's generators and increase its power output. The old cast-steel turbine runners installed in the 1930s have been replaced with stainless steel; one of the original runners now sits in Boulder City's Wilbur Square.

One of the most dramatic moments in Hoover Dam's history occurred in the summer of 1983. A heavy late-winter snow in the Rocky Mountains followed by a heatwave and heavy rain caused a runoff into the Colorado River more than double the norm. Lake Powell behind the Glen Canyon Dam upstream from Hoover filled for the first time early in June. The government released water through the Glen Canyon spillways, and by 2 July Lake Mead had risen to an unprecedented height. The bureau had to open Hoover Dam's spillways, and the resulting flood caused millions of dollars in damage to property along the river all the way into Mexico. When the dam's drum gates closed on 6 September, inspectors discovered that the 100-mile-an-hour rush of water had gouged tons of steel and concrete out of the tunnel's linings. When repairs commenced two years later, government engineers had to modify the original spillway design to prevent such damage in future floods.

The government has also rebuilt the roads and enlarged the tourist facilities on top of Hoover Dam. The hairpin curve that proved so dangerous when Curley Francis transported the penstock sections into the canyon during construction has been replaced by a new road that swings out over the canyon on a cantilever bridge. Completed in 1995 were a multilevel parking garage, express elevators, and a new visitor center and exhibit building overlooking Black Canyon.

Perhaps the most impressive change will be a new visitor's center and museum. Artifacts from construction days described by the men and women interviewed in this book will be displayed alongside photographs and restored motion picture film. The pen with which the Six Companies contract was signed will have a place of honor in the museum, but so will Six Companies employee badges, company scrip, reservation passes, bosun's chairs used by the high scalers, hard hats, and hip boots.

The Boulder Canyon Project's last milestone passed on 30 May 1987. On that day the original mortgage for Hoover Dam was paid off. For 50 years power customers paid $5.4 million dollars a year at 3 percent interest for the dam's construction as part of their monthly utility bills. On 1 June a new 30-year contract for sale of power took effect, and from that day the old Hoover Dam—the dam that brought hope to the dispossessed, that restored faith in American values, and that tamed an untamable river—passed into history.

To those who conceived the Boulder Canyon Project, individuals like Arthur P. Davis, Elwood Mead, Herbert Hoover, and Walker R. Young, Hoover Dam was a utilitarian undertaking designed to provide water, power, and flood control. To the New Dealers of the Roosevelt administration, the dam represented a showcase of government's ability to plan regional development, execute large public works projects, and work with private enterprise to stimulate economic recovery. For Americans crushed by the Great Depression, the dam offered hope. Even for those who had nothing to do with the dam, the project's success renewed their faith in American ingenuity, industry, and technology. The economy might be out of control, but nature was harnessed.

The dam bore a heavy symbolic burden. In 1931, as the depression worsened, the American Engineering Council published a report on the dam suggesting that success on the dam confirmed private enterprise, American democracy, and even national leadership:

> The execution of the plan was put into the hands of private enterprise with the full understanding that . . . individual initiative and responsibility have been a great force in the economic development of this nation. In other ages, a government would have executed such a work by autocratic compulsion with forced-labor wrung from a group living close to the margin of subsistence. . . .
>
> There is here being generated confidence and admiration in the nation's leaders. There is evidence that competitive industries can work together for a common goal. . . .
>
> The human factor here is the supreme factor, and the impelling motive is this understanding that they are doing something that counts.[3]

The report concluded that the dam was "the answer to the cynical protest which said 'it can't be done' for there is abundant proof that it is being done."[4]

The men and women whose stories are recorded here saw both the dam's practical character and its symbolic one. Some, like Curley Francis, said, "It wasn't no thrill. Just a job." Others realized they had been part of something important and unique. "I had an idea it was a project that would make history," said Bob Parker.

And he was right. Hoover Dam was a supreme human achievement, given its time and circumstances. It was a seminal work in every way: in its engineering and from economic, political, and social perspectives. Even the philosophies embodied in its design and construction, more than in any other project of its nature, lift Hoover Dam from the mundane to a special place in American history.

The dam offered evidence of the value of public works projects in times of economic upheaval. President Hoover realized the potential of public works to provide relief, and even in the prosperity of the early 1920s he argued that public works ought to be deferred until times of depression and unemployment. With the onset of the depression, he asked governors and mayors to accelerate public works to provide employment.[5] Late in 1930 he directed the Bureau of Reclamation to proceed with construction of the dam on the Colorado with the "utmost dispatch possible," even though it meant that work would begin before adequate housing was available for workers. The decision gave relief to those fortunate enough to get jobs, but it had the unfortunate consequence of bringing thousands of people to the southern Nevada desert with no place for them to live.[6]

Nevertheless, by lending government money for this public work Hoover hoped to show that economic recovery was possible without scrapping the old economic order altogether. Hoover Dam construction thus began under contracts that promised the government would recover its investment with interest through sale of generated power. Hoover Dam was the jewel of Hoover's efforts to relieve the financial crisis; however, while the project provided work for thousands of laborers directly and for tens of thousands more through concessions and subcontracts, it delivered too little relief to alleviate the general crisis.

Its greatest economic value may have been symbolic, since ironically the success of the Boulder Canyon Project stood as an affirmation of Roosevelt's first New Deal. Hoover Dam represented a rare continuity in the otherwise wrenching change from Hoover's administration to Roosevelt's. As a symbol of the success of national recovery programs, Hoover Dam made other such programs possible throughout the 1930s. An account of the dam written five years after construction began contended that "the American claim to democracy has governmentally advocated that individual enterprise linked with some competition is the best and speediest method for the promotion of progress. . . . The United States Government in undertaking this monstrous task—the Boulder Dam—did not throw a heavy burden of taxation upon the people of the nation, but on the contrary invested this enormous sum of money without recourse to taxation."[7]

Hoover Dam was a political prize, and since its construction spanned two presidential administrations, both tried to claim as much credit as possible. Hoover's visit to the damsite on 12 November 1932, just days after his defeat in the presidential election and days before the turning of the river through the diversion tunnels, gave him a last chance to take credit. He described the dam as "the greatest engineering work of its character ever attempted by the hand of man" and repeated his claim that the dam would pay for itself by generating electricity.[8]

Even though work on Hoover Dam had passed the halfway mark by the time Franklin Roosevelt won election to the presidency, he nonetheless put the stamp of his administration on the project. He criticized Hoover's veto of Senator George Norris's bill to have the government operate the Wilson Dam at Muscle Shoals on the Tennessee River and distribute its electricity.[9] Campaigning in Portland, Oregon, in September 1932, Roosevelt argued that the federal government ought not to turn over power from the dam on the Colorado to private interests as Hoover had planned and as he had done at Muscle Shoals. Rather, the government should control development of four great regional power projects: "the St. Lawrence River in the Northeast,

Muscle Shoals in the Southeast, the Boulder Dam project in the Southwest, and finally . . . the Columbia River in the Northwest." These projects, Roosevelt said, should "be forever a national yardstick to prevent extortion against the public and to encourage the wider use of that servant of the people—electrical power."[10]

Even the dam's name was political. That the dam should be named for President Hoover struck some as wildly inappropriate, while others thought it was a fitting tribute. When he announced the name in 1930, Secretary of the Interior Ray Lyman Wilbur suggested that the name Hoover would honor "the great engineer whose vision and persistence, first as chairman of the Colorado River Commission in 1922 and on so many other occasions since, has done much to make it possible."[11] But Hoover's name was not held in high regard by the time Wilbur named the dam. As the depression tightened its grip, critics even turned Hoover's accomplishments against him, and Hoover Dam was fair game. One barb complained that "the Great Engineer had quickly drained, ditched and dammed the country."[12]

On 13 May 1933, 10 weeks after Roosevelt's inauguration, Secretary of the Interior Harold Ickes issued an order that henceforth the dam would be known as Boulder Dam rather than Hoover Dam. He claimed that Secretary Wilbur had been out of line in naming the dam after a sitting president, that Wilbur had not had congressional authorization, and that the dam had already been known as Boulder Dam.[13] Hoover contended in his memoirs that he did not consider the name of the dam important, yet suggested that Presidents Theodore Roosevelt, Woodrow Wilson, and Calvin Coolidge had dams named for them even though they had taken "no more than a casual interest" in those projects, whereas he had been involved in the Boulder Canyon Project since chairing the commission that produced the Colorado River Compact early in the 1920s.[14] Hoover received his vindication in 1947 when Congress restored the name Hoover Dam.

Hoover Dam had its most immediate social impact by providing jobs. Once word was out that jobs were available, laborers came from all over to seek work on the Boulder Canyon Project. The government hired experienced Bureau of Reclamation employees first, and the bureau claimed to have a surplus in most job categories because of the recent completion of other projects. Veterans also received hiring preference, and although only 15 percent of applicants had been in the service, as many as 47 percent of those employed claimed veteran status. So many veterans received jobs that nonveterans complained of discrimination. Even before excavation of the riverbed began, the government boasted that every state but two had representation on the dam's work force.[15] In one month early in 1931, the government's employment office received 2,816 letters of application but placed only 82 men and 17 women. By September 1932 the Las Vegas employment office had more than 65,000 applications on file.[16]

The Boulder Canyon Project witnessed government-supported racism. The Boulder Canyon Project Act prohibited only "Mongolians" from being hired, but many others also had grievances. A complaint to the Nevada State Labor Commission alleged discrimination against job applicants because of "their physical stature, weight, color, character, and age."[17] In contrast, Scandinavians had reputations as skillful construction workers. Ray Lyman Wilbur remembered that most of the people who were "willing to be let down over the canyon and work in such blistering heat" were Scandinavians, and Tommy Nelson remembered a supervisor assuming that he knew how to operate a jackhammer because he had a "Scandinavian name, and most Scandinavians are pretty good hammermen." Wilbur's Interior Department hired Apache Indians because they were "natives of the desert area, [so they] might like to take up that sort of outdoor work and could stand it well."[18]

Blacks were the minority most targeted for discrimination: few blacks worked on Hoover Dam. Some workers remember Charlie Rose's crew, but few have recollections of other blacks on the project. Sims Ely prohibited blacks from living in Boulder City, and so the handful of black workers who were able to get jobs had to live in Las Vegas. Restaurants in Boulder City like the Green Hut refused to serve blacks. Blacks in Las Vegas complained that they were not being hired; Leonard Blood, who ran the Las Vegas employment office, responded that indeed they should not be hired, since their presence on the job could cause tension with white workers and because of the "difficulties of housing and feeding 'colored labor' and the cost of providing separate facilities for them."[19]

The Hoover administration had never shown concern for promoting the interests of blacks. In 1932 the National Association for the Advancement of Colored People (NAACP) and the National Urban League alleged that federal contractors at Hoover Dam and at the Mississippi River flood control project were denying jobs to blacks, or abusing those who had jobs. An investigation at Hoover Dam in May by William Pickering, field secretary for the NAACP, confirmed the charges, but the administration made no changes in its policies on the Boulder Canyon Project. W. A. Bechtel grudgingly pledged to hire blacks if they had "the necessary experience" and soon hired 10 black veterans to work in the Arizona gravel pits, one of the hottest and most remote jobs on the project.[20]

Roosevelt's New Deal brought little improvement for blacks at Hoover Dam. The black press and black voters continued to support Republicans in 1932, since nothing in New York governor Franklin D. Roosevelt's record suggested that a Democratic administration would be more sympathetic. Initially that judgment seemed accurate. Not until initiation of the programs of the Second New Deal in 1935 did the Roosevelt administration include requirements for hiring blacks on New Deal programs. Secretary of the Interior Harold Ickes was the foremost advocate for blacks in the Roosevelt cabinet, and after hearing complaints about discrimination in hiring and segregated facilities at the dam, he investigated. Although his findings verified the charges, the Six Companies contract blocked him from changing hiring practices. He did pry a concession from the Six Companies to allow blacks working on the project—less than 1 percent of the workforce—to live in Boulder City, but that promise was never fulfilled.[21]

The dismal economic climate of the early 1930s made it an employer's market. Despite horrible working conditions, low pay, inadequate housing in the early months of dam construction, and dictatorial control of life in Boulder City later, few workers protested. Those who did jeopardized their jobs. Although there were three strikes on the project, only the August 1931 strike was a significant challenge to existing labor-management relations. Much contributed to the failure of that strike, including decisive action by the Six Companies, reluctance of most workers to risk their jobs, and federal cooperation with Six Companies despite claims of neutrality in labor relations.

The August strike was also the last gasp of the IWW. The union's reputation for radicalism hindered its ability to gain support among most workers, even though its goals for the Boulder Canyon Project were moderate. Labor historian Guy Louis Rocha has shown that the strike's organizers were dedicated "to protecting the unskilled workers from exploitative contractors and bettering their immediate conditions, and not particularly in promoting class warfare and revolution." The strike was "one of the last important I.W.W.-related activities in America,"[22] and the reasons for the ultimate failure of the union are manifest in the Hoover Dam strike. The workers interviewed for this book expressed their sympathy for the grievances voiced by IWW organizers but also had pragmatic reasons for not supporting the strike.

Despite failure of the strike, the IWW was one of the most persistent critics of the collaboration between the federal government and the Six Companies. One article from the IWW paper referred to Leonard Blood of the Las Vegas employment office as "the blacklisting agent" and called the employment application a "blacklisting questionnaire." The article included a satiric description of the employment ordeal: "Blood looks the worker up and down much in the manner of a southern planter of ante-Civil War days inspecting a living piece of 'black ivory' in the slave market. . . . Having ridden the goat and been inducted into the Royal Order of the Dumb Bell, [the worker] is considered a third-degree Master Ox and given all the secret pass words and signs of the order, including a muck stick and pick. After a lot more running around, . . . he is ready for the big slaughter holes."[23]

But the IWW remained isolated, with little support even from the workers at the dam it sought to defend. Failure of organized labor to affect significantly the Boulder Canyon Project curbed union influence until after World War II.

Apart from the political, economic, and social impact of Hoover Dam, the structure presented in its design and technical execution a symbol for the prevailing philosophy of the time. Design features reflect the art deco style popular in the 1930s, a celebration of efficiency and technological achievement. The sculptures, bas-reliefs, and plaques of Oskar J. W. Hansen project the same themes. In his book *Sculptures at Hoover Dam*, Hansen explains the philosophy that guided his conception of the artwork at Hoover Dam: "The dam represents the building genius of America in the same sense as the Pyramids represent that of ancient Egypt, the Acropolis that of classical Greece, the Colosseum that of Imperial Rome, and Chartres Cathedral that of the brooding religious fervor which was Gothic Europe. . . . The building of Hoover Dam belongs to the sagas of the daring."[24]

Hansen's prose is florid, but his sentiment was sincere. He saw construction of Hoover Dam as an absolute humanistic triumph, and he produced his Winged Figures of the Republic on a heroic scale. At a time when faith in institutions and personal value was slipping away, Hoover Dam was an inspiring symbol for depression-weary Americans. Hansen's sculptures celebrate the dam's purpose—flood control, irrigation, and power production—but also honor the area's history, the workers who built the dam, and those who lost their lives during construction. Hansen wrote, "In such a place as the Hoover Dam, a monument becomes a universal as well as a personal experience." By laying a star map into the terrazzo describing the dam's dedication in astronomical time, Hansen fixed Hoover Dam's place in the universe.[25]

Other writers considered the building of the dam as a victory of the human spirit in a war against nature. George A. Pettitt, who in 1935 published one of the earliest accounts of the building of the dam, suggested that "the struggle to curb the Colorado River was truly a war—a war against the incorrigible and frequently barbaric forces of Nature."[26] Zane Grey's novel *Boulder Dam* portrays a construction worker approaching the damsite saying, "Boys, we're near the front now." Another replies, "You said it, buddy. War!" Grey's hero later sees dam workers in Herculean terms: "He scarcely included himself in a band of toilers who proved beyond doubt that heroism had not forsaken a modern world, that courage and sacrifice were as great as they had ever been, that labor of hands and body were the hope, the salvation, the progress of a race."[27] Secretary of the Interior Ray Lyman Wilbur expressed the same notion in less elaborate prose when he suggested that "for each of those who have struggled and worked for the Hoover dam it will be said, 'He builded better than he knew.' "[28]

Appendix A

The Language of Hoover Dam's Builders

The men who built Hoover Dam developed their own language. The following is a list of terms used by construction workers who worked on the dam.[1]

Banjo: An ordinary shovel

Big Bertha: The double-deck transports, having a capacity of 150 men

Blit: To annihilate a guy

Blue room: The room at the upstream end of Anderson's messhall, where the elite sit

Build it: A phrase used by men when they are stating the fact that they must again return to work

Bulldozer: A caterpillar tractor equipped with a horizontal blade which pushes dirt

Candy wagon: A light Ford truck

Cat: A caterpillar tractor

Catwalk: A narrow suspended footbridge

Cornbinder: An International truck

Cowdozer: A cat rigged up with a blade on the back to pull muck

Crutch: A long-handled shovel

Dinky: A small locomotive, usually propelled by gas

Double-ugly: A truck driver

Easy-dough: A boss

Gaffer: Another word for foreman or boss

Gertz: A group of cables

Goldbrick: A guy who doesn't put out much work

Gravy-train: A goldbrick's job

Glory hole: Territory between the two cofferdams and the two canyon walls

Getting a spot: Taking five, or a short lay-off

Hole: Down in the canyon

Juicer: An electrician

Joe McGee: A makeshift tool of any kind used on the job

Job: The Boulder Dam and appurtenant works

Jumbo: A large structure used in tunnels from which operations are carried on

King Kong: The government cableway, the largest in the world [at the time], with a capacity of 150 tons

Mud: Concrete ready to be placed

Muck: Loose dirt

Mucker: A man who handles muck

Monkey-slide: Two cableways, one of which travels on the downstream face of the dam, and the other of which travels on the upstream face of the dam

Perverted: An adjective applied to anything broken, or "out of kilter"

Stooge: A man who caters and apple-polishes his gaffer

Signal punk: One who relays signals from the signalman in the "hole" to the operator of the highline or cableway

Shay: A steam locomotive with a side eccentric, and a high gear ratio

Stiff-leg: A type of derrick

Twirp: One of the girls

Twidgett: Another of the girls

Whoopee: A Ford pickup

Wood-butcher: A carpenter

Appendix B

President Franklin D. Roosevelt's
Address at the Dedication of Boulder Dam
30 September 1935

Senator Pittman, Secretary Ickes, Governors of the Colorado's States, and you especially who have built Boulder Dam, this morning I came, I saw and I was conquered, as everyone would be who sees for the first time this great feat of mankind.

Ten years ago the place where we are gathered was an unpeopled, forbidding desert. In the bottom of a gloomy canyon, whose precipitous walls rose to a height of more than a thousand feet, flowed a turbulent, dangerous river. The mountains on either side of the canyon were difficult of access with neither road nor trail, and their rocks were protected by neither trees nor grass from the blazing heat of the sun. The site of Boulder City was a cactus-covered waste. The transformation wrought here in these years is a twentieth-century marvel.

We are here to celebrate the completion of the greatest dam in the world, rising 726 feet above the bed-rock of the river and altering the geography of a whole region; we are here to see the creation of the largest artificial lake in the world—115 miles long, holding enough water, for example, to cover the State of Connecticut to a depth of ten feet; and we are here to see nearing completion a power house which will contain the largest generators and turbines yet installed in this country, machinery that can continuously supply nearly two million horsepower of electric energy.

All these dimensions are superlative. They represent and embody the accumulated engineering knowledge and experience of centuries; and when we behold them it is fitting that we pay tribute to the genius of their designers. We recognize also the energy, resourcefulness and zeal of the builders, who, under the greatest physical obstacles, have pushed this work forward to completion two years in advance of the contract requirements. But especially, we express our gratitude to the thousands of workers who gave brain and brawn to this great work of construction.

Beautiful and great as this structure is, it must also be considered in its relationship to the agricultural and industrial development and in its contribution to the health and comfort of the people of America who live in the Southwest.

To divert and distribute the waters of an arid region, so that there shall be security of rights and efficiency in service, is one of the greatest problems of law and of administration to be found in any Government. The farms, the cities, the people who live along the many thousands of miles of this river and its tributaries—all of them depend upon the conservation, the regulation, and the equitable division of its ever-changing water supply.

What has been accomplished on the Colorado in working out such a scheme of distribution is inspiring to the whole country. Through the cooperation of the States whose people depend upon this river, and of the Federal Government which is concerned in the general welfare, there is being constructed a system of distributive works and of laws and practices which will insure to the millions of people who now dwell in this basin, and the millions of others who will come to dwell here in future generations, a just, safe and permanent system of water rights. In devising these policies and the means for putting them into practice the Bureau of Reclamation of the Federal Government has taken, and is destined to take in the future, a leading and helpful part. The Bureau has been the instrument which gave effect to the legislation introduced in Congress by Senator Hiram Johnson and Congressman Phil Swing.

As an unregulated river, the Colorado added little of value to the region this dam serves. When in flood the river was a threatening torrent. In the dry months of the year it shrank to a trickling stream. For a generation the people of the Imperial Valley had lived in the shadow of disaster from this river which provided their livelihood, and which is the foundation of their hopes for themselves and their children. Every spring they awaited with dread the coming of a flood, and at the end of nearly every summer they feared a shortage of water would destroy their crops.

The gates of these great diversion tunnels were closed here at Boulder Dam last February. In June a great flood came down the river. It came roaring down the canyons of the Colorado, was caught and safely held behind Boulder Dam.

Last year a drought of unprecedented severity was visited upon the West. The watershed of this Colorado River did not escape. In July the canals of the Imperial Valley went dry. Crop losses in that Valley alone totaled $10,000,000 that summer. Had Boulder Dam been completed one year earlier, this loss would have been prevented, because the spring flood would have been stored to furnish a steady water supply for the long dry summer and fall.

Across the San Jacinto Mountains southwest of Boulder Dam, the cities of Southern California are constructing an aqueduct to cost $220,000,000, which they have raised, for the purpose of carrying the regulated waters of the Colorado River to the Pacific Coast 259 miles away.

Across the desert and mountains to the west and south run great electric transmission lines by which factory motors, street and household lights and irrigation pumps will be operated in Southern Arizona and California. Part of this power will be used in pumping the water through the aqueduct to supplement the domestic supplies of Los Angeles and surrounding cities.

Navigation of the river from Boulder Dam to the Grand Canyon has been made possible, a 115-mile stretch that has been traversed less than half a dozen times in history. An immense new park has been created for the enjoyment of all our people.

At what cost was this done? Boulder Dam and the power houses together cost a total of $108,000,000, all of which will be repaid with interest in fifty years under the contracts for sale of the power. Under these contracts, already completed, not only will the cost be repaid, but the way is opened for the provision of needed light and power to the consumer at reduced rates. In the expenditure of the price of Boulder Dam during the depression years work was provided for 4,000 men, most of them heads of families, and many thousands more were enabled to earn a livelihood through manufacture of materials and machinery.

And this is true in regard to the thousands of projects undertaken by the Federal Government, by the States and by the counties and municipalities in recent years. The overwhelming majority of them are of definite and permanent usefulness.

Throughout our national history we have had a great program of public improvements, and in these past two years all that we have done has been to accelerate that program. We know, too, that the reason for this speeding up was the need of giving relief to several million men and women whose earning capacity had been destroyed by the complexities and lack of thought of the economic system of the past generation.

No sensible person is foolish enough to draw hard and fast classifications as to usefulness or need. Obviously, for instance, this great Boulder Dam warrants universal approval because it will prevent floods and flood damage, because it will irrigate thousands of acres of tillable land and because it will generate electricity to turn the wheels of many factories and illuminate countless homes.

But can we say that a five-foot brushwood dam across the head waters of an arroyo, and costing only a millionth part of Boulder Dam, is an undesirable project or a waste of money? Can we say that the great brick high school, costing $2,000,000, is a useful expenditure but that a little wooden school house project, costing five or ten thousand dollars, is a wasteful extravagance? Is it fair to approve a huge city boulevard and, at the same time, disapprove the improvement of a muddy farm-to-market road?

While we do all of this, we give actual work to the unemployed and at the same time we add to the wealth of the Nation. These efforts meet with the approval of the people of the Nation.

313

In a little over two years this work has accomplished much. We have helped mankind by the works themselves and, at the same time, we have created the necessary purchasing power to throw in the clutch to start the wheels of what we call private industry. Such expenditures on all of these works, great and small, flow out to many beneficiaries. They revive other and more remote industries and businesses. Money is put in circulation. Credit is expanded and the financial and industrial mechanism of America is stimulated to more and more activity.

Labor makes wealth. The use of materials makes wealth. To employ workers and materials when private employment has failed is to translate into great national possessions the energy that otherwise would be wasted. Boulder Dam is a splendid symbol of that principle. The mighty waters of the Colorado were running unused to the sea. Today we translate them into a great national possession.

I might go further and suggest to you that use begets use. Such works as this serve as a means of making useful other national possessions. Vast deposits of precious metals are scattered within a short distance of where we stand today. They await the development of cheap power.

These great Government power projects will affect not only the development of agriculture and industry and mining in the sections that they serve, but they will also prove useful yardsticks to measure the cost of power throughout the United States. It is my belief that the Government should proceed to lay down the first yardstick from this great power plant in the form of a State power line, assisted in its financing by the Government, and tapping the wonderful natural resources of Southern Nevada. Doubtless the same policy of financial assistance to State authorities can be followed in the development of Nevada's sister State, Arizona, on the other side of the River.

With it all, with work proceeding in every one of the more than three thousand counties in the United States, and of a vastly greater number of local divisions of Government, the actual credit of Government agencies is on a stronger and safer basis than at any time in the past six years. Many States have actually improved their financial position in the past two years. Municipal tax receipts are being paid when the taxes fall due, and tax arrearages are steadily declining.

It is a simple fact that Government spending is already beginning to show definite signs of its effect on consumer spending; that the putting of people to work by the Government has put other people to work through private employment, and that in two years and a half we have come to the point today where private industry must bear the principal responsibility of keeping the processes of greater employment moving forward with accelerated speed.

The people of the United States are proud of Boulder Dam. With the exception of the few who are narrow visioned, people everywhere on the Atlantic Seaboard, people in the Middle West and the Northwest, people in the South, must surely recognize that the national benefits which will be derived from the completion of this project will make themselves felt in every one of the forty-eight States. They know that poverty or distress in a community two thousand miles away may affect them, and equally that prosperity and higher standards of living across a whole continent will help them back home.

Today marks the official completion and dedication of Boulder Dam, the first of four great Government regional units. This is an engineering victory of the first order—another great achievement of American resourcefulness, American skill and determination.

That is why I have the right once more to congratulate you who have built Boulder Dam and on behalf of the Nation to say to you, "Well done."[1]

Appendix C

Boulder Canyon Project Fatalities

The following is a list of fatalities on the Boulder Canyon Project, including the date of death, name, employer, and cause of death.[1]

1922

**12/20	J. G. Tierney, U.S. Bureau of Reclamation (USBR)	Drowned

1931

5/17	Harry Large, Six Co.	Rock Slide
5/17	Andrew Lane, Six Co.	Rock Slide
5/18	Fred Olsen, Lewis Const. Co.	Premature Explosion
6/20	William Bryant, Six Co.	Explosion
6/20	J. P. Sweezy, Six Co.	Explosion
6/26	Ray Hapland, Six Co.	Heat Prostration
6/27	Pat Shannon, Six Co.	Heat Prostration
6/28	Mike Madzia, Six Co.	Heat Prostration
7/5	Joe Rolland, Six Co.	Drowned
*7/5	Martin Puluski, visitor	Drowned
7/8	Robert Core, Newberry Elec.	Heat Prostration
7/10	A. E. Meridith, Lewis Const.	Heat Prostration
7/11	Joe Lyons, Anderson Bros.	Heat Prostration
7/13	Earl Parker, Six Co.	Heat Prostration
7/15	John Swenson, Six Co.	Heat Prostration
7/20	Chase Allen, Six Co.	Heat Prostration
*7/22	A. A. McClurg, Int'l. Truck Co.	Heat Prostration
7/23	Tom Noonal, Six Co.	Heat Prostration
7/24	Joe Ganz, Anderson Bros.	Heat Prostration
7/26	Lew Starnes, Anderson Bros.	Heat Prostration
9/11	H. H. Kidd, Six Co.	Falling Rock
9/29	Jack Seitz, Six Co.	Fell 400 feet
10/2	Lauri Lehto, Six Co.	Falling Rock

10/17	Ralph Henderson, Six Co.	Falling Rock
10/17	M. C. Stuckey, Six Co.	Falling Rock
11/7	D. R. Elston, Six Co.	Struck by Truck
12/15	M. J. Sidmore, Six Co.	Premature Explosion
12/15	Frank Manning, Six Co.	Premature Explosion

1932

1/7	S. A. McDaniel, Six Co.	Fell
2/11	Joe Talbert, Six Co.	Power Shovel
2/25	Ben Johnson, Six Co.	Drowned in Tank
3/11	O. A. George, Six Co.	Crushed—Trucks
3/30	Frank Brady, Six Co.	Falling Rock
4/14	Carl Bennett, Six Co.	Explosion
4/21	H. H. Nightingale, Six Co.	Shovel—Crushed
4/26	L. N. McBride, Six Co.	Struck by Skip Line
4/27	Bert Lynch, Six Co.	Falling Rock
4/28	V. R. Moore, Six Co.	Struck—Concrete Skip
5/11	John Abercrombie, Six Co.	Transport Collision
5/20	B. S. Joyce, Six Co.	Falling Rock
5/30	H. A. Willis, Six Co.	Electrocuted
6/17	H. L. Scothern, Six Co.	Struck by Cable
7/25	Walter Hardesty, Six Co.	Struck by Crane
7/27	E. A. Bishop, Six Co.	Truck Went Overboard
7/29	Alexander Girardi, Six Co.	Fell from Wall
8/24	A. E. Wooden, Six Co.	Crushed by Form
8/31	E. H. Gammill, Six Co.	Premature Explosion
9/24	V. I. Kemnitz, Six Co.	Rock Fall
9/25	P. B. Hicks, Six Co.	Fell from Wall
9/28	James C. Roberts, Six Co.	Falling Rock
11/9	Louie Goss, Six Co.	Fell from Wall
11/16	Carl Soderstrom, Six Co.	Drowned
12/12	Dan Shovlin, Six Co.	Struck by Truck
12/23	Walter Hamer, Six Co.	Fell from Valve House

1933

1/1	F. C. Palmer, Six Co.	Fell from Valve House
1/10	Gus Enberg, Six Co.	Explosion
1/11	Howard Cornelius, Six Co.	Explosion
2/1	V. H. Blair, Six Co.	Fell from Truck
2/7	J. H. Powers, Six Co.	Truck fell on him
2/7	M. M. Kaighn, Six Co.	Rock Slide

3/12	Tome Markey, Six Co.	Fell
3/16	William Koontz, Six Co.	Run over by Truck
4/8	Dan Kalal, Six Co.	Gravel Slide
5/20	H. D. Bluhm, Six Co.	Struck by Shovel
5/22	Pete Savoff, Six Co.	Fell
6/23	Mike Landers, Six Co.	Falling Rock
6/26	L. W. Steele, Six Co.	Run over by Truck
7/1	F. B. Kassell, Six Co.	Premature Explosion
7/13	George Falkner, Six Co.	Falling Timber
7/19	J. M. Nelson, Six Co.	Fell from Form
9/15	V. O. Lee, Six Co.	Electrocuted
10/1	James Jackman, Six Co.	Falling Concrete Bucket
11/8	W. A. Jameson, Six Co.	Concrete Slide
11/8	James Tocci, Six Co.	Run over by Truck
12/6	L. E. Roach, Six Co.	Fell from Jumbo
12/29	P. A. Malan, Six Co.	Fell from Form

1934

1/22	George Good, Six Co.	Falling Material
2/1	Rosyn Grant, Six Co.	Fell
2/6	Kenneth Walden, Six Co.	Crushed by Concrete Bucket
2/26	Eugene Buckner, Six Co.	Falling Timber
3/10	George R. Robinson, Six Co.	Elevator Accident
3/23	Harry Morgan, Six Co.	Fell
4/14	Allen Jackson, Six Co.	Fell
5/16	G. D. McIsaac, Six Co.	Electrocuted
5/20	Howard Bently, Six Co.	Falling Rock
5/26	Samuel L. Carter, Six Co.	Hit by Concrete Dinky
5/26	Fred Deckmann, Babcock & Wilcox (B&W)	Fell
6/11	Grant Miles, Six Co.	Fell 60 feet walking thru drain. Not considered industrial by Six Co. as he did not accept furnished mode of transportation
6/24	Victor K. Auchard, Six Co.	Crushed under Jumbo
8/27	Harris Lange, B&W	Objects from Broken Sling
9/16	Frank A. Fritz, Six Co.	Electrocuted
9/26	John W. Rawls, Six Co.	Fell from Form
11/1	Paul L. Jordan, B&W	Fell from 30 foot Pipe
11/1	Richard M. Whelan, B&W	Penstock Car Ran Wild
11/1	Martin L. Hempel, B&W	Penstock Car Ran Wild

11/4	Alfred E. Foreman, B&W	Penstock Car Ran Wild
11/14	K. H. Rankin, USBR	Struck by Concrete Bucket

1935

1/3	J. W. Pitts, Six Co.	Struck by Concrete Bucket
2/19	Kenneth L. Wilson, Six Co.	Line broke—Fell 200 feet
2/21	B. R. Reaves, Six Co.	Fell into tunnel; drown
5/15	David C. Nixon, Six Co.	Crushed: Concrete Bucket
5/17	Verne Matson, B&W	Falling Pipe
6/21	Harold Koile, B&W	Falling Casting
8/14	William R. Skaloud, B&W	Fell
11/17	Albert G. Loper, Six Co.	Fell
11/24	Roy Stevens, Six Co.	Struck by Flying Object
**12/20	Patrick W. Tierney, USBR	Fell: Intake Tower, Lake

Summary

Company Name	Total Fatalities
Anderson Brothers	4
Newberry Electric	1
International Truck Co.	1
Babcock & Wilcox	9
Lewis Construction Company	2
Six Companies	91
U.S. Bureau of Reclamation	3
Visitors	1
Total Deaths	**112**

*Not on dam force; outsiders
**J.G. Tierney, the first man killed on the Boulder Canyon Project (12/20/1922), and Patrick W. Tierney, the last man killed on the Project (12/20/1935), were father and son.

Notes and References

Introduction

1. Marc Reisner, *Cadillac Desert: The American West and Its Disappearing Water* (New York: Viking Penguin, 1986), 108.

2. See Reuel Leslie Olsen, "The Colorado River Compact" (Ph.D. diss., Harvard University, 1926); Beverly Bowen Moeller, *Phil Swing and Boulder Dam* (Berkeley and Los Angeles: University of California Press, 1971); and Joseph Stevens, *Hoover Dam: An American Adventure* (Norman: University of Oklahoma Press, 1988).

Chapter 1

1. This was probably Murl Emery, who had lived on the Colorado River since 1917.

2. A small mining town several miles southeast of Black Canyon in the foothills of the Cerbat Mountains of Arizona.

3. Chairman of the Colorado River Board, 1928.

4. Prominent Colorado River explorer and chief engineer of the Panama Canal.

5. Dr. Roy Martin opened the first medical practice in Las Vegas in August 1905 and was president of the Las Vegas Chamber of Commerce during the 1920s; James Cashman, Sr., arrived in Las Vegas in 1904, owned several ferries on the Colorado River, and in 1920 was appointed to the Colorado River Commission; Edmund W. Griffith was first president of the Las Vegas Chamber of Commerce (1913–14; 1916–18), a Nevada state assemblyman (1917), and a Nevada state senator (1919–21).

6. This was Emmet Derby Boyle, Nevada's governor from 1915 to 1922.

7. Field engineer for the Boulder Canyon Project.

8. Construction superintendent for the Six Companies.

9. Director of construction for the Six Companies.

10. Warren A. Bechtel was president of the Six Companies until his death in 1933; his son Stephen D. Bechtel was director of audits, purchasing, and the warehouses.

11. Davis was an employee of Las Vegas's Oakes Photographic Studio from 1930 to 1941. His assignments included visual documentation of the Boulder Canyon Project.

12. Fort Callville was a Mormon commercial settlement founded on the Colorado River near the western end of Boulder Canyon in December 1864. Intended as a port for steamships, Fort Callville was abandoned in 1869. The ruins were covered by Lake Mead in 1935–36.

13. Ray Lyman Wilbur was president of Stanford University from 1916 to 1943. He took a leave of absence from 1929 to 1933 to serve as Herbert Hoover's secretary of the interior.

14. On 8 May 1933, shortly after Roosevelt took office, Ickes issued an order changing the name of Hoover Dam to Boulder Dam. On 30 April 1947 a House joint resolution changed the name back to Hoover Dam.

Chapter 2

1. Office engineer for the Boulder Canyon Project.

2. Named for Deputy U.S. Marshal Claude Williams, who had jurisdiction over the Ragtown settlement.

3. W. R. "Roscoe" Thomas was elected police commissioner of Las Vegas in 1929.

4. When Union Pacific shop employees walked off their jobs on 1 July 1922 in support of a nationwide railroad shop workers' strike, the railroad closed the Las Vegas repair shops. Hundreds were thrown out of work, and Las Vegas went into an economic decline from which it did not recover until construction of Hoover Dam began.

Chapter 3

1. Frank Moran was a bouncer at the Anderson Brothers Mess Hall.

2. The Southern Sierras Power Company, dba the Nevada-California Power Company, brought power in from southern California for Hoover Dam construction.

Chapter 4

1. The name "jumbo" is one of many terms that constituted the unique vocabulary of Hoover Dam construction workers. A compilation of these terms is given in appendix A. This list originally appeared in the *Las Vegas Evening Review-Journal* on 31 January 1934.

2. Liners were jackhammers mounted on the jumbos and supplied by air and water lines.

3. Small access tunnels that led to the main diversion tunnels and were used to supply ventilation.

4. An oiler was part of the mucking crew that cleaned the tunnels of the debris from blasts. Other members of the mucking crew were a shovel operator, a pitman, and a Cat skinner, who operated a Caterpillar tractor.

5. Sidewalls were the tunnel walls.

6. Herbert Hoover made three trips to Black Canyon: 22 November 1921, 12 November 1932, and 2 May 1933.

Chapter 5

1. The company store was operated by the Boulder City Company, a subsidiary of the Six Companies, and managed by V. G. Evans.

2. The Railroad Wye was a tent settlement on the west edge of Boulder City where the railroad to the damsite branched off from the spur that led into the town itself.

3. The first school on the reservation met in a small building in Ragtown that also functioned as a church. Classes opened on Monday, 28 September 1931. See *Las Vegas Evening Review-Journal*, 22 September 1931, 4:5.

4. *Six Companies, Inc., v. DeVinney, County Assessor*, 1933.

5. Dr. Toland performed the surgery on Dr. Haas.

6. Basic Magnesium began operations during World War II in Henderson, Nevada, midway between Boulder City and Las Vegas.

Chapter 6

1. Zane Grey included the story in his novel *Boulder Dam*.

2. The accident occurred on 19 February 1935.

3. These were actually brand-new dishpans, cut to hold light bulbs.

Chapter 7

1. Brothers Harold and Walter Anderson founded the Anderson Boarding and Supply Company in Salt Lake City in 1912. In 1931 Harold and his younger brother William founded the Anderson Brothers Supply Company of Nevada and won the contract to provide the commissary services for the Boulder Canyon Project. At the beginning of World War II, Anderson Brothers held the contract to provide commissary services for Basic Magnesium, Inc., at Henderson, Nevada.

2.   See *Las Vegas Evening Review-Journal*, 25 January 1935, 1:5, and 26 February 1935, 3:4.

3.   Marion A. Zioncheck represented Washington in the U.S. Congress from 1933 until his death on 7 August 1936.

4.   Charles "Pickpockets" Bollman died on 5 March 1935.

5.   *Boulder City Reminder*, 8 July 1939, 1:1.

6.   In 1978 the Bureau of Reclamation placed a plaque on the Nevada side of the dam that read: NIG, THE DOG THAT ADOPTED A DAM. BORN ABOUT MARCH 1932, DIED ABOUT JUNE 1936. (The actual date of the death was 21 February 1941.) To Clarence Kailin, a visitor to the dam from Madison, Wisconsin, the plaque had obvious racist overtones. He mounted a letter-writing campaign against the plaque, and several civil rights organizations joined in the protest. Senator Gaylord Nelson referred the complaint to the bureau, which removed the plaque early in 1979. Boulder City residents began a petition drive protesting the plaque's removal. Leroy Burt was one of those who objected, saying, "People aren't stopping to think what the dog meant to us folks that worked on the dam." But as Bob Parker explains, the bureau did not restore the plaque. (*Las Vegas Review-Journal*, 27 March, 1979, 1B:1–3 and 30 March 1979, 1B:2–5; *Boulder City News*, 22 March 1979, 1:1–3 and 12 April 1979, 3:1–8.)

Chapter 8

1.   The settlements in this area were known as Midway and Whitney.

2.   *Las Vegas Evening Review-Journal*, 26 March 1935, 6:1–3.

3.   Gambling was legalized in Nevada on 19 March 1931.

Chapter 9

1.   The spiders were struts that kept the penstock pipes from warping while they were moved and installed.

2.   Crescent-shaped steel beams with which the pipe sections were attached to the cableway.

3.   Wheatstone bridges are used to measure electric resistance.

4.   The spillways were used again during the summer floods of 1983.

5.   Men and women who were in Boulder City in 1931 or who have lived there for thirty-one years are eligible to join the Thirty-Oners, a group that holds annual reunions celebrating the early days of the city and the construction of the dam.

Chapter 10

1.   The initial shock of this quake registered a magnitude of 5 on the Richter scale and was felt over 9,000 square miles. Buildings in Boulder City were damaged,

and roads around Hoover Dam were blocked. Aftershocks over the next three days registered magnitudes of 3.5 to 4.

2. Roosevelt's train pulled into Las Vegas at 9.30 A.M. the morning of 30 September.

3. See appendix B for President Franklin D. Roosevelt's dedication speech.

4. Dave Laughery, a Boulder City ranger, Mrs. Voss's first husband.

5. Wyoming Street was the northern boundary of the Six Companies residential area. North of Wyoming stood the uptown business district, and beyond that, the government administration building and residential area.

6. In July 1936 the Bureau of Mines opened a station in Boulder City to develop methods for the electrometallurgical application of Hoover Dam power and the use of raw materials from the area.

7. On 19 August 1936 the Bureau of Reclamation entered into a Memorandum of Agreement with the National Park Service. The agreement turned control of the Boulder Canyon Project Federal Reservation over to the National Park Service, except for Boulder City and Hoover Dam, over which the Bureau of Reclamation retained control. The former reservation became the Boulder Dam Recreational Area, later known as the Lake Mead National Recreation Area.

Conclusion

1. U.S. Congress, Senate, *Boulder City, Nevada, a Federal Municipality: A Report of a Survey Made under the Direction of the Bureau of Reclamation of Problems Affecting Boulder City, Nevada*, 81st Cong., 2d sess., 15 June 1950, Doc. no. 196.

2. Dennis McBride, "Dragged into Democracy," *Nevadan*, 11 September 1988, 6–7, 12–13, and "Birthing Boulder City," *Nevadan*, 18 September 1988, 6–7, 12–13.

3. "Report on Hoover Dam Project and Present Status," Committee Appointed by the Associated General Contractors of America and the American Engineering Council, Bureau of Reclamation Archives, Boulder City, Nevada, 11, 14.

4. Ibid., 14.

5. Martin L. Fausold, *The Presidency of Herbert C. Hoover* (Lawrence: University Press of Kansas, 1985), 75, 120.

6. Guy Louis Rocha, "The I.W.W. and the Boulder Canyon Project: The Death Throes of American Syndicalism," in *At the Point of Production: The Local History of the I.W.W.*, ed. Joseph R. Conlin (Westport, Conn.: Greenwood Press, 1981), 214.

7. Ralph B. Simmons, *Boulder Dam and the Great Southwest* (Los Angeles: Pacific Publishers, 1936), 157–58.

8. Herbert C. Hoover, speech, 12 November 1932, Boulder City, Nevada, *Public Papers of the Presidents of the United States, Herbert C. Hoover, 1932–33* (Washington, D.C.: Government Printing Office, 1977), 810–13.

9. Fausold, *The Presidency of Herbert C. Hoover*, 136; Frank Freidel, *Franklin D. Roosevelt: Launching the New Deal* (Boston: Little, Brown, 1973), 162–65.

10. Franklin D. Roosevelt, "A National Yardstick to Prevent Extortion against the Public and to Encourage the Wider Use of That Servant of the People—Electrical Power," campaign address of public utilities and the development of hydroelectric power, Portland, Oregon, 21 September 1932, in *The Public Papers and Addresses of Franklin D. Roosevelt* (New York: Random House, 1938), 1:740.

11. Ray Lyman Wilbur, Silver Spike dedication speech, *Las Vegas Age* (September 18, 1930), p. 6.

12. Dixon Wecter, *The Age of the Great Depression* (New York: Macmillan, 1948), 45.

13. Joseph E. Stevens, *Hoover Dam: An American Adventure* (Norman: University of Oklahoma Press, 1988), 174.

14. Herbert C. Hoover, *The Memoirs of Herbert Hoover: The Cabinet and the Presidency, 1920–1933* (New York: Macmillan, 1952), 226–29.

15. Elwood Mead, "Information to Applicants for Employment at Hoover Dam, Boulder Canyon Project, March 25, 1932: Every State in Country but Two Represented at Boulder Dam," newspaper clipping (source unidentified), 1931; William Boyle, labor commissioner, to Betty Hanson, secretary, Central Labor Council, Las Vegas, 20 February 1933, Leonard Blood Papers, Special Collections Department, University of Nevada, Las Vegas.

16. "1,100 Men at Work on Dam, Figures Show," clipping, 25 May 1931; Leonard T. Blood, superintendent in charge, Las Vegas Office, Department of Labor, form letter to applicants, 2 September 1932, Leonard Blood Papers, Special Collections Department, University of Nevada, Las Vegas.

17. Central Labor Union of Clark County, Nevada, to William Boyle, Nevada state commissioner of labor, 8 October 1932; William Boyle, labor commissioner, to Betty Hanson, secretary, Central Labor Council, Las Vegas, 20 February 1933, Leonard Blood Papers, Special Collections Department, University of Nevada, Las Vegas.

18. Ray Lyman Wilbur, *Memoirs, 1875–1949* (Stanford, Calif.: Stanford University Press, 1960), 460.

19. Cited in Roosevelt Fitzgerald, "Blacks and the Boulder Dam Project," *Nevada Historical Society Quarterly* 24 (Fall 1981):259.

20. Donald J. Lisio, *Hoover, Blacks, and Lily-Whites* (Chapel Hill: University of North Carolina Press, 1985), 270; Stevens, *Hoover Dam*, 176.

21. Harvard Sitkoff, *A New Deal for Blacks: The Emergence of Civil Rights as a National Issue—The Depression Decade* (New York: Oxford University Press, 1978), 58–82; Stevens, *Hoover Dam*, 176–77.

22. Rocha, "The I.W.W. and the Boulder Canyon Project," 211.

23. "How Workers Ride the Goat at Boulder Dam," clipping, 20 December 1931 (?), IWW paper, Leonard Blood Papers, Special Collections Department, University of Nevada, Las Vegas.

24.   Oskar J. W. Hansen, *Sculptures at Hoover Dam* (Washington, D.C.: Government Printing Office, 1960), 2, 8.

25.   Richard Guy Wilson, "Machine-Age Iconography in the American West: The Design of Hoover Dam," *Pacific Historical Review* 54 (November 1985): 463–93; David Lavender, *Colorado River Country* (Albuquerque: University of New Mexico Press, 1982), 96; Bureau of Reclamation, "Hoover Dam: Fifty Years" (Washington, D.C.: Government Printing Office, 1985), 54; Hansen, *Sculptures at Hoover Dam*, 3. See appendix C for a listing of the men who died on the Boulder Canyon Project.

26.   George A. Pettitt, *So Boulder Dam was Built* (Berkeley: Press of Lederer, Street & Zeus [copyright by Six Companies, Inc.], 1935), 108.

27.   Zane Grey, *Boulder Dam* (New York: Harper & Row, 1963), 50, 117.

28.   Ray Lyman Wilbur, Silver Spike dedication speech, *Las Vegas Age*, 18 September 1930, 6.

Appendix A

1.   "Boulder Dam Builders Have a Language All Their Own, and How They Talk It," *Las Vegas Evening Review-Journal*, 31 January 1934, 3.

Appendix B

1.   "President Roosevelt Dedicates Boulder Dam, September 30, 1935: Text of Dedicatory Address," *Reclamation Era* 25 (October 1935): 193–94, 196.

Appendix C

1.   Bureau of Reclamation, Lower Colorado Regional Division, Boulder City, Nevada.

INDEX

Note: Entries in which the last name of interviewees are capitalized (as in BURT, Leroy) refer to their testimony; lower case references (as in Burt, Leroy) refer to instances in which others mention the individual.

329

YOUNG, Walker R. (*cont.*)
Canyon as the Hoover damsite, 6; in Boulder Canyon, 2, 6; on Boulder City design, 59; choosing Boulder City townsite, 57, 59; on Colorado River exploration [1902–1920], 1–2; on Saco Rink DeBoer, 59; on Sims Ely, 118; on heat studies, 46; on Hoover Dam dedication, 273, 276; in St. Thomas, Nevada, 2; on settling of foundations in Bureau of Reclamation houses, 69; on Woody Williams liquor arrest, 111–12

Younger, Harold, 201

Yuma, Arizona, 32

Ziemer, Serene: at dedication, 278

Zioncheck, Marion, 186, 324n3

The Authors

ANDREW J. DUNAR first saw Hoover Dam at the age of sixteen on a family trip to the West, and he has been fascinated by it ever since. He is a professor of history at the University of Alabama in Huntsville. The author of *The Truman Scandals and the Politics of Morality* and coauthor of *Power to Explore: The History of Marshall Space Flight Center, 1960–1990,* he is currently working on an oral history of The Farm, a long-lived hippie commune in Summertown, Tennessee. Dunar is editor of *The Oral History Review,* the journal of the Oral History Association.

Boulder City native DENNIS McBRIDE grew up hearing the stories related in this book and counts among his friends many of those interviewed. McBride founded the Boulder City/Hoover Dam Oral History Project, has written, researched, and produced several video documentaries on Hoover Dam, and has served as a historical consultant to the Department of the Interior. Formerly a technical writer for the Bureau of Reclamation, McBride wrote and revised the Standing Operating Procedures for all the dams on the lower Colorado River, including Hoover Dam. He is currently establishing a library and research facility for the Boulder City Museum and Historical Association. His most recent book is *Hard Work and Far from Home: The Civilian Conservation Corps at Lake Mead, Nevada,* and he has published several dozen articles on the history of Southern Nevada, Las Vegas, and the Boulder Canyon Project. McBride's work appears in *Nevada Magazine,* the *Nevada Historical Society Quarterly,* and the *Los Angeles Times,* and his current book project is *Life in the Neon Closet: A History of Gay Las Vegas.* He also publishes horror fiction in the United States and Europe as D. R. McBride.